PRIESTS AND PROGRAMMERS

PRIESTS AND PROGRAMMERS

TECHNOLOGIES OF POWER
IN THE ENGINEERED LANDSCAPE
OF BALI

With a new foreword by William C. Clark
and a new preface by the author

J. Stephen Lansing

PRINCETON UNIVERSITY PRESS
PRINCETON AND OXFORD

Copyright © 1991 by Princeton University Press
Foreword © 2007 by Princeton University Press
Preface to the 2007 Edition © 2007 by Princeton University Press
Published by Princeton University Press, 41 William Street, Princeton, New Jersey 08540
In the United Kingdom: Princeton University Press, 3 Market Place, Woodstock,
Oxfordshire OX20 1SY

First edition, 1991

Reprinted, with a new foreword and preface, 2007
ISBN-13: 978-0-691-13066-8
ISBN-10: 0-691-13066-3

The Library of Congress has cataloged the first edition of this book as follows

Lansing, John Stephen.
Priests and programmers : technologies of power in the engineered
landscape of Bali / J. Stephen Lansing.
p.   cm.
Includes bibliographical references (p.   ) and index.
ISBN 0-691-09466-7 (cl.) — ISBN 0-691-02863-X (pbk.)
1. Rites and ceremonies—Indonesia—Bali (Province).
2. Irrigation—Indonesia—Bali (Province)—Management.
3. Irrigation—Indonesia—Bali (Province)—Religious aspects.
4. Temples—Indonesia—Bali (Province).
5. Bali (Indonesia : Province)—Politics and government.   I. Title.
GN635.I65L35   1991
306.3′49—dc20   91-9993

British Library Cataloging-in-Publication Data is available

This book has been composed in Linotron Sabon

Printed on acid-free paper. ∞

press.princeton.edu

Printed in the United States of America

3   5   7   9   10   8   6   4   2

For Thérèse de Vet

The test case for a theory of rationality with which the modern understanding of the world is to ascertain its own universality would certainly include throwing light on the opaque figures of mythical thought, clarifying the bizarre expressions of alien cultures, and indeed in such a way that we not only comprehend the learning processes which separate "us" from them, but also become aware of what we have *unlearned* in the course of this learning.
(*Jürgen Habermas*, The Tasks of a Critical Theory)

om sarwa prani hitangkaram
(may all that breathes be well)
(*Balinese farmer's prayer*)

Contents

Figures

Tables

Foreword

STEVE LANSING began the work reported here, like many anthropologists before him, with the simple intention of exploring the intricate beauty of Balinese culture. Fortunately for those of us whose appreciation of cultural anthropology is more enthusiastic than professional, his curiosity led him to explore questions and deploy methods that reached beyond the boundaries of his native discipline. The result was an enormously rich study of how Bali's human institutions and environmental landscapes coevolved over the centuries to produce a complex adaptive system. That system proved to be sustainable in the face of volcanic eruptions, dynastic warfare, and colonial invasion. It took the well-intentioned but ultimately arrogant expertise of early Green Revolution reformers to push the system beyond its limits and into a mutually reinforcing downward spiral of ecological and social degradation. *Priests and Programmers* tells the story of how Lansing and his collaborators elucidated the interlinked geological, ecological, social, and religious processes that have shaped the Balinese landscape and, in so doing, became entrained in a process of social learning that helped the system to recover some of its previous resilience.

A wide range of scholars, students, and development practitioners has come to know and benefit from Lansing's story, assisted not only by the lucid writing style on display in this most welcome new edition of *Priests and Programmers*, but also through an excellent film, an accessible simulation model, and a series of follow-up studies, all available through his Web site (http://press.princeton.edu/titles/8394.html). I am one grateful beneficiary of the diverse perspectives Lansing has brought to bear on human-environment interactions in Bali, having used them for more than a decade in teaching a course on sustainable development at Harvard University's John F. Kennedy School of Government. My course uses four detailed case studies to explore how scholars, policy makers, and local practitioners have interacted in efforts to promote increases in human well-being without degrading the environmental life-support systems on which further development depends. I have kept the Bali story in an otherwise-changing set of course cases over the years simply because it is the one that elicits the most learning in my students, and the one they best recall when I talk with them as alumni. What makes Lansing's rendition of the Bali story such a pedagogical gold mine?

First, the Bali story is a specific instance of the much more general case of sustainable use of natural resources to support human well-being in the developing world. Half of the world's people still live in rural communities. A billion or so of those people are poor, with livelihoods more or less directly tied to the continuing productivity of natural resources. Often, as in the Bali case, sophisticated local knowledge of those resource systems and their limits has enabled societies to do quite well in utilizing them sustainably over centuries or longer. Increasingly, however, such traditional use systems have come under pressure from efforts to accommodate more people, increase yields, or respond to a globalizing economy. Distressingly often, the result has been catastrophic for both people and the resource systems they inhabit.

Lansing's work is especially valuable in illustrating the multiple forms that may be taken by the "local knowledge" that often turns out to be central to sustainable resource management. The individual villagers he interviewed in Bali clearly knew a great deal about planting rice, protecting it from pests, and building the irrigation systems that provided it with water. Some of this knowledge they could explain to him very articulately. Some was less explicit, consisting rather of the sort of "tacit" knowledge (or knowledge of practice) with which we all are familiar in our daily lives. Lansing's analysis, however, takes the reader far deeper into an understanding of the "local knowledge" that enabled sustainable human development of Bali's steep volcanic slopes. He shows that over the centuries, the value and thus the use of water had taken on not merely material but also spiritual significance for the Balinese. The religious structures, practices, and calendar that revered water for its own sake had evolved in ways that also served effectively to regulate and coordinate the sharing of limited water resources among farmers across entire watersheds. The "local knowledge" guiding sustainability thus consisted of what individuals knew and knew how to do, plus the physical system of irrigation canals and water shrines that such peoples' ancestors had constructed over time, plus the enduring religious beliefs that strongly shaped both individual and social action. The elegant systems models of water use and agriculture on Bali created by Lansing and his colleagues clearly show that each of these sorts of "local knowledge" is crucial for the sustainable use of the system. Though the forms of relevant local knowledge would clearly be different for other resource systems, the general teaching value of Lansing's work is in its compelling illustration that local knowledge matters more than we think, that it is more multidimensional than most of us would imagine, and that it is embodied in forms and places that most of us would not suspect.

This leads to what I, as a teacher, researcher, and occasional policy advisor, have found most valuable in Lansing's work: his demonstration that to most of us, most of the time, most of the knowledge relevant to the sustainable management of resource systems may be simply invisible. Through careful archival work, for example, he shows that the Dutch colonial administrators—though more sensitive than most to the intricacies of water management—"saw" only the irrigation hardware of the Balinese and missed entirely the "soft" role of water temples and related religious practices in regulating the use of the hardware. Similarly, Lansing demonstrates that the Green Revolution agronomists—even the Balinese among them—saw the *tika* calendar as an historical irrelevance, missing its crucial role in setting fallow schedules that resulted in effective pest management. Perhaps most strikingly, he illustrates that well-meaning policy analysts—raised in the modern science tradition—were unable to see in religious leaders' generally accurate diagnoses of the crisis conditions of the 1980s anything more than superstition. The cumulative force of these cases of selective blindness sets up one of the most powerful teaching "moments" I have experienced, letting me ask my students (and myself), "What potentially relevant sources of knowledge are *you* overlooking in your present work on sustainable development?"

The stand-and-deliver power of this question is substantially enhanced by Lansing's own demonstration that it can, in fact, be frankly confronted and dealt with. In *Priests and Programmers,* but even more in the associated film *The Goddess and the Computer*, we see Lansing and his collaborators grappling with the challenge of learning to "see" human-environment interactions through multiple lenses. They go further still, wrestling with the even more perilous task of creating shared frames of reference from which different actors—priests, programmers, and bureaucrats alike—can see, and understand, one another's views of the world. The use of computer models and graphics by the Lansing team to facilitate this essential "boundary spanning" role is as subtle and self-critical as any I have seen in a career of making and using models to inform resource policy.

This thoroughly delightful little book has long since become a classic in the emerging field of sustainability science. It elegantly illustrates the field's central tenet that complex human-environment systems can be more clearly understood and more effectively managed through the application of appropriate multidisciplinary concepts, methods, and models. It also reminds us of how important it is that those tools of the field be wielded by individuals who are not only careful scholars, but who also approach their work on the very real problems of sustainable development with appropriate empathy and humility. Its republication in this new edition is an occasion for celebrating the occasional ability of good people doing good scholarship to make the world a slightly better place.

William C. Clark
Harvard University
November 2006

THE READERSHIP that I anticipated when I began this book was the small community of anthropologists and other scholars interested in Indonesian cultures. The title I had in mind was *The Temple of the Crater Lake*, because I thought the most interesting story was the discovery that one of Bali's major temples played a hitherto-unnoticed role in managing the ecology of the rice terraces. But the editors at Princeton persuaded me to adopt a different title, so as to emphasize the contrast between Balinese farming systems and the new methods introduced by Western consultants. This proved to be good advice: the new title helped to bring the book to the attention of a wider readership with different interests than those of the Bali specialists. The editor's invitation to write a preface for a new edition gives me an opportunity to address some of the questions that both groups of readers have raised.

Priests and Programmers tells the story of well-intentioned but ultimately disastrous attempts by planners to reorganize farming systems on the island of Bali. I did not set out to investigate this topic; instead I stumbled onto it while pursuing more conventional anthropological questions. Like other anthropologists and artists before me, in the 1970s I had become fascinated by Balinese ideas about time, music, literature, and the theater, especially as they came to life in performances held in village temples. It seemed permissible to pursue these delightful topics because they were also very popular among the Balinese; this was a time when many Balinese were rediscovering the riches of their "traditional" culture.

It was in these luxurious circumstances that I began to take an interest in the temples connected with agriculture and the "Green Revolution." The agricultural rituals that take place in Balinese fields and water temples require each household to create gorgeous flower offerings to the gods; the calendar itself is also a thing of beauty, with intriguing connections to ideas about music and the human life cycle. These were the topics that initially captivated me. But as I learned from the farmers, the timing of these agricultural rites had been thrown off by the Green Revolution, which required them to plant new hybrid rice varieties as often as field conditions would permit. Some of the rituals of the "rice cult" could be rescheduled to fit the new accelerated timetable for Green Revolution rice. But others, like harvests, could not, because they were tied to the phases of the moon or other ritual calendars. Consequently, while the ancient stone temples were still regularly blanketed with flower offerings shaped into mandalic patterns, the timing of these rites no longer matched the growth of rice in the surrounding fields. And farmers wondered what the consequences might be.

A possible answer soon appeared, in the form of devastating outbreaks of rice pests and interruptions in the flow of irrigation water to the fields. Was there a link between these problems and the disruption of the temple calendars? *Priests and Programmers* opens with this question, which by the early 1980s was becoming a matter of acute concern for Balinese farmers and public works officials. But lurking behind this issue was an even more fundamental question:

WHY WASN'T THE FUNCTIONAL ROLE OF WATER TEMPLES A MATTER OF COMMON KNOWLEDGE?

In 1984, as I note in the introduction to *Priests and Programmers,* the head of the Irrigation Division of Bali's Department of Public Works reported that "study of the role of large-scale coordination of irrigation by temples is urgently needed." How was it possible that the Balinese engineer in charge of irrigation for the island could ask such a question? Or the dean of the faculty of agriculture at Bali's Udayana University? For that matter, if the temples really did play a functional role in water management and rice production, why was this not reported in the many studies of Balinese farming carried out by Dutch colonial researchers in the early years of the twentieth century?

I began to pursue these questions with the usual research methods of cultural anthropology: digging into the colonial archives and Balinese manuscripts; talking with farmers, extension agents, and water temple priests; mapping irrigation systems; and observing temple rituals. My starting point was Clifford Geertz's elegant analysis of the Balinese "rice cult," which showed how agricultural rituals were "symbolically linked to cultivation in a way that locks the pace of that cultivation into a firm, explicit rhythm."[1] This rhythm had been disturbed by the Green Revolution. But what exactly were the consequences? Were the effects limited to the domain of culture, or did they extend to the ecology of the rice paddies? This question led me to begin working with a systems ecologist, James Kremer, in 1983. Together we built a computer simulation model of irrigation at the watershed scale, which enabled us to mimic the patterns of coordination created by networks of water temples. Using the model, we could simulate the effects of the Green Revolution by depriving the temples of any functional role, and instructing the artificial farmers to plant rice as often as they could.

The results of these simulations closely resembled the actual patterns of pest outbreaks and water shortages that we observed in the fields. If all the fields within a sufficiently large area harvest at the same time, and the fields are subsequently flooded, rice pests are deprived of their habitat and their populations will decline. However, this technique requires all the farmers in the area to plant their crops at the same time. It also requires a lot of water to flood the fields and turn them into ponds. If too many farmers try to do this at the same time, there will not be enough water for their downstream neighbors. Our simulations showed that the temple networks sustain good harvests by finding planting schedules that provide enough water for everyone, but also permit pest control by synchronizing fallow periods for each block of terraces. Soon after the temples lost control of planting schedules, pest populations exploded. Indeed, one could think of the Green Revolution as a kind of experimental test of the functional role of water temple networks: remove them from control of irrigation schedules, and see what happens. This was not, of course, what the architects of the Green Revolution had in mind, and they were not particularly pleased to be shown simulations in which their policies drove down harvests by disrupting temple networks. But it did supply an answer to the question of why the functional role of water temples had escaped everyone's attention: before the Green Revolution, the very success of the temple networks in balancing water needs and sustaining good harvests made them nearly invisible.

ARE THE WATER TEMPLES OF BALI A UNIQUE CASE?

This question came up soon after Kremer and I began to publish our results. Could the Maya or the ancient Khmer have invented something like the Balinese water temples? But in the end, the most interesting comparison we found was much closer to Bali. And it had nothing to do with irrigation, temples, or rice.

In 1967, the year the Green Revolution began in most of Indonesia, another government program opened the forests of the Outer Islands to logging for export. Like the Green Revolution, this policy inadvertently set in motion an experimental test of the resilience of a tropical ecosystem. And like the Green Revolution, it produced immediate, spectacular results. By the early 1970s, logging exports were generating annual export earnings of over US$1.5 billion, eventually rising to as much as $6 billion.[2] As the Ministry of Forestry proclaimed in 1990,

[t]he logging industry is a champion of sorts. It opens up inaccessible areas to development; it employs people, it evolves whole communities; it sup-

ports related industries. . . . It creates the necessary conditions for social and economic development. Without forest concessions most of the Outer Islands would still be underdeveloped.[3]

By the 1980s, in response to indications of forest degradation from logging, the Ministry began to promote industrial tree plantations for the pulp and paper industry, supported by interest-free loans from the "Reforestation Fund" and international investment. Along with reforestation, the government also encouraged the creation of palm oil plantations on logged land. Sawmills, logging roads, and palm plantations proliferated in the 1990s, and exports of pulp, paper, and palm oil boomed. In 2002, export taxes on raw logs were eliminated and Indonesian firms were permitted to sell logs to anyone. Plans for biodiversity conservation were based on selective logging and reforestation, and the creation of national parks.[4]

The dominant canopy tree family in Borneo and Sumatra is the Dipterocarpaceae, which consists of some 267 tree species that make up over 85 percent of Indonesia's tree exports. The sustainability of the timber industry thus depends on the regenerative capacity of dipterocarp forests. In 1999, ecologist Lisa Curran and her colleagues reported the results of a comprehensive fourteen-year investigation of the ability of the dipterocarps to reproduce. Regrowth depends on the survival of sufficient quantities of seedlings. Many forest animals and birds are seed predators, so the trees are engaged in a continuous race to produce more seeds than the predators can consume. Curran found that long ago, the trees evolved essentially the same solution to the problem of controlling predation that was later discovered by the Balinese farmers: reproductive synchrony. Dipterocarp forests produce nearly all of their seeds and fruits within a very small window in time, in a phenomenon known to ecologists as "mast fruiting." For seed predators, this means that large quantities of dipterocarp fruits and seeds become available only in short, irregular bursts that occur every three to six years, triggered by the El Niño Southern Oscillation (ENSO). ENSO is a global climatic cycle that causes an extreme reduction in rainfall in Borneo from June to September. The ENSO dry spell is used by the trees as a signal to initiate flowering and reproduction. Seed predators respond by synchronizing their own reproductive cycles to ENSO years, and by moving across the landscape, far from their usual ranges, to feed on dipterocarp seeds.

Over the past three decades, the harvesting of timber caused widespread fragmentation of what had formerly been a vast contiguous expanse of dipterocarp forest in Borneo, disrupting regional reproductive synchrony. Once synchrony was lost, small-scale local masts could not produce enough seedlings to escape being eaten by predators. Curran's extensive observations and field experiments led to a single conclusion: "Seed escape, and thus regeneration, only occurred in major mast events when all dipterocarp species across large areas participated."[5] The parallel with the Balinese case is exact. In the rice terraces of Bali, disruption of the synchronized planting schedules formerly organized by water temple networks led to crop failure, as migrating pests moved across the landscape consuming one harvest after another. Similarly, in Borneo the mast synchrony of canopy trees depended on signals sent through the root system. When the forests became fragmented, it was no longer possible to overwhelm predators with a vast synchronized mast.

We now know that in both Bali and Borneo, large-scale reproductive synchrony emerged as a solution to the problem of controlling seed predators. But in both cases, this cyclical pattern was invisible to planners. In Bali, the farmers were able to respond in the nick of time and restore control to the temple networks. But the trees were not so fortunate. The latest research by Curran and her colleagues shows that the lowland forests of Indonesian Borneo have lost the capacity to regenerate, probably beyond hope of recovery. As a consequence, ENSO—formerly a great forest regenerator—has become a destructive regional phenomenon, triggering droughts and wildfires with increasing intensity. By the 1990s, much of Indonesian Borneo had been deforested, leaving logging debris in place of canopy trees. When ENSO arrived in 1998, forest fires raged across the island and four hundred million metric tons of carbon were released into the atmosphere. Even peat swamps caught fire, adding another two hundred million tons of carbon. (For comparison, the Kyoto target for reduction in carbon emission for the whole earth was five hundred million tons.)[6]

Thus in both Borneo and Bali, synchronized growing cycles emerged as a solution to the problem of controlling predator populations in the winterless tropics, imposing a clockwork pattern on the life cycles of many species. At least in this respect, the water temple networks of Bali were not unique. Might other, similar systems exist elsewhere? If so, would they always be driven by the need for predator control? How much of the functional structure of the water temple networks was directly tied to the ecology of Bali or the biology of pests?

In 1998 my colleagues and I published a paper in the *Journal of Theoretical Biology* suggesting that phenomena like water temple networks or the Borneo forest clock could emerge spontaneously as global solutions to local problems.[7] We argued that this process—the emergence of self-regulating structures from the bottom up—was not tied to the specific ecology of Balinese rice terraces. But such systems would be likely to fade into the background as long as they were functioning normally. Our thinking on this question was influenced by the work of ecologists on the emergence of self-organized systems, and we used "Daisyworld," a thought experiment created by the chemist James Lovelock, to make our case.[8] Daisyworld had several advantages for us: the biology is as simple as Lovelock could make it; the model shows precisely how small-scale local adaptations can produce an emergent global structure; and it also shows why such global structures can easily fade from view, becoming noticeable only when the system as a whole has been pushed near its limits.

Lovelock's model is simple and interesting enough to be included here. Daisyworld is an imaginary planet orbiting a star like the sun and at the same orbital distance as the earth. The surface of Daisyworld is fertile earth sown uniformly with daisy seeds. The daisies vary in color, and daisies of similar color grow together in patches. As sunshine falls on Daisyworld, the model tracks changes in the growth rate of each variety of daisy, and changes in the amount of the planet's surface covered by different-colored daisies. The simplest version of this model contains only two varieties of daisies, white and black.

Black daisies absorb more heat than bare earth, while whites reflect sunshine. Clumps of same-colored daisies create a local microclimate for themselves, slightly warmer (if they are black) or cooler (if white) than the mean temperature of the planet. Both black and white daisies grow fastest and at the same rate when their local effective temperature (the temperature within their microclimate) is 22.5°C, and they respond identically, with a decline in growth rate, as the temperature deviates from this ideal. Consequently, at the given average planetary temperature, black and white daisies experience different microclimates and therefore different growth rates.

If the daisies cover a sufficiently large area of the surface of Daisyworld, their color affects not only their own microclimate but also the albedo, or reflectance of the planet as a whole. Like that of our own sun, the luminosity of Daisyworld's star is assumed to have gradually increased. A simulation of life on Daisyworld begins in the past with a cooler sun. This enables the black daisies to spread until they warm the planet. Later on, as the sun grows hotter, the white daisies grow faster than black ones, cooling the planet. So over the history of Daisyworld, the warming sun gradually changes the proportion of white and black daisies, creating the global phenomenon of temperature regulation: the planet's temperature is held near the optimum for the daisies, as shown in figure P.1.

Imagine that a team of astronauts and planners is sent to investigate

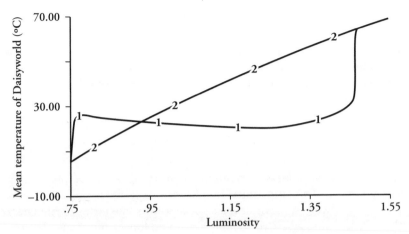

Figure P.1. Results of a simulation of temperature regulation on Daisyworld. As the sun ages and its luminosity increases from 0.75 to 1.5 times the present value (1.0), the temperature of a bare planet would steadily rise (line 2). In contrast, with daisies present, the temperature stabilizes close to 22.5° C (line 1).

Daisyworld. They would have plenty of time to study the only living things on the planet, and they would almost certainly conclude that the daisies had evolved to grow best at the normal temperature of the planet, 22.5° C. But this conclusion would invert the actual state of affairs. The daisies did not adapt to the temperature of the planet; instead they adapted the planet to suit themselves.[9] As we see in figure P.1, a Daisyworld without daisies would track the increase in the sun's luminance (line 2), rather than stabilizing near the ideal temperature for daisies (line 1). Only when the sun's luminosity becomes too hot for the daisies to control (~1.4 times the current value) will the daisy's former role in temperature stabilization become apparent.

Lacking this understanding, planners hoping to exploit Daisyworld's economic potential as a flower supplier would fail to appreciate the possible consequences of different harvesting techniques. While selective flower harvests would cause small, probably unnoticeable tremors in planetary temperature, clear-cutting large contiguous patches of daisies would create momentary changes in the planet's albedo that could quickly become permanent, causing temperature regulation to fail and daisy populations to crash.

Daisyworld and the dipterocarp forests of Borneo are simpler systems than the water temple networks of Bali. While daisies and dipterocarps have only one parameter to manage (respectively, temperature and pests), the temple networks need to adjust the balance between water sharing and pest control at multiple sites in large, interdependent and interconnected irrigation systems. This is a much more complicated problem, which inevitably produces temporary winners and losers as environmental conditions fluctuate. But the very simplicity of Daisyworld's flowers and Borneo's trees may help to clarify the more subtle dynamics of the water temple networks.

WHAT'S HAPPENING NOW?

Priests and Programmers recounts the history of our attempts to convince planners of the functional importance of water temple networks. In the end we were successful: today, except for some farms located near urban settlements, where the temple system no longer functions, the control of cropping cycles has returned to the temple networks, and farmers are no longer urged to plant rice as fast as they can. Indeed, the agricultural extension service in Bali has become a strong advocate for the temple system. Pesticide use has also declined, as pest populations were brought under control by the system of regional fallow periods. But one key component of the Green Revolution package remains in place, causing needless ecological damage at a high cost to the farmers, and threatening the long-term productivity of the rice terraces.

Green Revolution plants are bred to make efficient use of chemical fertilizers. When the Green Revolution began in Indonesia, fertilizer production was expanded and farmers were instructed to purchase "technology packets" containing seeds, fertilizers, and pesticides on credit.[10] The fertilizer contained in these packets included all of the nitrogen, potassium, and phosphate needed by the plants. But phosphate and potassium are naturally abundant in the volcanic soil of Bali.[11] Monsoon rains falling on the island leach these minerals from the earth, and irrigation canals transport them to the rice paddies. This natural system of fertilization was ignored by the designers of the technology packets. Working with staff from the agricultural extension service and the soil science department of Udayana University, Kremer and I measured nutrient concentrations in the paddies and irrigation canals, before and after fertilization. We found that most of the superfluous fertilizer flows out of the paddies and back into the rivers, accumulating to very high levels before reaching the coast.[12] Isotopic analysis of coral shows increases in nitrogen from fertilizer, and reefs located near agricultural drainages are often blanketed with destructive macroalgae.[13] One of our Balinese colleagues, Dr. Alit Artha Wiguna of the Ministry of Agriculture, carried out dissertation research on fertilizer use along an entire river in western Bali. He found that the cost of fertilizer for one hectare of rice in 2004 was approximately $101, of which $69.60 is superfluous (unused by the rice).[14] Moreover, soil fertility was much reduced in these paddies, compared to the paddies located in remote upstream locations that continued to plant native Balinese rice and rely on natural (organic) fertilizer. Artha Wiguna is now leading a campaign to reduce the use of chemical fertilizers and return to traditional methods of organic farming. The alternative is to accept continuing needless damage to the terrestrial and marine ecology of Bali.

IF SUCH SELF-ORGANIZING PROCESSES ARE INDEED COMMON, WHY HAVEN'T WE NOTICED THEM?

In the past two decades, ecologists have become interested in the ways that patterns can emerge from multiple processes occurring at different scales. In one of the most cited papers on this topic, Simon Levin observes that patterns are often generated by the collective behavior of smaller-scale units, which "operate at different scales than those on which the patterns are observed."[15] Ecological journals are filled with examples of such processes, with a growing emphasis on global-scale phenomena such as climate change. But these ideas have been slow to spread to the social sciences. Karl Marx famously dismissed the peasants as a "sack of potatoes," and for most social scientists, it is still true that one piece of countryside looks much like the next. Even anthropologists are seldom inclined to search for the kinds of pattern-and-scale interactions that Levin describes. Consider, for example, anthropologist James Scott's *Seeing Like a State: How Certain Schemes to Improve the Human Condition Have Failed*. This book begins with an analysis of the ecological disaster created by the beginning of "scientific forestry" in eighteenth-century Germany. The replacement of natural forests with orderly rows of commercially valuable trees soon led to pest outbreaks and "forest death." Scott goes on to explore the appearance of new practices designed to improve the "legibility" of the countryside for state bureaucracies, such as cadastral surveys, surnames, censuses, and the promotion of procedures deemed to be scientific (objective, precise, and universally valid) at the expense of local knowledge. Scott characterizes local communities as repositories of *metis*, a Greek term that he borrows from the classical scholars Marcel Detienne and Jean-Pierre Vernant. As these authors show, *metis* was a term favored by Greek poets to describe the craft, cunning, or clever adaptability of heroes like Odysseus.[16] Scott uses *metis* to describe the knowledge and practices of local communities, and offers a spirited defense of *metis* as it is embodied in practices like shifting agriculture.

Metis, then, is ad hoc, local, ingenious, and colorful. But it is not systematic, patterned, or emergent. One might easily view Balinese farming practices or water temples as particularly rich examples of *metis*, as treasuries of accumulated lore. Indeed, each community might be expected to have its own local stock of *metis*. This is precisely what I expected to find when I began my research on the water temples, and were it not for my collaboration with Dr. Kremer, it is probably all that I would have noticed. My point is not to critique Scott's book, which is after all focused on the behavior of states as instigators of development schemes. Instead, I wish to emphasize how easy it can be, even for an anthropologist, to fail to recognize the kinds of multiscale interactions that ecologists have trained themselves to see. *Priests and Programmers* describes how my colleagues and I gradually came to recognize the water temples as more than repositories of *metis*. But to borrow Scott's metaphor, our ability to see—to recognize emergent patterns in water temple networks—required a learning process. The temple networks came into view partly as a result of the Green Revolution, which exposed their ecological role, and partly through our expanding familiarity with the properties of complex adaptive systems like Daisyworld. Indeed, the enduring message of *Priests and Programmers* may be how easy it was to miss the significance of the temple networks—just as planners failed to appreciate the functional significance of the forest clock in Borneo.

NOTES

1. Clifford Geertz, *Negara: The Theatre State in Nineteenth Century Bali* (Princeton, N.J.: Princeton University Press, 1980), 82.

2. "Over the past two decades, the volume of dipterocarp timber exports (in cubic meters) from Borneo (Kalimantan, Sarawak and Sabah) exceeded all tropical wood exports from tropical Africa and Latin America combined." L. M. Curran et al., "Lowland Forest Loss in Protected Areas of Indonesian Borneo," *Science* 303 (2004): 1000–1003.

3. Situation and Outlook of the Forestry Sector in Indonesia. Jakarta: United Nations Food and Agriculture Organization and Directorate General of Forest Utilization, Government of Indonesia, 1990.

4. Paul K. Gellert, "The Shifting Natures of 'Development': Growth, Crisis and Recovery in Indonesia's Forests," *World Development* 33 (8) (2005): 1345–64.

5. L. M. Curran and M. Leighton, "Vertebrate Response to Spatiotemporal Variation in Seed Production of Mast-Fruiting Dipterocarpacae," *Ecological Monographs* 70 (1): 102.

6. Curran estimates that by 2005, less than 35 percent of the lowland forests (<500 m a.s.l.) were still standing, most of them already degraded (personal communication).

7. J. Stephen Lansing, James N. Kremer, and Barbara B. Smuts, "System-dependent Selection, Ecological Feedback and the Emergence of Functional Structure in Ecosystems," *Journal of Theoretical Biology* 192: 377–91.

8. James E. Lovelock, "A Numerical Model for Biodiversity," *Phil. Trans. R. Soc. B* 338 (1992): 383–91.

9. Peter T. Saunders, "Evolution without Natural Selection: Further Implications of the Daisyworld Parable," *Journal of Theoretical Biology* 166 (1994): 370.

10. Frederick C. Roche, "The Technical and Price Efficiency of Fertilizer Use in Irrigated Rice Production," *Bulletin of Indonesian Economic Studies* 30 (1) (April 1994): 59–83; James J. Fox, "Managing the Ecology of Rice Production in Indonesia," in Joan Hardjono, ed., *Indonesia: Resources, Ecology, and Environment* (New York: Oxford University Press, 1991), 61–84.

11. G. E. Wheller, R. Varne, J. D. Foden, and M. J. Abbot, "Geochemistry of Quaternary Volcanism in the Sunda-Banda Arc, Indonesia, and Three-component Genesis of Island-Arc Basaltic Magmas," *Journal of Volcanology and Geothermal Research* 32 (1987): 137–60.

12. J. S. Lansing et al., "Volcanic Fertilization of Balinese Rice Paddies," *Ecological Economics* 38 (2001): 383–90.

13. Guy S. Marion et al., "Coral Skeletal δ15 Reveals Isotopic Traces of an Agricultural Revolution," *Marine Pollution Bulletin* 50 (9) (Sept. 2005): 931–44.

14. I. W.A.A. Wiguna, "Kontribusi sisetm usahatani padi sawah terhadap pengkayaan hara nitrogen, fosfor dan kalium aliran permukaan pada ekosistem subak di Bali" (PhD diss., Environmental Sciences, Bogor Technical University, Indonesia, 2002).

15. Simon A. Levin, "The Problem of Pattern and Scale in Ecology," *Ecology* 73 (1992): 1943–67.

16. Marcel Detienne and Jean-Pierre Vernant, *Cunning Intelligence in Greek Culture and Society* (Atlantic Highlands, N.J.: Humanities Press, 1978).

Acknowledgments

I BEGAN this research with a grant from the National Science Foundation (# 53-4804-9827) that enabled me to spend ten months in Bali examining the role of water temples in irrigation management (1983–84) and a month at the International Rice Research Institute in the Philippines learning about the Green Revolution in rice. Film and sound recording equipment for use in the Philippines and Indonesia was provided by the Center for Visual Anthropology of the University of Southern California. In 1986, I returned to Bali for four months to study the Temple of the Crater Lake with support from a Fulbright regional research fellowship and a small grant from the National Science Foundation (NSF) (BNS #53-4804-2751). The following summer, a Social Science Research Council fellowship enabled me to spend a month in the Netherlands examining the colonial archives on Balinese irrigation and colonial administration. I then returned to Bali to begin a collaborative study of the role of water temples in terrace ecology with my friend and colleague Dr. James N. Kremer, a systems ecologist. Our work was also sponsored by the National Science Foundation (#BNS-8705400).

In the fall of 1987, Thérèse de Vet and I returned to Bali at the request of the temple priests to film the Panca Wali Krama ceremony at the temple. In the summer of 1988, James Kremer and I returned to Bali with a graduate student, Kevin Arrigo, to continue our work on the ecological role of the water temples. We were joined by the English anthropologist and filmmaker Dr. André Singer, who created a one-hour documentary film, "The Goddess and the Computer." The film crew included Mike Thomson (camera) and Margaret Wiener, who acted as sound recordist, Balinese interpreter and translator for the film crew, and anthropological consultant.

Field research was sponsored in Indonesia by the Lembaga Ilmu Pengetahuan Indonesia and Udayana University. The film projects in conjunction with the research were sponsored by the Departemen Penerangan of the Republic of Indonesia.

Several colleagues have read whole drafts of this manuscript, often more than once, and I have greatly benefited from their advice: Thérèse de Vet, Nicholas Dirks, Gary Seaman, André Singer, Lucien Taylor, Valerio Valeri, and Margaret Wiener. Patsy Asch, Timothy Asch, Janet Hoskins, James Kremer, Carol Lansing, Peter Lyman, Nancy Lutkehaus, Daniel Marks, and G. Alexander Moore have helped me struggle with various chapters. Most of the maps and illustrations in the book were originally created for the computer simulation model described in chapter 6 (specifically, for the Hypercard interface) by the Project Jefferson Team at the University of Southern California: Tyde Richards, Rick Lacey, and Dave Vronay.

In Bali, this research began as an individual effort and gradually evolved into a collaborative project. At Udayana University in Bali, I greatly benefited from the advice and assistance of Prof. I Gusti Ngurah Bagus of the Anthropology Department and Dr. Nyoman Sutawan of the Faculty of Agriculture. I also worked closely with several engineers and hydrologists working on irrigation and hydrology in Bali: Ir. I Made Sudiarsa and Ir. Cokorde Raka of the Proyek Irigasi Bali; Drs. Made Sukardja and Drs. Sumertha of the Hydrology Division of the Department of Public Works; and the current head of Public Works, Ir. I Ketut Kaler, along with his predecessors, Ir. Jelantik Sushila and Ir. Ktut Mandera. Dr. Putu Budiastra, the head of the Bali Museum and a fellow student of the Temple of the Crater Lake, has generously shared his manuscripts and insights into the temple's historical role. At the temple itself, I am greatly indebted to several individuals for countless hours of patient explanations: the Jero Gde Mekalihan, Jero Penyarikan Duuran, Guru Nengah Tekah, Guru Badung, Jero Balian, Jero Mangku Cri, and Kaki Djewati. Thanks also to my old friend Ida Bagus Ktut Sudiasa of the Griya Taman Sari Sanur for help with translations and analysis of lontar manuscripts. For help in understanding the practical aspects of irrigation management I am especially indebted to Wayan Pageh of Sebatu, Ida Bagus Beretha (Perbekel Sukawati), Rasman of Kedewatan, I Gde Suarja, Dewa Gde Adi Parwata, I Made Cakranegara, and Ni Made Tutik Sri Andayani, along with many others.

I am also indebted to Harold Conklin, Robert Hunt, Stuart Plattner, and John Daly for advice on how to study irrigation systems; to C. J. Grader for guidance in interpreting the colonial records; to Kristina Melcher for much warm hospitality during her tenure as American consular agent in Bali; and to Dr. A. A. M. Jelantik for many kindnesses and for curing my daughter's dengue fever. Finally, I would like to express my sincere appreciation to several people at Princeton University Press. Walter Lippincott persuaded me to try to aim for a broader readership than I had originally anticipated and helped me reshape the manuscript with this goal in mind. Mary Murrell, Beth Gianfagna, and Virginia M. Barker made many useful suggestions and helped speed the manuscript through its final revisions and preparation for publication. The Koninklijk Instituut voor Taal-, Land- en Volkenkunde graciously granted permission to publish various documents from their archives. My thanks to all, with of course the usual caveat that responsibility for any remaining errors or omissions is mine alone.

PRIESTS AND PROGRAMMERS

The Gods of the Countryside

felix qui potuit cognoscere causas. . . .
fortunatus et ille deos qui nouit agrestis
(Happy is one who has learned
the causes of things. . . .
Fortunate too is he who has found
the gods of the countryside)
(Virgil)

I FIRST became curious about water temples in the mid-1970s, when I was gathering materials for a study of the historical evolution of temples in Bali. One of the peculiarities of Balinese temples is their anonymity: most temples look exactly alike, and except for a few days each year when festivals are held, they are generally left empty and abandoned. The functions of the temple, and the identities of the gods worshiped within, are often known only to the temple's congregation. In a landscape dotted with hundreds of nearly identical temples, it is not a simple matter to work out their histories and purposes. The existence of a separate class of "water temples" is not mentioned in the scholarly literature on Bali, and I doubt that I would have become aware of the existence of the water temples but for the fact that my period of fieldwork happened to coincide with a phenomenon that seemed at first to have nothing whatever to do with temples: the onset of the "Green Revolution" in Balinese agriculture.

The term "Green Revolution" refers to the replacement of native rice with hybridized high-yielding varieties that require the use of chemical fertilizers and pesticides. The Green Revolution began in the laboratories of the International Rice Research Institute in the Philippines in the 1960s and spread swiftly across Asia, gaining a firm foothold in Indonesia by the early 1970s. In Bali, the Green Revolution was accompanied by new government agricultural policies that promoted continuous cropping of the new rice in an effort to boost rice production. Farmers were encouraged to plant rice as quickly as possible, without regard for traditional irrigation schedules. But the immediate gains in rice yields produced by this policy soon began to be offset by water shortages and unprecedented outbreaks of rice pests and diseases.

I learned of these concerns in conversations with farmers at Er Jeruk, a magnificent old temple located in the midst of the rice terraces near the sea at Sukawati. I had come to the temple to investigate the legends surrounding its creation. But the local farmers were much more interested in talking about the temple's current problems. I was told that in the time before the Green Revolution this temple had set a complicated rotational irrigation schedule for all the fields in its vicinity, in all nearly 500 hectares of rice terraces. But as a result of the new policy of continuous rice cropping, the temple had lost control of the irrigation schedule. Everyone was trying to grow rice as quickly as possible, so that as soon as one crop was harvested, another would be planted.

The idea of temples as irrigation managers was intriguing in light of the long controversy in Balinese studies over the historical role of Balinese kings in irrigation management. Both Marx and Wittfogel had proposed Bali as an example of their theories of "Oriental despotism": the idea that the power of Asian kings derived from their control over irrigation.[1] But the evidence from Bali had always been equivocal. Clifford Geertz had recently argued that Balinese kings had very little to do with irrigation.[2] Yet if the kings did not control irrigation, who did?

In 1983, I received support from the National Science Foundation for a study of the water temple system. En route to Bali, I spent a month at the International Rice Research Institute in the Philippines, trying to learn more about the Green Revolution and the technical aspects of growing paddy rice. A preliminary review of the literature on Balinese irrigation confirmed that little was known from an engineering standpoint about irrigation management in Bali. The studies that had been done concentrated on the smallest scale: the allocation of water between farmers in small water-user groups called *subaks*. Most *subaks* consist of about one hundred or so farmers who obtain their irrigation water from a common source, usually a main canal. The efficiency of the *subaks* as water-user groups had already made them famous in the irrigation literature. But as many as a hundred *subaks* might depend on a single river for irrigation. A microstudy of individual *subaks* might not detect higher-level systems of coordination, if indeed they existed.

Elsewhere in Asia, there was evidence that in earlier times temples had played an important role in ancient irrigation systems. In Cambodia, the work of Bernard Groslier showed that temples had been an important element in the grand irrigation systems of the Khmer.[3] In northern Thailand, Lando, Potter, and Moerman describe irrigation systems in which a pantheon of spirits are associated with irrigation control.[4] Nearer to Bali, Pigeaud's classic *Java in the Fourteenth Century* described sacred sources of power in the mountains and religious worship at the source of a river by the royal court.[5]

But was it really possible that a system of water temples was still functioning in Bali? When I arrived in Bali in 1983, I was surprised to learn
that this question was under study, not by a fellow scholar, but by engineers in the Balinese Department of Public Works. Because the public
works and agriculture departments in Bali are largely staffed by Balinese,
it seemed strange that they should have been previously unaware of the
significance of water temples. But it appeared that the Green Revolution
had taken them by surprise, creating "chaos in the water scheduling system" and "an explosion of pests and diseases."[6] Formerly, these agencies
had been occupied with taxes and engineering projects, not with the active management of irrigation. But the failures of the Green Revolution
compelled them to take a much more active interest in irrigation, which
ultimately led to the discovery of the water temple system. What the bureaucracy had discovered was not the existence of agricultural rituals or
water temples, but the fact that the temples exerted a form of hierarchical
control over irrigation. The Department of Public Works commissioned
a study of water temples and irrigation by the agricultural school of Bali's
Udayana University, which concluded that "the relationship between the
hierarchical system of subak temples and their connections to inter-subak
coordination of rituals and irrigation is not yet clearly understood. A
deeper and more thorough investigation of these topics will greatly assist
efforts to improve conditions."[7] Similarly, the head of the Irrigation Division of the Department of Public Works wrote in 1984 that "study of
the role of large-scale coordination of irrigation by temples is urgently
needed."[8]

Such reports confirmed that water temples exercised some forms of
control over irrigation. But the precise nature of this control proved very
difficult to define. Whether or not the authority of the temples overlapped
with that of government bureaucracies depended on which aspects of irrigation were in question. For example, the government claimed the right
to settle disputes over water rights and to grant permission for new irrigation systems. Were such rights called into question by the claim that all
irrigation waters belonged to the Goddess of Waters? So long as the bureaucracy contented itself with collecting taxes and replacing earthen
weirs with concrete structures, the temple system could easily be over-
looked, as much a part of the natural landscape as the rivers and the terraces themselves.

RITUAL TECHNOLOGY

The starting-point for my research, from an analytical standpoint, was
Georges Condominas's concept of "ritual technology." In *Nous avons*

mangé la forêt (We have eaten the forest) and subsequent essays, Condominas criticized the commonsensical distinction made by social scientists between ritual, particularly agricultural rituals, and the material technology of traditional farming. His fieldwork among the Mnong Gar, a Montagnard community in the central highlands of Vietnam, led Condominas to see ritual as an integral component of the technology of farming. Precise observation of the affairs of daily life (Lévi-Strauss calls him "the Proust of ethnology") persuaded Condominas that agricultural work is not merely a sequence of technical tasks; it is a meaningful series of interactions between social groups and the natural world. The field rituals that accompany each stage of agricultural labor form a kind of commentary on the productive process. Moreover, the rituals of work in the fields may be "performative," in that they call forth particular social groups to engage in activities such as planting or harvesting. Agriculture, in short, is a social as well as a technical process, which is structured by the sequence of agricultural rites.

Recently, Condominas has speculated that his concept of ritual technology might better be phrased in terms of a theory of work, and for several reasons I am inclined to agree. The word "technology" derives from *technē*, a Greek word that originally referred to the labors of the smith and other craftsmen. The analogous Greek word for the labors of the farmer is *erga* or "work," as in Hesiod's *Works and Days*. *Erga* could also mean farm lands: tilled fields, or lands that had been worked, but not virgin fields or forests. Thus fishing is the *erga* of the sea, while in another sense, honey is the *erga* of bees. This distinction between *technē* and *erga* is relevant to a theory of the special characteristics of agricultural rites.

For the Greeks, the smith was a solitary figure, whose *technē* was a jealously guarded secret connecting him to the powers of the underworld through the god Hephaestus. In contrast, the *erga*, or work, of the farmer was public, involving the whole of society and most of the gods. Both activities (smithing and farming) involved ritual, but in the case of *technē* the rituals were secret and individual, whereas *erga* are public and collective. Indeed, the calendar of agricultural rites is the master social calendar, for (as Condominas says of the Mnong Gar) "annual and agricultural cycles are one and the same."[9]

To the extent that the agricultural cycle of rites becomes the master calendar of social life, the analysis of one is equivalent to the analysis of the other. *We Have Eaten the Forest* describes the ritual cycle of a single village, which farms one small patch of forest after another. The major agricultural rituals are connected with transforming forest into agricultural land, a process that requires "welding into one collectivity all of the social beings of the Mnong Gar world," including the village, the spirits of the ancestors and the forest, and the Rice Mother.[10] Here, the social universe consists of only a single village and its collective farmlands. But a similar pattern may also be found on a much larger scale elsewhere. For example, Valerio Valeri has recently analyzed the relationship between agricultural rituals and the politico-religious structure of kingship in the ancient kingdoms of Hawaii. The Hawaiian case is interesting, because it highlights the most puzzling aspects of agricultural rites in Bali. Consider this contrast:

When Captain Cook arrived in Hawaii, each of the major islands was a separate kingdom. Each island kingdom was subdivided into districts ruled by lesser chiefs. These districts were called *ahupuaa,* from the word for temple altar (*ahu*). Each district had an altar, where the inhabitants presented firstfruits offerings to their local overlord or chief. As Valeri explains, "each holder of a land title gives the firstfruits of his land to the individual from whom he holds his title. These presentations follow the hierarchical route until they reach the king, who consecrates them to the major gods."[11] Such offerings legitimized the rights of chiefs and people to the land. As head of the temple hierarchy, the king dedicated the fruits of the collective labors of his subjects to the gods. In this way, agricultural rites were absorbed into the rituals of kingship and the symbolic representation of society. Structurally, the power of chiefs to rule was bound up in their relationship to the productive process.

The first European visitors to Bali also described annual cycles of agricultural offerings. But the organization of these offerings differs in an interesting way from that of the Hawaiian kingdoms. The island of Bali is a little larger than the largest Hawaiian island. Before its conquest by the Dutch, Bali was fragmented into half a dozen or more major kingdoms. These kingdoms were often subdivided into tiny quasi-autonomous principalities, whose rulers add new shades of diminution to the term *princeling.* The political boundaries of Balinese kingdoms were constantly changing as a result of warfare, alliances, and dynastic politics. But the crucial point, for our present purposes, is that the rituals of the agricultural cult essentially ignored the boundaries of these kingdoms and principalities and followed instead the natural boundaries of rivers and watersheds. Because no single kingdom controlled an entire river, delegations of farmers journeyed across the boundaries of kingdoms to perform rituals in chains of temples extending from the mountain lakes to the seacoast.

The physical separation of the agricultural cult from the boundaries of kingdoms was mirrored on a symbolic level. The Balinese cult of kingship involves a special class of rituals, which are distinct from the rituals of the agricultural cult. Agricultural rites invoke an imagery of power that transcends kingship: a mandala of waters in the mountain lakes and a goddess who dwells in them; gods who inhabit irrigation dams and springs; the Rice Mother and her sister goddess of the marketplace; and plague-bearing demons from the sea. Altogether, this is quite a different world from that of ancient Hawaii, one in which the *erga* of the farmers is not directly linked to the powers of kings.

It is not, perhaps, altogether astonishing that the Balinese contrived to organize their kingdoms, temples, and agricultural rituals differently from those of the ancient Hawaiians. But more fundamental issues are involved in these differences than may be apparent at first. In general, ethnographic analyses of non-Western societies like Bali or Hawaii have had little influence on mainstream social theory. Although this may be partly due to Orientalist prejudices, as some scholars have recently claimed, there are also deeper reasons. Social theory has been primarily concerned with the historical forces producing the modern secular and rational social universe. Jürgen Habermas puts it neatly: in premodern societies, the "lifeworld . . . is coextensive with society."[12] Where social formations are entirely embedded in the lifeworld, there is no historical subject. Ethnographic analyses of societies classed as premodern, therefore, have little bearing on mainstream social theory because by definition they lie outside the historical process. These societies enter history only as a result of European imperialism—a point originally made by Hegel and Marx, reiterated in Lévi-Strauss's distinction between *hot and cold* societies, and reaffirmed most recently by Eric Wolf in *Europe and the Peoples without History.*[13] From the standpoint of social theory as it is presently constituted, Balinese history begins with the arrival of the Dutch.

But the water temples of Bali do not fit easily into the Procrustean opposition between premodern and modern social formations for the very reasons we have been exploring. Basic to the definition of traditional society is the idea that social institutions are undifferentiated, that the domains of politics, religion, and economics form a unified whole. In contrast, modern or modernizing societies are characterized by structural differentiation. Yet here was a complex institutional system that transcended political boundaries.

Still, if this were the only distinguishing feature of the water temples, they would provide little more than an interesting footnote to the history of an exotic society. Of potentially greater significance is the observation that the water temples inhabit a world that is largely outside the domain of social theory as it is presently constituted. To define the water temple system, to bring the temples forward, will require us to broaden the perspective from which we view social institutions, and in this way to challenge the Eurocentric focus of Western social theory.

THE ENGINEERED LANDSCAPE

"The interaction of labor, techniques and resources proceeds at once by the laws of nature and the intentions of culture," according to Marshall Sahlins in *Culture and Practical Reason*. Sahlins seems to be following a reasoning similar to that of Condominas, stressing the symbolic significance of production in social life. But Sahlins also raises new questions concerning the relationship between symbolic structures and the logic of production, which are crucial for our analysis.

Sahlins is arguing against materialist or naturalistic theories of culture, for which "culture is organized in the final analysis by the material nature of things." From this perspective, the symbolic logic of culture is "subordinated to the instrumental, within production and therefore throughout society." But according to Sahlins, "there is no material logic apart from the practical interest, and the practical interest of men in production is symbolically constituted." The symbolic logic of culture is not a mere reflection or commentary on material-productive relationships, because "the material forces taken by themselves are lifeless" and acquire form and meaning only within the context of a symbolic system.[14] These points are well taken, and the reader who wishes to follow the complete exposition may be referred to *Culture and Practical Reason*.

But if we accept the argument that productive systems embody a cultural or symbolic logic, new questions appear when we move from theory to ethnography. The problem is a variant of the "excess of meaning" argument, which has often surfaced in cultural analysis. Simply put, the question is the relationship between symbolic systems, such as the agricultural rites of the water temples, and productive relationships. What is the match between practices and rites? Obviously, agricultural rites do not serve only to define productive relations, and Sahlins does not claim that material relations are the tertium quid of symbolic systems. But how are we to interpret the relationship between them?

Consider a simple ritual act, such as a farmer pouring a vial of holy water into his fields when the rice begins to flower, while he speaks a mantra naming half a dozen deities. What is the cultural logic or symbolic meaning of this act? Does the ritual define the meaning of the flowering of the rice, or the farmer's intentions?

There are several obvious solutions to this problem. We might choose to try to explicate the farmer's intentions or to trace the direct symbolic referents of the ritual. But these solutions—or others we might propose—lose coherence as soon as we accept the principle of the multivocality of ritual symbolism. The problem is magnified when we confront the true complexity of both the ritual and productive systems, for the productive system is not a single field but a vast engineered landscape of rice terraces and irrigation systems, of markets and market shrines, irrigation tunnel builders, and threshing societies. And the symbolic system includes an even more dauntingly complex system of rites, whose symbolic referents include not only the fields and flowers but more immaterial or transcendental concepts.

The multivocality of symbols and the lack of strict boundaries to the symbolism of material production are fundamental obstacles to a structuralist analysis. Rather than postulating a totalizing cultural logic, a perfect link between symbolic systems and material practices, the task becomes a search for relationships, which can only be discovered by tracing the logic of particular symbols and practices. But what kinds of relationships ought we to look for? Does *erga* have intrinsic symbolic significance?

There is, of course, one theorist for whom the answer to this question is a clear affirmation. The German translation of *erga* is *Arbeit*, "work" or "labor." For Marx, *Arbeit* is "a condition of human existence that is independent of all forms of society, a perpetual necessity of nature in order to mediate the material exchange between man and nature."[15] Marx's analysis of labor provides a frame of reference for an analysis of *erga* in Bali and at the same time situates the Balinese materials within the context of classical social theory, for as Eric Wolf observes, "It has been said, with reason, that the social sciences constitute one long dialogue with the ghost of Marx."[16]

Fortunately, our present concern is not with the whole corpus of Marx's writings but only with his theory of the symbolic meaning of labor. This is a subject that Marx often addressed in passages that remain remarkably consistent from his early writings to the "mature Marx" of the *Grundrisse* and *Capital*. For Marx, labor is "above all a process between man and nature, a process in which man through his own actions mediates, regulates and controls his material exchange with nature."[17] This insight was the basis of Marx's concept of a "mode of production" *(Weisen der Produktion)*, which he defined as the "production of man through human labor . . . so that nature as it develops in industry, even if in alienated form, is true anthropological nature."[18] The natural world is the stage on which human history is enacted and also the storehouse of raw materials that society reshapes into a "humanized nature."[19] The argument is neatly summarized by Jürgen Habermas:

> Only in its process of production does the species first posit itself as a social subject. Production, that activity which Marx apostrophizes as continuous sensuous labor and production, gives rise simultaneously to the specific formations of nature with which the social subject finds itself confronted, and

the forces of production that put the subject in a position to transform historically given nature in its turn, thereby forming its own identity.[20]

Thus for Marx, each succeeding generation acquires its concept of society through an awareness of historical process by observing the physical evidence of the labors of its predecessors. "It is as clear as noon-day," according to Marx, "that man, by his industry, changes the forms of materials furnished by Nature, in such a way as to make them useful to him."[21] External nature *(sinnliche Aussenwelt)*, or nature untouched by human society, exists today "nowhere except perhaps on a few Australian coral islands."[22] In reality, "nature" is the countryside of a civilization at a given epoch.[23] As Anthony Giddens explains, "In Marx, nature appears above all as the medium of the realisation of human social development. . . . Marx emphasizes that social development must be examined in terms of an active interplay between human beings and their material environment."[24]

Thus time becomes the medium through which societies define themselves, and nature the visible record of historical development. Like his contemporaries, what Marx saw in nature was evolution—a continuous linear process of growth. For Marx, the evolutionary progress of society was a scientific reality, which could be read from the social landscape just as Lyell could read geological history from the stratigraphy of Scotland.[25] Society was to be explained, not as the product of a fixed and unchanging human nature but as the end-product of a sequence of historical phases. Hence the importance of the distinction between historical societies, in which time means linear progress, and static cultures, where time is cyclical or even "reversible." Giddens summarizes: "By 'historicity' is meant a definite kind of time-consciousness, namely that human social energies can be actively controlled to promote progressive social change in a 'linear' fashion across time. This stands in strict contrast to what Lévi-Strauss calls 'reversible' time, characteristic of 'cold cultures.' "[26]

This argument leads to a seeming paradox, however, when we consider the Balinese case. On the one hand, there could scarcely be a better example of Marx's "humanized nature" than the engineered landscape of Balinese rice terraces. Although the gardens of Condominas's Mnong farmers are swallowed up by the forest in a year or two, the farmers of Bali look out on a landscape that has taken shape over the centuries through the carefully directed labor of generations of their predecessors. But on the other hand, the images of society that the Balinese see in their terraced valleys do not reflect the progressive linear order that Marx understood as "history." The Balinese have devised several mathematically sophisticated systems of time-reckoning that involve several different calendars that track both social and natural cycles. But what appears to be missing from the Balinese representation of time is the Marxist (or modernist) conception of society as undergoing linear progressive growth. Instead, Balinese time-reckoning systems provide tools to record the duration of natural cycles, such as the lunar synodic period or the growth of a rice plant from germination to flowering. The Balinese, one might say, have a biological view of time, in contrast to an industrial one.[27]

Marx's concept of linear progress emerged in the context of the discovery of geological time and the techniques of stratigraphy in the nineteenth century. Just as each geological age laid down new deposits, so each stage of human society left its traces in the rubble of the past. Industrial society was simply the latest stratum, Lamarck's "spearpoint of evolution," the most recent phase in the evolution of life on earth. Marx's concept of linear historical time was essentially a projection into the future of a Lamarckian view of developmental change. Nature was at once a museum of the past, and a storehouse of raw materials to be fashioned by human industry.

But a nonindustrial society that depends for its very existence on managing the natural productivity of the landscape might be expected to have quite a different view of nature. For the Balinese, virtually the whole of nature is a perpetual resource, not merely a museum of the past. The productivity of nature, not industry, is the basic social resource. In such a world, the relationship between society and nature is not stratigraphic but interdependent. Although Balinese society depends upon the productivity of the rice terraces, the reverse is also true: the terraces are a social creation, an artificially constructed ecosystem, sustained by continuous human management.

It is possible, of course, to lump the Balinese with the Mnong Gar, as "cold" or static societies whose concepts of nature are based on the simple rhythms of the agricultural year rather than the awareness of historical progress. Yet there are fundamental differences between them. As Condominas shows, for a Mnong Gar village each new year is like the last. The pattern of shifting cultivation is endlessly repeated and does not lead to cumulative changes in either the forest or the village. Each new generation of farmers confronts the forest anew.

Balinese farmers, in contrast, labor on terraces and irrigation works inherited from their predecessors. In the vocabulary of Marxist theory, these engineered structures do not represent "nature" but the "congealed labor" of prior generations of farmers. Each new year is not identical to the last, for over the course of many generations the primeval landscape of forested hillsides has been transformed into a productive system of terraces, tunnels, and irrigation systems. Further, the requirements of managing this engineered landscape shape social relationships for each new generation. As we will see in this book, the need for effective cooperation in the management of water links thousands of farmers in hierarchies of productive relationships that span entire watersheds.

Yet these productive relationships are simply invisible from within the horizons of classical Marxism. The distinguishing characteristic of Asian villages, according to Marx, is the absence of change. As Marx wrote in *Capital*, "The simplicity of the organization for production in these self-sufficing communities that constantly reproduce themselves in the same form, and when accidentally destroyed spring up again on the spot and with the same name—this simplicity supplies the key to the secret of the unchangeableness of Asiatic societies."[28]

In a letter to Engels, Marx actually referred to Bali as an example of the "stationary character of this part of Asia."[29] Marx's analysis was based on the idea that traditional Asian societies were divided into "villages . . . each of which possessed a completely separate organization and formed a little world in itself." Marx commented, "I do not think anyone could imagine a more solid foundation for stagnant Asiatic despotism." In India, these "stereotyped primitive forms" were broken up by British imperialism, but "in Bali, an island off the east coast of Java, this Hindoo organization, together with Hindoo religion, is still intact."[30]

Marx, of course, was not the first social theorist to emphasize the contrast between the timeless East and the progressive West. In his *Lectures on the Philosophy of History*, Hegel described the Orient as "a phenomenon antique as well as modern; one which has remained stationary and fixed."[31] Whereas Hegel merely commented on the unhistorical nature of Asiatic society, Marx attempted to provide an explanation. This explanation was based on two premises. First, Marx drew attention to the static and undialectical nature of farmer's labor. As the Marxist scholar Avineri notes, for Marx "history means man's process of changing his environment; where there is no change, there is no history."[32]

Second, Marx pointed to the concentration of power in the state, based on the control of irrigation, "This prime necessity of an economical and common use of water . . . necessitated in the Orient . . . the centralizing power of Government."[33] The result of this concentration of power in the state, coupled with the changelessness of village life, was a society lacking the internal dynamics to create historical change. From this analysis follows Marx's celebrated conclusion that European colonialism was the means by which Asiatic societies entered history. With colonialism came plantations, wage labor, the breakdown of the sealed and changeless village society. History begins when the labor process starts to shape new social relationships. Or as Avineri concludes, "Since Oriental society does not develop internally, it cannot evolve toward capitalism through the dialectics of internal change, [so Marx] necessarily arrives at the position of having to endorse European colonial expansion as a brutal but necessary step."[34]

Marx's analysis rests on two premises: the power-centralizing effects of hydraulic irrigation and the unique failure of agricultural labor to create productive relationships that extend beyond the boundaries of the village. As I shall try to show in this book, both premises are challenged in Bali by the existence of a hierarchical system of water management controlled by farmers. The issue here is not merely that Marx failed to accurately describe the complexities of irrigation management in Asia, which is neither surprising nor particularly significant. Instead, the Balinese case shows us that agricultural labor can build up complex structures of productive relationships in ways unforeseen by Marx.

These structures of productive relationships are the subject of this book. To investigate them, we will be obliged to tack back and forth between different levels of the system: from ritual symbolism to social practices; from the imagery of agricultural deities to quarrels between villages. Yet the concept of productive relationships as *systematic* is not merely a rhetorical device or the author's invention: I learned this perspective from the priests of the Temple of the Crater Lake. Thousands of farmers come to this temple each year to seek assistance with agricultural rituals and also with practical questions about water rights and irrigation management. The priests described their role to me with diagrams of rivers and irrigation networks, with mandalas of power and interlocking ritual cycles. It is this integrated system of ritualized ecological management that I hope to convey in this book, both in terms of its own internal dynamics, and its relationship to the wider society.

PLAN OF THE BOOK

The book is organized around four themes or topics. The first is the relationship between the traditional system of water temples and the irrigation bureaucracies implanted by the Dutch after their conquest of Bali in the nineteenth century. A great deal of what we know about water temples comes from the colonial archives on Bali. But irrigation was not a neutral topic for colonial authors, and indeed it played an important role in Dutch concepts of sovereignty and colonial rule. The physical reconstruction of Balinese irrigation works was accompanied by a symbolic reconstruction of royal irrigation management in the journals of colonial scholarship. The symbolic reconstruction of Balinese irrigation by the Dutch is a vivid example of what has been called the "invention of tradition."[35] There are, in particular, interesting parallels between the colonial reconstruction of Balinese society and the reformation of kingship in

South India by the British, as recently analyzed by N. B. Dirks.[36] Although my account is mostly based on research in the Dutch archives, I also draw on the recent work of H. Schulte Nordholt and C. Geertz on Balinese kingship and J. Rush on the colonial opium monopoly.[37] As Ann Stohler recently observed, colonial capitalism "by turns destroyed, preserved, and froze traditional relations of power and production, and as frequently reinvented and conjured them up."[38] In this case, we must be concerned not only with what was created by colonial rule but also with what was effaced or submerged.

Second, there is the question of the dynamics of power in the water temple system, more particularly, the relationship between the social and technical aspects of terrace management. From an ethnographic point of view, this is the heart of the book, the result of nearly two years of fieldwork with farmers, temple priests, and irrigation engineers. For the technical aspects of the role of temples in irrigation and terrace ecology, my evidence is based on a collaborative investigation I have carried out since 1987 with Dr. James Kremer, a systems ecologist. Appendix B describes Kremer's simulation model of Balinese irrigation systems, which I draw from to analyze the ecological functions of water temple networks.

With regard to the social and ritual dimensions of water temples, I hope to add a further dimension to Clifford Geertz's analysis of agricultural rituals in *Negara: The Balinese Theatre State in the Nineteenth Century.* In Bali, Geertz wrote, "A complex ecological order was both reflected in and shaped by an equally complex ritual order, which at once grew out of it and was imposed upon it."[39] Geertz emphasized the performative functions of ritual, particularly the timing of the ceremonies of the rice cult, which he saw as "symbolically linked to cultivation in a way that locks the pace of that cultivation into a firm, explicit rhythm." While acknowledging (and I hope, enriching) Geertz's analysis of the performative significance of agricultural rites, my major emphasis is on another dimension of ritual symbolism, which might be called sociogenic: the ability of ritual to bring forth, define, and empower social relationships in the context of the productive process.

My analysis of the sociogenic aspects of temple rituals picks up themes from many recent studies of ritual and society. In particular, there appear to be close parallels between the world of the water temples and that of mountain villages in eastern Java as described in Robert Hefner's recent book *Hindu Javanese: Tengger Tradition and Islam.* Shared themes include the symbolism of mountains and lowlands, the ritual preoccupation with fertility and the flow of water, mandala ritual classification, and the construction of priestly authority. I have also drawn from Judith and Alton Becker's ideas about the cultural construction of time and much recent work on Balinese ritual including Hobart, Guermonprez, Vickers, Stuart-Fox, Forge, Schulte Nordholt, Schaareman, Emigh, Duff Cooper, Howe, Hinzler, and Boon, as well as the classic works of Wirz, Korn, Goris, Grader, Hooykaas, Pigeaud, Moertono, van der Meij, Moojen, Zoetmulder and Liefrinck; along with recent studies of water temples by Balinese scholars including Ngurah Bagus, Putu Budiastra, and Sutawan.

A third theme is the relationship between the representation of power in the rituals of water temples and the royal cult of divine kingship. At the pinnacle of the water temple system, the Temple of the Crater Lake claims powers that intersect in various ways with the powers of kingship. Many scholars since Durkheim have shown that ritual reflects the social order. But I shall try to show that different ritual systems within a single society may construct competing images of the social universe. For this analysis, I draw primarily from my own fieldwork and the Dutch and Balinese archives.

Fourth, we return to the question of the contest of rationalities between water temples and the state, a contest brought to a head by the development plans of international agencies to "modernize" Balinese agriculture. Here I draw on the recent literature on the social and ecological effects of the Green Revolution, notably Zurbuchen and Poffenberger's analysis of the Green Revolution in Bali along with the work of Balinese scholars and administrators such as Jelantik Sushila and Nyoman Sutawan. This modern conflict has its origins in the colonial period, when the instrumental logic of Western bureaucracies was first brought into juxtaposition with the social and ecological constructions of the water temples.

The idea of a historical contest between modes of rationality I borrow from Foucault, who advises the human sciences to abandon Habermas's goal of a universal standard of rationality and "limit the sense of the word 'rationalisation' to an instrumental and relative use . . . and to see how forms of rationalisation become embodied in practices, or systems of practices."[40]

It is this contest with which the book begins.

CHAPTER ONE

"Income to Which No Tears Are Attached"

> Now the kingdoms have been defeated, fated by
> the All-Powerful.
> There was a sign, the palace of the rajah of
> Badung,
> at the temple of Suaragiri was inundated by rains.
> The shrine collapsed, and the place of the gods at
> Uluwatu
> likewise was destroyed by a thunderbolt.
> The Hall of Audience at the palace of Pemetjutan,
> blown apart by the winds.
> The beautiful beringan tree of Tabanan enveloped
> in spider's webs,
> so that it turned white, a sign of great danger.
> *(Ida Pedanda Ngurah of Mengwi,*
> *Bhuwana winasa, 1918)*

IN THE YEAR 1938, on the date the Balinese call *Galungan* when the spirits of the ancestors are believed to descend into the temples, an unprecedented ceremony took place at the supreme temple of Besakih, under the auspices of the colonial government. Eight Balinese aristocrats, draped with Dutch medals and Balinese gold, were consecrated as rulers (*Zelfbestuurder*) of the territories that the Dutch recognized as the eight former kingdoms of precolonial Bali. Balinese kingship, which had been obliterated by naval gunfire a generation earlier, was thus reconstituted in a ceremony that mingled the ritual paraphernalia of Balinese kingship and high colonial office. The cosmological significance of this event for the Dutch officials who organized it is signaled by their choice of time and place. Nineteenth-century Balinese kings were not consecrated at Besakih, or in any temple, but in their own palaces. But the Balinese believe that on the feast of Galungan, the supreme gods and the deified spirits of ancient kings descend to the temple of Besakih. The spirits that had guided Bali in the past were thus called on to witness the restoration of an enlightened monarchy. It was a moment of profound self-definition for the colonial civil service, carried out in the invisible presence of the glorious kings of ancient Bali. The civil service itself was not left out of the ceremony, for above each *Zelfbestuurder* was placed a Dutch officer, a *controleur*, whose task was to help the kings gently guide their realms into the twentieth century. Balinese sovereignty, having once been destroyed, was to be revived as a colonial fetish.

The ethnography of Bali, like that of every conquered people, begins not with the Balinese but with the written observations of colonial administrators. For these men, the act of writing about Balinese society was inevitably an act of self-definition. The Dutch had assumed complete control and with it, complete responsibility—the power to reshape any aspect of Balinese life. Thus, "scholarly" investigations into the nature of the Balinese caste system led to new policies that exempted high-caste aristocrats from compulsory labor service. The study of village law led to a new system of magistrates. And to write about kingship was inevitably to adopt an attitude towards the sovereignty of the Dutch. For men whose "paternal" authority was unbounded, who could create and enforce regulations concerning any aspect of Balinese life, there were no neutral topics, no issues outside the scope of colonial authority.

For reasons that will soon become apparent, the Balinese system of irrigation management quickly became a favorite topic for colonial authors. Because irrigated rice terraces were the economic foundation of Balinese kingdoms, when these kingdoms became Dutch possessions it was necessary for the colonial government to define a role for itself with respect to irrigation. The study of irrigation could not fail to be rewarding, because any improvements to the existing irrigation systems would simultaneously generate increased government revenue from agricultural taxes and make a lasting contribution to social welfare. Undoubtedly the Dutch, whose own country was a triumph of hydraulic engineering, could do a better job with irrigation than the former kings of Bali.

The attractions of irrigation as a topic for colonial authors were further enhanced by the unspoken comparison with the second major source of government revenues—opium. The imposition of a government opium monopoly on Bali was a principal motivation for the final attacks on the Balinese kings. And when the last king had been defeated, it was opium, not rice, that provided the larger share of the government's revenues from Bali. But on the subject of opium the journals of colonial scholarship are silent.

To understand why this should be so, it is necessary to understand the intended relationship between scholarly investigations and colonial policy at the time of the Dutch conquest of Bali. Beginning in the 1880s, the "*Adat* law" school of scholar-administrators came to prominence in the colonial service. The *Adat* law school taught that field officers should acquire a professional competence in native languages and *volkenkunde* (what we would now call ethnography), to equip them to undertake studies of Indonesian societies that would provide a firm foundation for colonial policy.[1] Field officers were encouraged to publish the results of their investigations in scholarly journals, where they would be subjected to the rigorous tests of professional scholarship. Irrigation was a subject admirably suited to this type of investigation—a better understanding could be translated immediately into more effective policies. In this way, it could be shown that colonial rule meant progress: steady improvements in the economic foundations of Balinese society. But such a case could hardly be made for the other major source of government revenues, the sale of millions of guilders' worth of opium to the Balinese. As W. F. Wertheim, a prominent Dutch historian and former colonial civil servant, wrote in a foreword to a recent study of opium in the Dutch colonies, "At the turn of the century, hardly had a colonial war ended before the first building would go up in the conquered territory—the office of the government opium monopoly!"[2] But on the subject of opium, as distinct from irrigation, the journals and archives of colonial scholarship are silent.

The Dutch archives provide endless quantities of descriptive material on Balinese irrigation systems from the days when independent kingdoms still existed on Bali. But to understand what colonial administrators in Bali chose to report, it is necessary to understand the larger significance of irrigation for the civil service. And so our story really begins with the arrival of the Dutch.

THE CONQUEST

Toward the middle of the nineteenth century, Dutch imperialism began to evolve from a mercantilist to an imperial-annexationist phase. The "native states" of the Indies put up what resistance they could, and several of the worst colonial wars were fought in Bali. In 1846, the Dutch launched the largest military expedition they had yet dispatched against any of the "native states" to conquer north Bali. The failure of this expedition led to a second in 1848 and an even larger one in 1849.[3] The Third Expedition did succeed in conquering north Bali, although at heavy cost. But the invasion of the southern kingdoms began to founder. Shortly after petitioning Batavia for reinforcements, the supreme commander of the Dutch forces was killed. When reinforcements finally arrived, the new commander declined to press the attack and contented himself with a series of treaties with the "sovereign kingdoms" of Bali: Klungkung, Gianyar, Bangli, Tabanan, Karangasem, and Djembrana. The key agreement was signed with the ruler of Klungkung, whom the Dutch recognized as the *emperor* of Bali. In return for pledges not to enter into agreements with other "white men," to refrain from interference with Dutch shipping, to provide assistance to shipwrecks, and to allow Dutch representatives to remain permanently on the island, the Dutch promised not to "interfere with the governance of the Emperor," "The Government of the Dutch Indies states that so long as the Emperor in the lands of Klungkung complies with the above agreements, the Government shall not in any way attempt to establish itself in this land or interfere with the governance of the Emperor."[4]

But despite these assurances, having established themselves in the north of the island, the Dutch searched for ways to extend their power over the southern kingdoms. A Dutch controleur was placed in charge of the administration of North Bali in 1855. For a few decades, although the Dutch made no further attempts at territorial conquests, strategies for completing the conquest of the island formed the chief topic of the administrative correspondence between the controleur of north Bali and his superiors in Batavia.[5] In the 1880s, a new phase of imperial expansion began with the creation of a residency for Bali and Lombok. Lombok is an island to the east of Bali, which was conquered by the east Balinese kingdom of Karangasem in the eighteenth century and subsequently ruled by the Balinese princes of Karangasem. In 1894, the Dutch Resident persuaded his superiors to embark on an invasion of Lombok.

As it was intended to do, the invasion of Lombok provided a dress rehearsal for the conquest of the kingdoms of south Bali. In November, a large Dutch force landed on the beaches of south Lombok. But the expedition met unexpectedly determined resistance and lost so many casualties that the army commander, General Vetter, sought permission to return to Batavia. Instead, he was sent reinforcements and ordered to attack. On November 18, 1894, he destroyed the main palace of Cakranegara, suffering 166 casualties among his own men and killing approximately two thousand Balinese. The palace strong rooms yielded a fortune in treasure—230 kilograms of gold, 7,299 kilograms of silver, and three cases of jewels and ornaments, which were shipped back to Batavia.[6] The king survived the destruction of his palace but died in exile six months later.[7]

With the fall of the Balinese princes of Lombok, the east Balinese kingdom of Karangasem also passed into Dutch control. Soon two more of the southern Balinese kingdoms, Bangli and Gianyar, signed treaties by which they acquiesced to Dutch imperial sovereignty. But three of the Balinese kingdoms remained defiant: Badung, Tabanan, and Klungkung. In 1904, J. B. van Heutz became governor general of the Dutch East Indies, determined to complete the conquest of the last remaining native states. Within a few months, Van Heutz appointed a new Resident for Bali and Lombok. In his memoirs, the new Resident describes his first interview with the governor general, who led him to a map of Bali and "running his hand across the principalities of South Bali said no more than 'this all has to be changed.' "[8]

In a matter of months, a military expedition was assembled to complete the conquest of Bali.[9] It seemed possible that a mere show of force would compel the surrender of the Balinese kings, who could not hope to prevail against a modern army. War correspondents from the major Dutch newspapers joined the expedition to record the inevitable triumph of a force that included battalions of infantry, batteries of field artillery, and even a detachment of cavalry.

After a short sail from Surabaya, the Dutch warships carrying the expeditionary force positioned themselves off the southern coast of Bali and began to fire explosive projectiles into the royal palaces. But the Balinese kings remained defiant, choosing to transform their defeat into a spectacle, the final act of the last great Balinese dynastic chronicle. When the army marched inland and reached the gates of the burning palaces of Badung, they found themselves facing the entire court, dressed in their most elegant garments and armed with swords and lances. Balinese princesses hurled their jewels at the Dutch soldiers and demanded to be shot. The king of Denpasar was seen to assume the posture of semadi meditation before he was struck by rifle fire. According to a Balinese chronicle, the ladies of the court "advanced like white ants, but the bullets of their enemies were like fire, so as they came forward and fell, their bodies piled up, a mountain of corpses in a sea of blood." The Dutch officer in charge of the cavalry reported that "the wives of the rajah bent over his corpse, and many wounded had dragged themselves to him to cover him. His body was buried under bodies, and out of this mass here and there gilded points of spears protruded."[10]

With the exception of a few women who were wounded but survived, the entire court was killed and the palace burned to the ground. In the afternoon, the same drama unfolded at the neighboring palace of Pamatjutan. The scene was one which even hardened colonial infantry could hardly stomach. According to the memoirs of the Dutch cavalry commander, "After the expedition, when the plan was proposed to put small memorials on those places where there had been massacres, this idea as far as I could see was greeted with sympathy by the army."[11]

But the worst was yet to come. A few weeks after the fall of Badung, the Dutch army marched on Tabanan, a prosperous kingdom to the west. The king of Tabanan chose not to sacrifice his army in a suicidal attack but came to treat with the Dutch himself. But the Dutch took him prisoner and demanded an unconditional surrender. That night, the king cut his own throat with a blunt knife, and the crown prince took poison.[12] Of the eight sovereign states of mid-nineteenth century Bali, only Klungkung was left. On April 28, 1908, the palace of Klungkung—the largest, oldest, and most sacred of all Balinese palaces—was blown to rubble by Dutch artillery, and the last king and his entire court chose death rather than surrender.

OPIUM AND RICE

The defeat of the Balinese kings gave the Dutch unchallenged mastery of the island; the era of clever plots and invasions was over. On May 4, 1908, when the first reports of the fall of Klungkung began to come in, a leading newspaper in Batavia editorialized, "It seems clear to us that the government will switch over to direct government of the whole of Bali."[13]

As the civil service took possession of Bali, several tasks loomed large. The first, of course, was to assure the profitability of colonial rule. The bankruptcy and collapse of the Netherlands East India Company at the close of the eighteenth century made frugality a paramount virtue in subsequent colonial administrations. New colonial governments were expected not only to pay for themselves but to generate profits for Batavia. In Bali, from the time of their earliest conquests, the Dutch obtained nearly all of their revenue from two sources: opium and rice. To understand what the Dutch had to say about the apparently innocuous topic of rice, one needs to be aware of what they did not say about opium.

In the Balinese kingdoms of North Bali ruled by the Dutch in the nineteenth century, the income from taxes on opium amounted to approximately two-thirds of the total annual revenues, with taxes on rice accounting for most of the remainder.[14] Important as the opium revenues were, they were soon to play an even greater role in colonial policy. In 1894, the year the Dutch invaded Lombok, the colonial minister of finance suggested a new plan designed to greatly increase government revenues from opium throughout the empire. Formerly, opium was sold by private traders called *opiumpachters,* and the government obtained revenues by taxing opium imports. The finance minister proposed that the government put the opiumpachters out of business and assume direct control over all aspects of the opium trade as a government monopoly. This *opiumregie* (government opium monopoly) was tried in Madura in 1894, yielding revenues to the government of 17,500,000 guilders. In the following year, the opium monopoly was extended to all Dutch possessions. The profits were immense: by 1914, the opium monopoly had generated total revenues amounting to nearly half a billion guilders.[15]

It is clear from the internal correspondence of senior Dutch officials that in the first decade of the twentieth century extending the opium monopoly to each of the newly conquered Balinese kingdoms and ultimately to the whole island was a principal goal of the colonial government. In a secret report to the governor general written from his residency in Singaraja (North Bali) on December 26, 1907, De Bruyn Kops wrote, "I think it is legitimate to use force if necessary—and be assured that only in the most necessary case will weapons be used—to persist with the installation of the opium monopoly on the island of Bali."[16]

The complete plan for Bali, drawn up by the chief inspector for the opium monopoly in Batavia and forwarded to the governor general on January 13, 1908, called for the sale of government opium over the whole of Bali. Packaged opium would be supplied from a central depot in Singaraja to 124 salesmen, under the supervision of 5 assistant collectors. Altogether, 127 permanent "points of sale" were to be established for the sale of opium in Balinese villages.[17]

The government attempted to impose the opium monopoly on Bali in the spring of 1908. As far as the major newspapers in Batavia were concerned, it was Balinese resistance to this plan that prompted the massacre of the court of Klungkung. Klungkung fell on April 28. A week later, as the first reports began to filter back, the *Bataviaasch Nieuwsblad* reported:

> At the establishing of the opium monopoly troops were sent without warning (into Klungkung) to look for clandestine opium. It was the advent of these troops which made the population go for its arms. This information seems in accord with the passage in our report from yesterday, which says that it is not so much the king himself who wants war as the population. . . . The role of the opium monopoly in this rebellion becomes even clearer when one learns that after the departure of our officer van Schauroth from Klungkung to the coast, all of the salesmen of the opium selling points were murdered.[18]

In the remainder of 1908, after the fall of Klungkung, the colonial government obtained revenues of Fl 273,000 from Bali. Soon afterwards, as the opium monopoly took root in Bali, the profits to the government became enormous. In 1911, the Dutch sold three and a half million guilders' worth of opium in Bali and Lombok.[19]

It will come as no surprise that the opium monopoly was not a favorite topic of colonial scholarship, particularly by government officials. In 1914, H. van Kol, an irrigation engineer, wrote bitterly about the government's attitude, "Anywhere the monetary interests of the government are involved or those of the European entrepreneurs who consider it bait for obtaining coolies, the damages of opium sales are often denied and attempts are made to excuse it because of the small amounts used."[20]

Critics like van Kol argued that in the long run opium was an economic as well as a moral disaster for the Dutch government and called for an end to the opium monopoly: "The loss of opium monies will be recompensed by the increasing prosperity of the population whose productive force will no longer be paralyzed, and the enormous amounts presently spent on this juice will be used for the purchase of necessities which will increase tax income. Moreover, this will be income to which no tears are attached."[21]

But the merits of opium compared to agriculture as sources of government revenue were not openly debated in the colonial literature. As W. F. Wertheim, a prominent Dutch historian and former colonial civil servant, recently observed, "One almost has the impression that since the turn of the century, there has been a taboo of silence on the subject of the politics of opium in the Netherlands Indies."[22]

Consider, then, the attractions of rice—in Bali, the second most valuable source of government income. The colonial archives overflow with observations, theories, and descriptions of irrigation and rice. Nearly all Balinese rice is grown in wet-rice paddies (*sawah*), which depend upon effective irrigation systems. As far as the Dutch were concerned, responsibility for the effective management of irrigation rested with the government. If Dutch engineers could improve the irrigation works, if Dutch officials could devise a more efficient managerial system, if taxes on rice lands could be spread more equitably, truly well-earned income would flow into the government's coffers, and Bali would prosper. How these ends might best be accomplished was a subject that attracted many authors from the ranks of the colonial civil service.

Van Kol was a liberal and an irrigation engineer by profession. But the structure of the colonial administration in Bali ensured that irrigation would become an important topic for virtually all Dutch officers. In each of the conquered kingdoms, the Dutch moved quickly to establish a new government that was grafted onto the existing political structure as much as possible to minimize administrative costs. In the princedoms that had chosen not to go to war with the Dutch, considerable local autonomy was preserved. But each realm was placed under the authority of a Dutch controleur. To do their jobs well, controleurs needed to become experts on what we would now call the ethnography of their little kingdoms. In these small agrarian states, the main productive activity was wet-rice cultivation. The controleurs and Residents accordingly were obliged to take a strong interest in land rights and systems of agricultural taxation.

Almost from the beginning, prudent officialdom could foresee that the question of government involvement in irrigation management could not long be postponed. Hence the question, What was the usual role of Balinese kingdoms in irrigation? The question arose soon after the troop ships of the victorious Third Expedition departed for Batavia, leaving the Colonial Service with the task of creating a new government for the conquered territories of North Bali.

KINGS AND TAXES

Following the conquest of Buleleng, a Dutch controleur was appointed to supervise the reorganization of the kingdom into a regency. The first controleur was van Bloemen Waanders, who established himself in Singaradja in 1855. A second controleur was appointed to the adjacent, sparsely populated territory of Djembrana in 1856. As soon as the political-military situation was stabilized, the controleurs turned their attention to the question of potential sources of revenue for the colonial government. The first step was to appropriate the revenues generated by the existing system of taxation, which was estimated at 12,650 Dutch guilders in 1859.[23] From the point of view of the colonial government, these revenues were absurdly small, and van Bloemen Waanders set about finding ways to increase them. The income from "trade licenses" was primarily generated by opium imports: for a small annual fee of 4,200 guilders, the king granted the right to control trade to a Chinese "harbormaster" and opium trader (opiumpachter). The colonial government decided to increase both the quantities of opium imported and the amount of the import tax.[24] By 1902, shortly before the invasion of the south, the government's annual income from the sale of opium in Buleleng was over one hundred thousand guilders.[25]

After opium, the second most promising source of revenue was agriculture. Van Bloemen Waanders initiated surveys of productive lands and soon began to levy new taxes on most agricultural products. At first, the intent of the land surveys seems to have been simply to provide information on which to base the new systems of taxation. But this soon led to the question of whether the government could substantially increase production by playing a more active role in agricultural affairs, particularly irrigation. Investigations were set in motion, and an energetic controleur named F. A. Liefrinck undertook a "survey of the economic situation in those areas under direct rule of the Dutch government during the last few years with the object of establishing a basis for a system of taxation."[26]

"For centuries," he wrote, "the inhabitants of Buleleng have spared no effort to convert the seawards-sloping ridges into fertile sawahs, the major obstacle being that the water needed for irrigation flowed in streams through the valleys often hundreds of feet below." According to Liefrinck, "the explanation of the amazingly high standard of rice cultivation in Bali is to be found in Montesquieu's conclusion that 'the yield of the soil depends less on its richness than on the degree of freedom enjoyed by those who till it.' " This seems at first an ironic sentiment for a colonial officer who played an important role in the violent overthrow of the independent kingdoms of Bali and Lombok.[27] But the legitimacy of the colonial government was enhanced by portraying the Balinese kings as decadent and ineffectual despots, whose replacement was in the best interests of the Balinese people. Liefrinck concluded that in traditional Balinese kingdoms, the king had little to do with the creation of irrigation systems.[28] Whatever influence the king had over irrigation was exerted through a royal official called the *sedahan agung*: "The sedahan agung is at the head of the administration concerned with the sawahs. In previous times he was more or less a royal major domo, for he controlled the stocks furnished by the sawah levies, and he had to have always on hand a sufficient supply not only of rice and kepengs (copper cash) but also of fruits and other foodstuffs as well as betel quids to meet the needs of the prince's household."[29]

Liefrinck paid close attention to the sedahan agung because the issue of the degree of royal control of irrigation appeared to hinge on the scope of his authority. The title itself (*sedahan agung*) provides a first clue as to his overall function. *Sedah* is the high Balinese term for betel nut, which is commonly the first refreshment offered to guests. *Agung* means simply "great" or "superior." Thus the *sedahan agung* is the "great provisioner," the one who ensures a prince's readiness to provide hospitality—or, as Liefrinck aptly says, a "royal major-domo." "In addition," says Liefrinck, "he was in charge of the royal ricefields and other royal lands, and he arranged the reception of ambassadors from other principalities and of all guests visiting the prince."[30]

As Liefrinck noted, for geographical reasons the rulers of Buleleng were in a position to exercise greater direct control over irrigation than most other Balinese kingdoms.[31] The kingdom of Buleleng consists of a very narrow strip of coastline, and "most of the rivers in Buleleng do not traverse the territories of any other principalities." In the rest of Bali, nearly all rivers used for irrigation pass through several sovereign or semisovereign principalities. Thus in southern Bali, no single ruler was in a position to exercise control over an entire watershed.[32] In fact, as Liefrinck noted, elsewhere the princes were often more likely to be destroyers than creators of irrigation systems:

> Where the rivers in Bali traverse the territories of different principalities disputes often arise over the use of the water. Moreover, it is customary in the frequent wars between the principalities for the rulers of the higher inland regions to divert the rivers supplying the ricefields nearer the coast or to block the streams at a given point and then release a flow of water that destroys all the dams on the river below that point. Incalculable damage has been caused by these stratagems, as in 1884 when the ruler of Bangli caused the failure of most of the crop in Gianyar in order to enforce his claim to the district of

Apuan. Only recently the inhabitants of Mengwi ruined much of the crop in Badoeng by this means.[33]

Liefrinck concluded that even in Buleleng most aspects of irrigation were not managed by the royal courts but at the local level by a unique Balinese institution, the *subak* association. There had been brief references to the *subak*s in earlier accounts from travelers and colonial officers, but this was the first major study that established the model of the *subak* system for colonial (and later) students of Bali. "The complexes of ricefields obtaining water from the one conduit or from the one branch of a conduit are called in Balinese *subak*, and the owners of the ricefields making up such a complex constitute a subak association, or *sekehe subak*. From the foregoing description it can be seen that the subak consists of a stretch of ground divided into allotments sharing a single system of irrigation and drainage."[34]

In describing the workings of the *subak* system, Liefrinck distinguishes between the secular and religious obligations of *subak* members. The secular obligations, he says, "can be said to derive from the common access to water from the subak conduit, for the most important features of the work performed collectively are the maintenance of the dams and conduits of the subak irrigation system and the patrolling of the conduits to safeguard against theft of water. The extent to which each individual member is obliged to participate in the collective labor is assessed according to the distribution of water in the subak."[35] This work includes (1) maintenance of the dam and conduits and the various installations; (2) inspection and patrolling of the conduits; (3) maintenance of roads and culverts; (4) policing the subak and assisting the *klian* (subak head); (5) construction and maintenance of buildings.

In addition, *subak* members might infrequently be called upon to perform labor for the ruler.[36] The *subak* was thus an institution separate from the village because the membership consisted of all the farmers who obtained their irrigation water from a common source, usually a single large canal. Someone who farmed lands in two irrigation areas belonged to two *subak*s. Liefrinck described the *subak*s as efficient, democratic organizations that managed irrigation more effectively in the absence of royal interference.

Liefrinck devoted considerable space to the religious aspects of the *subak* system, describing both water temples and *subak* rituals. He noted, for example, that "the building and maintenance of temples erected near dams is similarly shared by several subak associations when one dam provides water for several subaks."[37]

But his analysis presupposed that managerial control of irrigation was a secular matter, which rested with the *subak*s and, to a limited extent, with the *sedahan agung* on behalf of the ruler. Henceforth, the religious activities of the *subaks* remained outside the domain of irrigation planners. The activities of water temples were often noted by later colonial officials, as we will see in chapter 6. But the basic distinction between the practical and religious aspects of *subak* affairs that Liefrinck established was never subsequently challenged.

Liefrinck's analysis of the secular aspects of water control had direct policy implications: if the state had formerly managed the irrigation systems through the *sedahan agung*, then it would probably be necessary for the Dutch to increase their involvement in agricultural affairs. But Liefrinck's report suggested that there was no need for the colonial government to play an active role in irrigation or land management. The system functioned very well without direct government control. However, the rate of agricultural taxation could be significantly increased. By the end of the century, taxes on rice lands in Buleleng were worth Fl 150,000 per year to the colonial government.

FEUDALISM

The conquest of southern Bali put an end to the laissez-faire attitude of the colonial government towards irrigation in Bali. A greatly expanded colonial administration set about finding ways to boost revenues from Balinese agriculture. The policies adopted for Bali were first tried out on the neighboring island of Lombok, after the conquest in 1896. The Lombok campaign was much more costly than had been anticipated, and in the aftermath, the Dutch moved aggressively to seize all royal property "by right of conquest." "Royal lands" (*domeingrond*) in Lombok were seized outright, and all taxes formerly collected in the king's name were declared to be the property of the colonial government.

Ingela Gerdin has recently investigated the origins of this policy of land annexation in Lombok, which provided the initial basis for colonial land policy in the conquered kingdoms of South Bali. As her analysis shows, even at this early stage, the need for a legal basis for colonial land policy put the officials in the field in an awkward bind. On the one hand, as a practical matter, they needed to understand the existing system of taxation and land rights. But both the practical and the legal requirements of creating a new administration involved reinterpreting these rights in terms of a workable administrative system, with clearly defined ownership and tax obligations.[38] When the Dutch invaded South Bali in 1906, the apparently simple task of identifying "royal lands" and the sources of royal tax revenues proved unexpectedly complicated. To begin with, the notion of discrete territorial *kingdoms* proved to be illusory, as noted in this 1924 report:

> The territory of the present administrative district of Badoeng before the year 1906 was mostly occupied by the kingdoms of Badoeng and Mengwi. The kingdom of Badoeng in turn consisted of three power rings: Denpasar, Pamatjutan and Kesiman. These were areas without special borders, that ran into each other, and at the head of each there was a Tjokorde (prince). The Tjokorde of Pemetjoetan was in lineage and respect the most important of the three, but he and his colleague the Tjokorde of Kesiman were under the supremacy of the Tjokorde of Denpasar, who was generally looked upon as the king of Badoeng.[39]

In other words, on closer inspection the supposed *kingdom* of Badoeng disintegrated into three amorphous "power rings" (*gezagskringen*), "areas without special borders, that ran into each other." Any solution would be arbitrary, so the Dutch took advantage of the situation and appropriated as much land belonging to all three ruling houses as possible.[40]

But what of the remaining productive lands? The colonial service chose to describe these lands in the terminology of European feudalism as royal *appanages*. According to this conception, the holders of "appanage lands" were feudal lords bound to pay taxes of one sort or another to their king. Based on this imaginary political structure, the Dutch proceeded to divide Balinese rice lands into two categories: land belonging to the king and lands held by his feudal retainers. Permanent fixed boundaries were established by the government land survey. Furthermore, once the territorial boundaries had been mapped and recorded, the same irrigation districts that passed taxes up the administrative hierarchy could be used to carry managerial decisions downwards. Quite soon after the land surveys, the Dutch began to experiment with taking control of the irrigation systems in this way.

And so, half a dozen feudal kingdoms came into existence in South Bali. According to the fiction adopted by the Colonial Service, each of these kingdoms had formerly been ruled by a king-regent, supported by feudal lords with their own vassals and appanages, with clearly defined territorial boundaries. Because the new classification of land laws and of taxation, once instituted, became the political reality, in time the regencies did indeed begin to resemble the idealized feudal principalities on which the model was based. It is not surprising that later colonial officers often became quite muddled about which arrangements were "old Balinese custom" and which were legal fictions. The very heart of the confusion lay in the question of agricultural taxes because the legitimacy of Dutch claims depended on projecting the feudal-kingdom model into the precolonial past. The debate over whether Balinese irrigation was centralized or decentralized, which has continued to the present, owes its origins to this historical legerdemain, for the Dutch did their best to reorganize Balinese irrigation as a centralized, territorially organized administrative system managed by the *sedahan agungs*. The legitimacy of government *rights* to land and agricultural taxes depended on the fiction that the Dutch were reestablishing the sovereign rights of the rulers of Bali.

The heart of the new colonial irrigation and land policy was the reorganization of the *sawah*s into units called *pangloerahan*, territorial units created by the Dutch on the basis of the land surveys.[41] Each *pangloerahan* consisted of a number of *subak*s, and each *subak* was required to appoint an official called a *pekaseh*. The *pekaseh* "has to file full reports on his activities to the pangloerah in question, who if necessary consults further with the sedahan agung," according to a 1907 Dutch report.[42] In this way, the Dutch attempted to impose an hierarchical, territorial, and bureaucratic system of organization on the *subak*s of Badoeng, while still retaining many of the forms and titles of the precolonial past. The artificiality of the new system was occasionally commented upon by later colonial officials, as in this assistant resident's report for Badoeng written in 1937:

> The area was divided into 12 clearly marked and boundaried irrigation areas, which contained the subaks that had a common conduit. The heads of these areas, the pangloerahs, were in charge of the following: equitable water sharing among the subaks; taking care of the waterworks; supervision of the collection of the sawah taxes; and acting as umpires when there were disputes among the people. *At the head of the sawah government, they put a sedahan agung, who at the same time was sub controleur of taxes. This job was unknown in the time of the kings* [emphasis mine].[43]

The system of management developed in Badung was extended to Klungkung soon after the conquest. The Resident of Bali wrote: "A division between irrigation personnel and government personnel is urgently required, so a division of irrigation areas under pangloerah (or sedahan) must be designed. The subaks must be united into larger units since too many pekasehs (subak heads) will make government supervision more difficult."[44]

Eventually, in all of the former kingdoms, a *sedahan agung* was placed in charge of the *pangloerahan*s, in an attempt to create a new centralized administrative system for irrigation.[45] The new system gave the Dutch outright ownership of the royal lands, and the right to collect taxes on all other irrigated lands. Government surveyors mapped out the boundaries of the new kingdoms, while political officers created an administrative structure for taxes and irrigation management.

The reorganization of the *subaks* into *pangloerahans* was coupled with an investigation into the "royal systems of taxation" prevailing before the conquest. The situation in Badoeng, which as the first regency in South Bali established the basic precedents for later administrations, was particularly troublesome. In Badoeng, the prime—indeed the only—candidate for the role of a royal system of taxation was something called the *soewinih*. In several ways, the *soewinih* seemed to be just what was needed, a royal tax on *appanage* lands. According to the reports of colonial officers, the *soewinih* was assessed only on appanage lands, on the basis of the quantities of irrigation water used, and was collected annually by the *sedahan agung*. It might, therefore, plausibly be described as a royal tax on irrigation water on the (feudal) appanages. But problems arose with this interpretation of the *soewinih*. First, there was a certain territorial confusion: "It was very seldom that all the djaba sawah owners were all living in a certain area and owed soewinih to one and the same lord. For instance the Tjokorde of Denpasar also counted soewinih payers among the inhabitants of Kesiman and Pamatjoetan, and the other way around, both of those Tjokordes had soewinih owed to them by people living in Denpasar."[46]

Moreover, it appeared that the *soewinih* usually did not go into the royal treasury but "was spent by the king mostly in offerings in water temples. Only where a king had given himself the trouble to construct water works was the *soewinih* paid to him, but used for offerings."[47] In the kingdom of Bangli, the *soewinih* was not given to the rajah "but to the foremost subak temples."[48] Altogether, the observations of colonial officials suggest that the *soewinih* was less a royal irrigation tax on appanage lands than a form of contribution to water temple festivals.[49] Indeed, at one point Van der Heijden describes the *soewinih* as a "counter-prestation for the use of the water that belongs to the gods."[50] But the civil service needed to see the *soewinih* in a different light, as a royal irrigation tax that could be appropriated by the colonial government. Thus Van der Heijden argued that the soewinih must formerly have been a more substantial source of revenue, which no longer fulfilled its proper purpose—maintenance of the irrigation system and, indirectly, the king's authority—because the kings had gradually relinquished control of taxation (the right to get *soewinih*) to family members and dependents. In this way, the institution of kingship had been weakened over the centuries. This theory had the desirable implication that the Dutch conquerors were simply restoring a strong centralized government to the degenerate "kingdom of Badoeng." In particular, the "revived" *soewinih* "royal irrigation tax" could be used to fund improvements in the irrigation system in the manner of the kings of old.

As evidence for this theory, Van der Heijden pointed to the sheer impressiveness of the irrigation systems: "But there are great difficulties associated with the construction and maintenance of regular sawah irrigation systems of this kind, of such a nature that is suspected they would not have begun to build them before the continuous spread of cultivation made it necessary to construct larger and more permanent irrigation works. It is sure that the larger dams came into existence through the influence and cooperation of the king, whose power only became more prominent in later centuries."[51]

Van der Heijden argued that the Balinese system of irrigation had originated at the village level. Gradually, the kings began to interest themselves in the construction of larger dams. The growth of centralized irrigation systems led to corresponding increases in the power of the rulers. Eventually, a process of decline was set in motion by the dispersal of the royal irrigation water tax (the *soewinih*) to the king's relatives, whose descendants developed rival power centers. The absence of historical evidence for this theory was awkward, but as an explanation of how things might have been, it provided the needed rationale for colonial policies. Not long afterwards, this thesis was articulated as a genuine historical explanation for the evolution of the Balinese state, by the leading twentieth-century Dutch ethnographer of Bali.

ENLIGHTENED MONARCHS

In 1932, a former controleur named V. E. Korn published an encyclopedic study of Balinese society entitled *Het Adatrecht van Bali*, which was immediately recognized as a landmark in Balinese studies. For Korn, the "great failing" of the Balinese state was "the lack of a powerful government over the whole realm." Inevitably, this was linked to the question of centralized control over irrigation. Korn summarized a dispute between two irrigation engineers, Groothof and Happé, on the question of the centralization of irrigation in the time of the kings:

> Although engineers Groothof and Happé agree on the sophistication of the Gianyar irrigation system of old, technically as well as administratively, they differ in opinion on the meaning of the big dam areas, pangloerahans, at the head of which there is an official called the pangloerah. Happé represents it as if . . . irrigation was instituted under the leadership of a royal agrarian employee, the pangloerah, who as the king's representative was invested with absolute power. . . . The pangloerah developed into the head of an irrigation

system, the "waterschap." Groothof does not speak of these "waterschaps" at all, and considers the pangloerah as merely a royal employee.[52]

Korn dismissed Happé's theory as a "fantasized creation of history." But although he saw irrigation as largely in the hands of the subak, he was prepared to believe that the kings constructed the largest irrigation works: "The royal interference is not to be regarded as the beginning of the whole system, but as the completion of an existing system of irrigation." That is, "in old Bali the irrigation system was a village matter . . . the popular societies (e.g., *subaks*), bound as they were by their borders, must have known a system of small irrigation. The king saw greater possibilities by the construction of greater irrigation works, by which the rivers in the plains gave the opportunity." For Korn, this helped to explain why small mountainous kingdoms such as Bangli had no irrigation taxes, no *sedahans*, and no apparent royal role in any aspect of irrigation, whereas in the coastal kingdoms, such as Badoeng, there were larger dams and supposed traces of a more active irrigation administration. Thus Korn concurred with Van der Heijden: the large dams must have been the work of powerful kings. The fact that *Badoeng* at the time of its fall was not a unified kingdom, but only three "power rings" ruled by sovereign princes, meant only that the irrigation system must have been built at some time in the past, when Badoeng was a stronger, unified kingdom. Despite Korn's cautionary notes, this hypothetical scenario was soon accepted as historical fact.[53]

Thus by the 1930s, the theory that more powerful irrigation-based kingdoms had existed in the past had become firmly embedded in the colonial discourse on the state. The search for such kingdoms became a central problem for Dutch scholarship in the years following the publication of Korn's monograph. The idea that Bali had once been ruled as a single glorious kingdom, which had gradually fallen apart and was now in its senescence, held great attractions for civil servants who saw themselves as having rescued Bali from decadent and irresponsible kings. The Dutch were encouraged in their search for powerful kings in the past by the many Balinese legends of glorious ancient kingdoms. With the decipherment of old Balinese script, it became possible for archaeologists to investigate the structure of ancient Balinese kingdoms dating from the eighth through the fourteenth centuries.[54] Unfortunately for the Dutch, the evidence uncovered by the inscriptions provided little support for the decline-from-greatness theory of Balinese kingship and no evidence for a centralized irrigation system in ancient Bali.[55]

The only well-documented case of a royal court playing a major role in irrigation is provided by the court of Mengwi, which was the most powerful kingdom in southern Bali for much of the nineteenth century. In a recent study, H. Schulte Nordholt links the rise to power of the Mengwi dynasty to the creation of a new dam:

> Of the first king of Mengwi it is said that he, in cooperation with the lord of Blayu, constructed a dam in the river Sungi, to the west of Blayu, and then expanded the sawah area around the desa of Mengwi. By so doing the village became situated right in the middle of a wide fertile sawah plain, where food for the royal center was grown. The allied lord of Blayu was in charge of guarding the dam. A not unimportant side effect was that the king, by constructing the dam near Blayu, could influence the water supply of the sawahs of Kaba-Kaba situated to the south. In the most extreme case he could even divert the river Sungi by which Kaba-kaba would become virtually dry.[56]

But as Schulte Nordholt also noted, "The king could not control all irrigation systems in the area in this way. A number of satellites had their own irrigation systems outside the king's reach. Examples of this are the puris (dynasties) of Penarungan and Kapal which got their water from a different river, the Penet, where they had their own dams. Also the line of Puri Sibang owned their own dam in the river Ayung."[57] As we will see in later chapters, most Balinese rivers support several dozen dams and irrigation systems. Yet even the king of Mengwi—for much of the nineteenth century, the richest and strongest Balinese ruler—effectively controlled only a single dam. Lesser princes, nominally subordinate to the king, in fact retained considerable autonomy in irrigation as in other domains. Thus in real Balinese principalities—as distinct from the imaginary kingdoms constructed by the colonial service—only fragments of irrigation systems came under the control of even the most powerful princes.

In 1938, after prolonged debate, the colonial government proceeded with the installation of Balinese princes as "self governors" (*Zelfbestuurder*) of the eight territories that the Dutch had tried so hard to redefine as former sovereign states. Set above each new ruler was a Dutch controleur and below him, a "Council of State" (*Rijksraad*). And so, the essence of Liefrinck's original policy was restored: the colonial government withdrew from most aspects of administration. The ritual by which the princes were installed as *Zelfbestuurder*s marks the end of the long Dutch quest for a proper Balinese king. Now, at last, each realm was to be a kingdom, each kingdom with its own proper king. The orderly structure that the archaeologists had been unable to discover at the beginning of Balinese history, the Resident would impose at its end. That the new monarchs would indeed be both powerful and enlightened could also be assured by the colonial service, which saw to it that members of the royal families learned Dutch and were encouraged to go to school in Java or in Holland. Moreover, the tax and land laws were so arranged that the ruling houses greatly increased their land-holdings.

In return for these privileges, the new monarchs had two responsibilities. The first was, of course, to ensure the smooth functioning of colonial administration. The second, less obviously but I believe indisputably, was to accept a certain role within the colonial imagination: the Dutch image of Balinese kingship would finally become tangible reality in the persons of these cultivated Dutch-speaking aristocrats. Henceforth, they were to preserve Bali as a museum of pre-Islamic high culture. As defenders of *Adat* law and religion, patrons of art, and enlightened managers of the village republics and the *subak*s, these fairy-tale kings would gently guide Bali into the modern age under the wise tutelage of their personal controleurs. In a letter written in 1940 to Korn, who had recently retired, Assistant Resident Cox wrote with satisfaction that "Young Bali develops very well, but fortunately Old Bali has things still under firm control."[58]

Eighteen months later, the Japanese arrived.

SOVEREIGNTY

Nineteenth-century Dutch officials found little evidence for centralized royal control over irrigation. But in the twentieth century, for reasons of its own, the colonial administration did its best to create an hydraulic bureaucracy and argued that in so doing they were merely restoring an ancient system that had fallen into decay during the nineteenth century. Colonial archaeologists searched for evidence that the spectacular terracing and irrigation works—"strips of silver in the green mountains"— were the work of ancient kings, which had been sadly neglected by the latter-day monarchs the Dutch had just overthrown. The *restoration* of a powerful irrigation bureaucracy would not only increase tax revenues, it would provide an attractive justification for colonial rule. When it became obvious that no centralized royal system of irrigation management existed in any of the conquered principalities, the Dutch did their best to invent one. Fragments of administrative structures drawn from different regions of Bali were reassembled into a new system of agricultural management, and the tax-collecting *sedahan*s were transformed into royal irrigation managers.

Both the administrative reorganization and the archaeological investigations were driven by the need to legitimize colonial policy, to provide a conservative civil service with a mission beyond the sale of opium and extraction of agricultural taxes. But both efforts ended in failure. The archaeologists found no evidence for centralized royal control of irrigation. And by the mid-1930s the government quietly abandoned most of its attempts to intervene directly in water management, confining its activities to replacing temporary weirs and irrigation works with permanent structures. Once again, the *sedahan*s were relegated to the role of agricultural tax collectors. But this history would hardly have made an appealing subject for an essay in the *Koloniale Studiën!*

As for the water temples, we have already seen that there is evidence that the Dutch were aware of the existence—and even some of the practical functions—of the temples associated with farming and water control. But it appears that once the temples had been pigeonholed as religious institutions, their practical functions became invisible. Although the colonial archives provide useful observations of the workings of the water temple system, the system itself was not detected because it rested on a system of power relations so ephemeral, from the point of view of a colonial administration, as to be imperceptible—"an external whisper, a beating of wings that one has difficulty in hearing in the serious matter of history."[59]

CHAPTER TWO

The Powers of Water

WE HAVE DONE, for the moment, with the history of colonial scholarship on Bali. Our concern is no longer with the development of the colonial discourse on the state but with what this discourse failed to discover. With the collapse of the Dutch empire after World War II, one might imagine that the question of the role of the state in Balinese irrigation would vanish into the limbo that had already claimed such topics as the morality of the opium monopoly. But by that time, Balinese irrigation had already entered the literature of Western scholarship as a case in point for one of the most enduring debates in political theory.

For over a century, materialist social theory has proclaimed a link between the management of hydraulic irrigation and the centralization of power. For Marx, as we have seen, "The prime necessity of an economical and common use of water . . . necessitated in the Orient . . . the centralizing power of Government."[1] But Marx was faced with the difficulty, pointed out to him by Engels, that his model of an "Asiatic mode of production" could not apply to existing states then under European rule. Marx replied that an "intact example" might still be found on the island of Bali.[2] A century later, Karl Wittfogel found himself in a similar bind: his model of "Oriental despotism" described early states, not those of the twentieth century. Like Marx, he suggested that a still-functioning example could be found on Bali.[3] But the evidence from Bali was contradictory. Some colonial authors, like Liefrinck, portrayed Balinese irrigation as a decentralized system managed by hundreds of *subaks*. Others, like Happé, maintained that the Dutch were merely restoring a strongly centralized royal irrigation system that had fallen into decay in the nineteenth century. Thus it proved difficult to decide whether Bali actually supported the basic thesis that the technical requirements of irrigation management encouraged the centralization of power in the state.

Fieldwork by anthropologists in the postcolonial era led to a renewed emphasis on the role of the *subaks* in irrigation management. Indeed, thanks largely to the work of Clifford Geertz, the *subak* system became a celebrated example of local-level irrigation control.[4] But because of the controversy over irrigation in the colonial era, questions remained concerning the role of centralized irrigation management. As recently as 1976, those conducting a cross-cultural comparative study of irrigation and power concluded that the evidence for centralized control of irrigation in Bali remained ambiguous.[5]

Part of the difficulty in answering this question was due to uncertainty about the actual technical requirements for the management of water in Balinese irrigation systems. Were the *subaks* "melons on a vine," each drawing water as needed from a constant source? In other words, could each *subak* function as an autonomous unit? In this chapter, we will evaluate the practical requirements for water management in Bali as a necessary prelude to an analysis of the social relations of production.

ARTIFICIAL ECOLOGY

Every year, several thousand new articles are added to the scientific literature on rice. The tremendous sustained productivity of wet-rice paddies has made rice the single most important food crop for human beings and enabled civilizations like Bali to develop. One of the earliest known writings in the Balinese language, a royal edict from the eighth century A.D., refers not only to rice harvests but to irrigation tunnel builders.[6] The oldest human settlements in Bali are concentrated in the best rice-growing areas, where it appears that some terraces have been under continuous cultivation for a millennium or more. By contrast, all other systems of irrigated agriculture are subject to a gradual decline in productivity as a consequence of salinization and loss of soil fertility.

The Balinese do not build irrigation tanks or storage dams, so irrigation is dependent on the seasonal flow of rivers and springs. About half of the 162 named streams and rivers on the island flow only during the rainy season, which lasts from November through April. Bali is a relatively ancient volcanic island, located in a region of heavy monsoons. Nearly all Balinese rivers do not flow at ground level, where irrigation would be easy, but in deep channels on the flanks of the volcanos. Gaining access to such rivers for irrigation poses a difficult engineering challenge. Most Balinese irrigation systems begin at a weir (diversionary dam) across a river, which diverts part of the flow into a tunnel. The tunnel may emerge as much as a kilometer or more downstream, at a lower elevation, where the water is routed through a system of canals and aqueducts to the summit of a terraced hillside. In the regions where rice cultivation is oldest in Bali, irrigation systems can be extraordinarily complex, with a maze of tunnels and canals shunting water through blocks of rice terraces. Because the volume of water in the rivers during the wet season can be ten times greater than the dry season flow, the irrigation system has to cope with conditions ranging from a trickle to flash floods. Irrigation systems originating at different weirs are often interconnected so that unused water from the end of one irrigation system can be shunted into a different block of terraces or returned to a neighboring stream.

To appreciate the level of precision required for the system to work, it is necessary to understand something about the basic dynamics of the paddy ecosystem. In essence, the flow of water—the planned alternation of wet and dry phases—governs the basic biochemical processes of the terrace ecosystem. A general theory in ecology holds that ecosystems which are characterized by steady, unchanging nutrient flows tend to be less productive than systems with nutrient cycles or "pulses."[7] Rice paddies are an excellent example of this principle. Controlled changes in water levels create "pulses" in several important biochemical cycles. The cycle of wet and dry phases alters soil pH; induces a cycle of aerobic and anaerobic conditions in the soil that determines the activity of microorganisms; circulates mineral nutrients; fosters the growth of nitrogen-fixing algae; excludes weeds; stabilizes soil temperature; and over the long term governs the formation of a plough pan that prevents nutrients from being leached into the subsoil. Potassium, for example, is needed for rice growth and depends largely on drainage. Phosphorus is also essential and may be increased more than tenfold by submergence.[8]

The main crop produced is, of course, rice. But in addition, the paddy also produces important sources of animal protein, such as eels, frogs, and fish. Even the dragon-flies that gather over the rice to hunt insects are themselves hunted by little boys, who roast and eat them.[9] Most paddies support a large population of ducks, which must also be carefully managed because they will damage young rice plants if left untended. After each harvest, flocks of ducks are driven from field to field, gleaning leftover grain and eating some of the insects, like brown planthoppers, that would otherwise attack the next rice crop. Traditional harvesting techniques remove only the seed-bearing tassel, leaving the rest of the stalk to decompose in the water, returning most of its nutrients to the system. Depending upon the danger from rice pests, after harvesting farmers may decide to dry the fields and burn the stalks, thus killing most pests but losing some of the nutrients in the harvested plants. Alternatively, they may flood the field and allow the rice stalks to slowly decompose underwater.

As a method of pest control, the effectiveness of drying or flooding the fields depends on cooperation among all of the farmers in a given block of terraces. For a single farmer to try to reduce the pests on a field without coordinating with neighbors is useless because the pests will simply migrate from field to field. But if all of the fields in a large area are burned or flooded, pest populations can be sharply reduced. Both kinds of fallow periods—burnt fields or flooded—are effective techniques for reducing the population of rice pests, but both depend on synchronizing the harvest and subsequent fallow period over many hectares. How large an area must be fallow, and for how long, depends on the species characteristics of the rice pests. Major pests include rodents, insects, and bacterial and viral diseases.

Just as individual farmers manage their paddies by controlling the flow of water, so larger social groups control pest cycles by synchronizing irrigation schedules. The role of water in the microecology of the paddy—creating resource pulses—is duplicated on a larger scale by irrigation cycles that control pest populations by flooding or draining large blocks of terraces.

WATER CONTROL

Until quite recently, rice scientists were unaware of the existence of this method of pest control. Studies of traditional Asian systems of wet-rice cultivation assumed that pest control was beyond the capability of traditional farmers until the advent of chemical pesticides. The little research that was done on the sociological aspects of rice production focused not on the ecological effects of traditional systems of irrigation management but on how to educate farmers in the effective use of agrochemicals. New agricultural policies based on these ideas were introduced in Bali in the 1970s as a means to increase rice production. Farmers were required to plant high-yielding varieties of rice, and very large quantities of pesticides were applied to the fields, with disastrous results. World Bank officials concluded in a recent study that pesticides have already "pervasively polluted the island's soil and water resources."[10] We will have more to say about this history in chapter 6. But for the moment, the point is that the social systems of water management that sustained the ecological productivity of Balinese rice paddies for centuries do not function automatically. It is perfectly possible to grow rice with chemical fertilizers and pesticides and ignore the biochemical cycles that sustain rice growth in traditional paddies. Indeed, on a short-term basis, extensive use of agrochemicals make it possible to dramatically increase crop yields, if sufficient water is available. Thus the answer to the question of the types of social control required for irrigated rice production will differ drastically, depending on whether one approaches the question from the point of view of a biologist studying traditional farming systems or an agronomist studying systems dependent on chemical inputs. From the latter perspective, all that is needed from the irrigation system is a sufficient supply of water. The timing of irrigation is not thought to have any influence on productivity. Instead, how much rice is grown depends on the rice variety and the amounts of fertilizer added. But for the systems ecologist, the timing of irrigation appears to be the key influence on the growth of the rice plants and other food species and maintenance of the high productivity of traditional wet-rice paddies.

One could argue, then, that the requirements for social control of irrigation in Bali have become much simpler now that agrochemicals and high-yielding rice varieties are available. But the problem is not quite so simple. In response to the threat of severe toxic contamination from pesticides and gradual loss of soil fertility, the government of Bali now strongly supports the use of traditional techniques of coordinated fallow periods as the primary method of pest control. Perhaps more importantly, the need for closely coordinated irrigation planning is built into the engineering structure of most Balinese irrigation systems.

As mentioned earlier, the rugged topography of Bali strongly influences the design of irrigation works. In a different sort of physical environment, with large rivers flowing through broad, flat rice plains, small groups of farmers might be able to tap directly into main irrigation canals without worrying very much about their neighbors. But in Bali, virtually every farmer depends on an irrigation system that originates several kilometers upstream and flows in fragile channels through the lands of many neighbors before reaching individual fields. A brief interruption in the flow will destroy a farmer's crop, and an unexpected downpour of rain may wreck terraces and irrigation works unless it is quickly shunted away. Even the largest irrigation structures are highly vulnerable. The weir in the river that provides the water for the main canals is likely to be made of earth, logs, and stones and may easily be washed away by flash floods. Moreover, the amount of water that reaches the weir in the dry season may be strongly affected by the cropping schedules of upstream neighbors.

For all these reasons, it is clear that the productivity of traditional Balinese rice terraces depends upon precise control of irrigation on the scale of several hundred hectares. The social units controlling irrigation must, at a minimum, include all of the *subak*s that share water from the same weir. But is there a need for more widespread cooperation from one weir to the next?

We can explore this question with a brief survey of hydrological relationships among three weirs located on the upper reaches of the Oos River. The map in figure 2.1 shows the location of the weirs that provide water for farmers from the villages of Taro, Bresela, Bukian, Kliki, and Klutug. Furthest upstream after the tiny weir of Taro kaja is the Taro irrigation system, which contains seven *subak*s and 162 hectares of rice

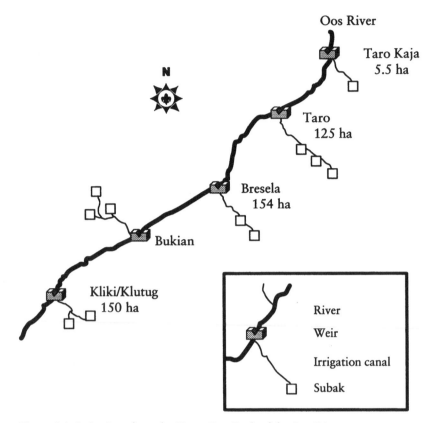

Figure 2.1. Irrigation along the Upper East Fork of the Oos River

terraces. River flow and irrigation requirements for Taro are given in table 2.1.

The variation in the river flow is five-fold from January through August. During the rainy season (roughly November through April), the problem is not water shortage but overabundance: fields and irrigation works must be protected from damage by flooding. During the dry season, Taro usually has enough water. But if excess water is not returned to the irrigation system feeding the villages downstream, they may suffer a shortage during the dry season. As shown in table 2.2, there would be a shortage of irrigation water from May through July, were it not for the release from the Taro irrigation system.

Thus from May through August, the flow from the Bresela weir would be inadequate to meet the irrigation demands of Bresela without the surplus water released from the Taro *subak*s upstream. The same story is repeated downstream in the *subak*s of Kliki and Klutug, which receive an

TABLE 2.1
Taro Irrigation (flow × 10,000 m²)

Month	Inflow	Actual Intakes	Irrigation Demand
January	268	9.2	8.0
February	220	7.4	6.5
March	257	22.0	19.2
April	190	47.8	41.6
May	115	55.0	47.9
June	104	38.5	33.5
July	54	27.4	23.9
August	47	13.1	11.4
September	73	14.7	12.8
October	115	9.5	8.3
November	195	29.9	26.0
December	223	30.8	26.8
Totals	1,861	305.3	265.9

Source: Department of Public Works, Irrigation Division, Sangglah, Bali.

TABLE 2.2
Bresela Irrigation (flow × 10,000 m²)

Month	Release from Taro Irrigation	Inflow from Bresela Weir	Total Flow	Irrigation Demand	Deficit
January	258.9	112.5	317.4	13.1	0
February	212.2	92.2	304.4	10.6	0
March	234.8	111.7	346.5	31.6	0
April	142.0	79.7	221.7	68.1	0
May	60.3	48.5	108.8	78.6	− 30.1
June	65.7	43.8	109.5	55.0	− 11.2
July	26.5	22.7	49.2	39.3	− 16.6
August	33.4	19.5	52.9	17.3	0
September	57.8	30.5	88.3	13.4	0
October	105.9	48.5	154.4	9.0	0
November	165.5	82.1	247.6	42.6	0
December	192.5	93.8	286.3	44.2	0

Source: Department of Public Works, Taro Irrigation Project in Taro, Gianyar, Bali.

important share of their water from Bresela (and thus indirectly from Taro).

The release from the Bresela weir is the principal component of the total flow for the irrigation systems of Kliki and Klutug. Altogether, four separate weirs provide irrigation for three villages, and there is also an

TABLE 2.3
Villages of Kliki and Klutug Irrigation (flow × 10,000 m²)

Month	Release from Bresela	Inflow from Weir	Total Flow
January	356.3	121.8	478.1
February	292.2	99.8	392.0
March	310.2	116.6	426.8
April	148.4	86.3	234.7
May	18.4	52.4	70.8
June	46.2	47.4	93.6
July	4.0	24.5	28.5
August	33.0	21.1	54.1
September	72.9	33.0	105.9
October	144.0	52.4	196.4
November	198.7	88.7	287.4
December	235.5	101.5	337.0

Source: Department of Public Works, Bali Irrigation Project.

intermediary weir between Bresela and Klutug, which provides water for three *subak*s lying on the opposite side of the river. Hydrological interdependency extends beyond individual *subak*s and weirs to include all of these irrigation systems.

WATER TEMPLES

By now it should come as no surprise that the social units that set cropping patterns and irrigation schedules are usually not individual *subak*s but regional water temples, like the Masceti temple, Er Jeruk, located in the rice terraces below the village of Sukawati. The village of Sukawati receives irrigation water from three dams on two rivers, the Oos and Petanu. In all three cases, the main irrigation canals irrigate other fields upstream before reaching the 403 hectares of terraces in the Sukawati terraces. The congregation of the Masceti temple includes thirteen small *subak*s, which are divided into three groups for the purpose of rotational irrigation.

The role of the temple is described by the head of the village, who is also a farmer.

VILLAGE HEAD: The Pura Er Jeruk is the largest temple hereabouts, that is, the temple whose congregation includes all the farmers of the village of Sukawati. Now below this temple there are also

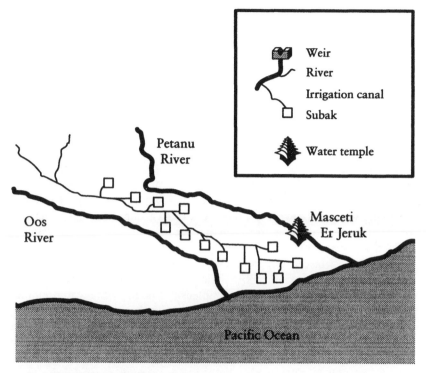

Figure 2.2. Sukawati Irrigation System

smaller temples, which are special places of worship for the *subaks*—each *subak* has its own. There are fourteen of these temples, fourteen *subaks*[11] all of which meet together as one here. They meet at the Temple Er Jeruk. Every decision, every rule concerning planting seasons and so forth, is always discussed here. Then, after the meeting here, decisions are carried down to each *subak*. The *subaks* each call all their members together: "In accord with the meetings we held at the Temple Er Jeruk, we must fix our planting dates, beginning on day one through day ten." For example, first *subak* Sango plants, then *subak* Somi, beginning from day ten through day twenty. Thus it is arranged, in accordance with water and *Padewasan*—that is, the best times to plant. Because here time controls everything. If there are many rodents and we go ahead and plant rice, obviously we'll get a miserable harvest. So we organize things like this: when the rodent population is large, we see to it that we don't plant things they can eat, so that they will all die—I mean, actually, that their numbers will be greatly reduced pretty quickly.

LANSING: Is there a fixed schedule of meetings?

VILLAGE HEAD: Once a year. Each new planting season, there is a meeting. If the planting schedule is not to be changed, there is no meeting. Of course, the ceremonies held here go on regardless—there are two temple festivals here, a one-day festival every six months, and a three-day festival every year. . . . This place is the home of the spirits of those who have preceded us, who built this temple—I would call this temple the fortress of the farmers hereabouts.

All three groups plant rice at least once a year in the rainy season. During the dry season, there is a rotational system. One group is guaranteed water for a second planting of rice, and one group plants a vegetable crop, receiving water once every five days. The third group will plant either rice or vegetables, depending upon whether the amount of irrigation water is judged adequate for rice. By setting the cropping pattern and irrigation schedule, the Masceti temple attempts to optimize water sharing while establishing a widespread fallow period to reduce pest infestations.

A slightly more complicated example is provided by the water temples of Kedewatan, located about midway up Mount Batur (see map 3). Here, seven *subak*s share water from a single large canal originating from a major weir nearly 4 kilometers upstream. Where the water first enters the terrace complex, there is a major temple called Ulun Swi (Head of the Ricefields). About 100 meters downstream from this temple, the main canal splits in two, and there is a Masceti temple alongside the upstream

TABLE 2.4
*Subak*s Attached to Masceti Temple Er Jeruk

Subaks	Area (ha)	Members (1985)
Abasan	31.66	96
Babakan	20.18	66
Bubun	38.41	120
Cau Beten	31.74	97
Cau Duwur	19.29	63
Juwak	33.35	99
Langge/Landep	34.49	62
Laud	34.92	84
Lebo	30.05	92
Palak	72.62	198
Sanga	36.28	108
Somi	20.93	65
Sungguhan	33.35	75

branch canal. A second Masceti temple is located about a half kilometer downstream, where the second branch canal enters the second set of terraces. The two Masceti temples form the congregation of the Ulun Swi Temple.

Each *subak* thus belongs to the congregation of the Ulun Swi and to one or the other of the Masceti temples:

The congregation of the Ulun Swi temple thus includes seven *subak*s with a total of 1,775 members, farming 558.04 hectares of ricefields. All *subak* members share equally in the responsibility to maintain the main

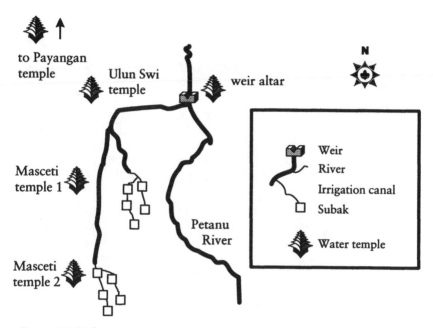

Figure 2.3. Kedewatan Irrigation System

TABLE 2.5
Water Temples of Kedewatan (Terraced area in hectares)

Ulun Swi Temple			
Masceti Temple #1 (first main canal)		*Masceti Temple #2 (second main canal)*	
Lungsiakan	54.82	Mas	38.74
Kibul Bebek	28.37	Sindhu Jiwa	94.59
Pacekan	133.41	Mandi	126.26
		Tebungkan	81.85
Subtotals	216.60		341.44

canal and weir. During the rainy season, the whole Ulun Swi unit plants the same variety of rice at the same time, ensuring a uniform fallow period after harvest to control pests.[12] For the second planting, each Masceti acts as a unit, choosing the crops to be planted and assigning rotational irrigation if needed. Each *subak* (or in the case of large *subak*s like Pacekan, each *tempek* unit) takes turns in both maintenance of the irrigation works and performing the annual rituals at the Masceti and Ulun Swi temples. Thus the practical management of irrigation is embedded within the hierarchical structure of the water temples.

SOCIAL CONTROL

We were concerned with two fundamental questions in this chapter: the kinds of managerial control required for wet-rice terraces in general and specific requirements for the management of irrigation along two Balinese rivers. Previous studies have assumed that the function of irrigation is simply to supplement rainfall. But as we have seen, in rice paddies water is used to construct an artificial pond ecosystem, which imposes far more stringent constraints on water management. The cycle of wet and dry phases governs the basic biochemistry of the paddy ecosystem, accounting for its extraordinary long-term productivity.

Along the Oos and Petanu rivers the monsoonal climate and rugged volcanic terrain create further constraints on irrigation control. A very few of the smallest *subak*s, located at the highest elevations, obtain all of their water directly from a single weir or spring and so are not obliged to cooperate with their neighbors in setting irrigation schedules. But the majority of the 172 *subak*s along these rivers depend on the release flow from upstream neighbors for an important fraction of their irrigation water. Hydrological interdependency is built into the very engineering structure of the irrigation systems, with long and fragile systems of weirs, tunnels, canals, and aqueducts threading their way down the mountainsides. Thus the physical constraints of Balinese irrigation require a system of control extending well beyond the *subak* level, connecting weir to weir and watershed to watershed.

The Balinese technique of pest control via coordinated fallow periods establishes a further set of constraints for water management. Even *subak*s that belong to separate irrigation systems may attempt to synchronize their harvests to minimize pests. This method, in turn, requires synchronized cropping patterns and irrigation schedules, which must balance the requirements of water sharing and pest control. For the fallowing system to have a real effect on pest populations, cropping patterns must be tightly synchronized over hundreds of hectares.

Altogether, it is clear that the productive process involves intricate systems of social control extending over hundreds, even thousands, of hectares of irrigated terraces. To evaluate the specific managerial functions of particular local hierarchies of water temple management is a complex question to which we will return in chapter 6 with the aid of a computer simulation model. But for the moment, other issues are more pressing. Although the temples play a practical role in irrigation management, they are essentially social and religious institutions, for as Condominas reminds us, agriculture is at once a social and a technical process. In chapter 3, we shift our attention from the technical effects of temple management to an exploration of their role in defining the productive process.

CHAPTER THREE

The Waters of Power

IN *Negara: The Balinese Theatre State in the Nineteenth Century*, Clifford Geertz described the cult of divine kingship as the basis of power in traditional Balinese kingdoms, "The whole of the negara—court life, the traditions that organized it, the extractions that supported it, the privileges that accompanied it—was essentially directed towards defining what power was; and what power was was what kings were."[1]

The cult of divine kingship, as Geertz explained, claimed unlimited, godlike power for each ruler. A king must be a "universal monarch, the core and pivot of the universe." These claims were somewhat diluted by the sheer numbers of would-be divine monarchs who "dotted the landscape . . . each quite aware that he was not alone."[2] But in the rituals of his own royal cult—in the prayers spoken by his court priests—each king was, indeed, "what power was."

The subject of this chapter is a different constellation of powers that originate in the *erga* of the farmers and find expression in the rituals of water temples. For the most part, these powers lie outside the domain of politics, which also kept them from coming into focus for the Dutch, for whom the water temples remained lost in the hazy background of agricultural rituals and folk beliefs. Yet as we saw in the last chapter, the technical requirements for managing irrigation in Bali are anything but hazy. Now that we are somewhat acquainted with the nature of these requirements, it becomes possible to appreciate the kinds of controls and powers exerted by the water temples.

But to understand the role of water temples, it is necessary to begin with a more general appreciation of the relationship of temples to society in Bali. The key point is that all traditional Balinese social units, from households to kingdoms, possess their own altars or temples, where regular offerings are made to the gods concerned with their affairs—market gods in the market temple, village ancestors in the village temples. In other words, each social unit forms the congregation of a specific temple or shrine, which symbolically defines its place in the Balinese social universe. This principle has survived into the modern era, as banks, government offices, and even tourist hotels construct small temples on their grounds, which superficially establish their identity. However, modern institutions like office buildings have no immediately obvious relationship to particular deities, and so it is difficult to know which gods should be invited to their festivals. If one examines these new-building temples more closely, it becomes clear that they are empty shells, and their very blankness serves to highlight the precisely defined symbolic roles of traditional Balinese temples.

For unlike all traditional Balinese temples, these new-building temples possess no shrines to particular deities. Instead, they typically include only a single shrine, a throne (*padmasana*) for the abstract deity Sang Hyang Widi. Until the arrival of Christian missionaries in the nineteenth century, Sang Hyang Widi was one of the most obscure and esoteric Balinese gods, a paradoxical concept of formless divinity to beguile Brahmanic theologians. The first Christian missionaries to Bali selected Sang Hyang Widi to represent the Christian God. But this proved to be a poor choice because in the context of Balinese polytheism Sang Hyang Widi is definable only negatively as the essence common to all the gods. Throughout the colonial era, the missionaries had little success with Sang Hyang Widi as a vehicle for Christianity. But after Indonesian independence in 1947, it became politically important for the Balinese to define their religion as *monotheistic*. In the effort to stave off Islamic proselytizers, Balinese theologians brought Sang Hyang Widi to the fore, this time as a Balinese equivalent of Allah. It was at this stage that shrines to Sang Hyang Widi began to be attached to new buildings, from tourist hotels to banks and government offices. These new temples may best be described as shrines to divinity in the abstract.

By contrast, all traditional Balinese temples consist of a collection of altars and shrines for specific deities, which express in a well-defined symbolic vocabulary the social role of the temple. For example, all Balinese markets have temples. The principal deity enshrined is Maya Sih, mistress of illusions, but there are also small shrines to other deities like the Rice Goddess. These shrines help situate markets in the meaningful context of Balinese cosmology, partly by articulating the link between the market temple and other temples elsewhere. Thus markets are not only places where the mistress of illusions holds dominion. They are also important to the Rice Mother in her specific incarnation as mistress of the "Head-of-the-Ricefields" temples. For although most rice goes directly from the fields to the rice barns, some is sold in the market before it reaches someone else's rice barn, and so the Rice Mother is obliged to take an interest in markets. Her shrines in the market temples are relatively minor, but they link the market temple to the "Head-of-the-Ricefields" temples and in this way help to define the significance of market activities.

In a similar way, every water temple has an array of shrines identified with a specific collection of anthropomorphic deities that expresses the social and cosmological role of the temple. This is precisely what the shrines to Sang Hyang Widi in the new-building temples fail to do: to *read* the symbolism of the new-building temples is to read an empty page. In the language of Balinese ritual, a temple to Sang Hyang Widi fails to define any specific way in which the institution relates to society. Instead, on the anniversary of the building's completion, generic offerings are made to the generic deity, Sang Hyang Widi. In time, perhaps, Maya Sih (the mistress of illusions) or some other deity may find a new niche in the temples for banks or hotels. But for the present, banks remain unconnected to society—as it is defined by the symbolism of temple rituals.

I draw attention to this contrast because it helps to define what I would like to call the *sociogenic* aspects of water temple rituals. By this I mean that rituals at a water temple provide a deep reading of what the institution is about—its specific relationship to the social microcosm. Temple rituals literally call into existence the task groups that manage the terraces for economic production. These groups have no separate existence apart from the water temple system. In this sense, the temples provide a vehicle to achieve voluntary social cooperation in the management of the irrigation on which each village—and society as a whole—is utterly dependent. Each village obtains its water from a fragile weir and irrigation works that lie in the territory of other villages upstream. In the absence of a "hydraulic bureaucracy" to manage irrigation, the temple system itself must maintain a kind of "hydraulic solidarity," by persuasively articulating the common interest in watershed management. The symbolism of temple rituals is driven by a powerful logic, and it is to the principles of this logic that we now turn.

THE TEMPLE SYSTEM

Nadi tirtha-taya priye,
om tirtha-nadi ta kumbhas-ca

(River, dear because thou art Holy Water!
River of Holy Water, as well as receptacle)[3]

We begin with a simple equation: water temples define connections between productive groups and the components of the natural landscape that they seek to control. Each shrine or temple is associated with some particular component of the irrigated landscape. A local irrigation system begins with a spring, or, more often, a weir in a river, which diverts part or all of the flow of water to an irrigation canal. Beside each weir or spring is a shrine. The congregation of the weir shrine or spring shrine consists of all the farmers who use the water originating from this source. The principal deity to receive offerings at the weir shrine is called the

"Deity of the Weir" (bhatara empelan). Offerings are also made at the weir shrine to the Goddess of the Temple of the Crater Lake, who is said to make the rivers flow.

The irrigation canal that takes off from the weir eventually reaches a block of terraces. This spot is usually a kilometer or more downstream from the weir and is marked by a major water temple, the "Head of the Rice Terraces" temple (Pura Ulun Swi). The congregation of this temple is the same as that of the weir shrine: it consists of all farmers who grow rice in the terraces irrigated by this particular canal system. The principal deity of the Ulun Swi temple is called Ida Bhatara Pura Ulun Swi, the "Deity of the Ulun Swi Temple," whose influence extends to all of the terraces watered by the canal. The temple itself is simply a walled courtyard containing a shrine where farmers can make offerings to this deity. Additional shrines provide a place for offerings to other gods and goddesses, such as the Deity of the Weir and the Goddess of the Temple of the Crater Lake. These offerings at the Ulun Swi temple acknowledge the dependency of farmers on the flow of waters into their terraces, which in turn depends upon the flow at the weir and ultimately upon the flow in the river.

Other water temples and shrines follow a similar logic. All water temples are physically located at the upstream edge of whatever water system they purport to control. Chains of water temples articulate the hydrologic of each irrigation system. Temples and shrines are situated in such a way as to exert influence over each of the major physical components of the terrace ecosystems, including lakes, springs, rivers, weirs, major canals, blocks of irrigated terraces, subaks and individual fields. The temples link these physical features of the landscape to social units according to a logic of production: the congregation of each temple consists of the farmers who obtain water from the irrigation component controlled by the temple's god.

There are thus two aspects to the hydro-logic of irrigation dependency. The first is the link between a temple, its congregation, and the component of the ecosystem that it represents. Thus the Deity of the Weir dwells in the weir and requires offerings from every farmer who benefits from the water flowing through it. The weir is the origin of an irrigation system that has both physical and social components. The concept of an anthropomorphic "weir god" draws attention to the ways in which these components are related, for the weir is a man-made structure, a shared responsibility, which is also part of the physical landscape. For as long as the weir exists, a relationship of interdependency links the farmers who receive its waters. The weir shrine institutionalizes this relationship: particular farmers may come and go, but the social unit defined by the waters from the weir persists. Like the irrigation waters, this social unit originates at the weir. The concept of the weir god evokes this collective social presence in the weir, where free-flowing river water becomes controlled irrigation water.

The idea of a collective presence leads to the second type of relationship expressed by water temple rituals: the interdependency of temples along an irrigation system. For example, the Deity of the Weir and the gods of other upstream water temples may be invited to descend into the Head of the Rice Terraces temple at the time of its major festival, to receive offerings. All water temples enclose an array of shrines and offerings platforms, in which homage may be offered to numerous deities. Because many of these deities are known by such names as "Deity of the Weir" or "Deity of the Masceti Temple," it is clear that they are essentially symbolic representations of other water temples. To do them honor is to acknowledge a relationship between the host temple and the temples of the gods they represent.

If one looks at the system from the bottom up, each farmer has a small shrine (*bedugul*) located at the spot where irrigation water first enters his fields. This "upstream" corner of his fields is considered sacred; it is here that he makes offerings to the Rice Goddess incarnate in his crop. At harvest time, the rice that grows closest to the water inlet is used to create a sacred image of the Rice Goddess herself, which is not eaten, but carried to the rice barn and given offerings.

Upstream from the farmer's field shrine, the next water temple is usually the *subak* temple, representing a block of irrigated terraces with a common water source. Several *subak*s make up the congregation of an Ulun Swi temple, associated with a large canal, and a weir or spring shrine. Several weirs typically form the congregation of a Masceti regional water temple. Finally, each spring, lake, and the headwaters of each river have shrines or temples. The largest water temple is furthest upstream—the Temple of the Crater Lake, associated with Lake Batur, which is considered to be the source of all irrigation waters within its river boundaries.[4]

At the downstream terminus of irrigation systems, important temples are located, which are classified as Masceti regional water temples. Upstream and downstream temples have very different functions associated with two different symbolic properties of water. Upstream water is associated with the nourishing, or life-giving, effects of water and is regarded as a gift from the Goddess of the Lake. In contrast, downstream water is cleansing water—water used to purify, to wash away pollution. It is not collected in sacred vessels, like upstream water, but is left running in the rivers. Impurities such as the ashes from sacrifices are thrown directly into the rivers, which bear them to the sea. This is the basis of a powerful symbolic contrast: whereas the waters high above in the crater lake represent the mystery of water as life-giver, the waters of the sea are associated with the equally potent mysteries of dissolution and regeneration. Downstream Masceti temples are located at the downstream edge of the last block of rice terraces irrigated by major rivers, along the sea coast. By the time they reach the sea, the rivers are considered to be brimming with impurities—the ashes of burnt sacrifices, the discharge from village and fields. The sea dissolves them all, removing their human content as impurities, and returning them to a wild, elemental, natural state.

SACRED WATER

om Apsu deva-pavitrani

(The gods in the waters are the purifying agents)

The hydro-logic of upstream and downstream dependency is imposed on the course of every river by the regional systems of water temples, which mark out the paths traced by the waters of the goddess as they simultaneously cause growth and cleanse the land of pollution. But the paths of the rivers are fixed, and there would be little point in a symbolism that could only reflect the unchanging logic of irrigation systems. Although the physical location of water temples suggests important clues about their meaning, the concept of "holy water" provides a vehicle to express more complex relations than simple irrigation dependency.

The importance of this concept for the Balinese is hinted by the very name of their religion: *Agama Tirtha*, "the religion of holy water." *Tirtha* (holy water) is the one indispensable element common to all Balinese rituals, not only those that take place at water temples. "*Matirtha*," the verbal form of the word for holy water, is the name for the culmination of every act of worship, in which—after one has concluded one's offerings and prayers—a blessing of holy water is sprinkled on one's head, and one drinks a few drops. Libations of *tirtha* are poured over offerings, sacrifices, buildings, and ricefields and into irrigation canals. Holy water fuses the symbolic qualities of upstream and downstream: it is at once a blessing and a purification.[5]

The sacredness recognized in these properties of water—its ability to cause growth and to purify and cleanse—derives in part from the human uses of water. It is only controlled water that can cause growth or bear away impurities. The particular potencies attributed to different varieties of holy water are symbolically associated with the original source of the water. Holy water must originate from an upstream source, and in most instances the more upstream a source is, the more potent the holy water that can be made from it. This appears to be a general principle true for all temples rather than only water temples. For example, David Stuart-

Fox has recently completed a detailed study of Pura Besakih, often described as the supreme temple of Bali.[6] The holy water for Besakih comes from several springs located above the temple on Mount Agung. According to Stuart-Fox, a simple rule governs the potency of these waters: the higher in elevation the spring, the more sacred are its waters.

We are thus led to ask, What is it about the quality of "upstreamness" that sanctifies water for the Balinese? The answer must surely begin with the relationship of farmers to upstream water. An example with which we are already familiar is the upstream source of irrigation water marked by a weir shrine. Here, "wild" flowing water becomes upstream irrigation water. As it enters the main canal, the flow is undivided. Downstream, it will encounter a series of water dividers that will ultimately channel it to individual fields and farmers. But upstream, at the weir, no one has yet laid claim to his portion of the flow. Thus although downstream water belongs to individuals, the undivided flow of water upstream at the weir belongs to the collective.

To create "holy water" at the weir, a cup of water drawn from the main canal at the weir is set at the foot of the weir shrine and offerings are made to the weir god, who is asked to sanctify the water. Although the water is physically removed from the canal, its upstream quality—its ability to signify the collective—remains intact, for it is now holy water. The ritual simply abstracts the qualities associated with the upstream flow of the weir—the association of the water with the social unit that originates from it. Henceforth, this holy water will be carefully labeled as to its origin and will always signify whatever qualities are associated with it as an upstream flow.

For this reason, holy water is regularly requested by downstream groups from upstream water temples. For example, holy water from the Bayad weir on the upper Petanu River is sought each year by farmers belonging to the Ulun Swi temple Celeng Patas (see map below), who mix it with holy water from their own temple.

The farmers of Celeng Patas obtain their irrigation water not from the Bayad weir but from the Manuaba weir. However, the Bayad weir lies directly upstream from the Manuaba weir, so the amount of water reaching the farmers of Celeng Patas largely depends on the release from the Bayad weir. Thus, holy water from the Bayad weir shrine is of great significance to the congregation of the Celeng Patas temple. Each year, a delegation from the Celeng Patas temple ascends the river to the Bayad weir altar, where a Bayad *subak* priest receives their offerings and prepares the holy water for them. Returning to their temple, they mix the Bayad holy water with the waters from their own temple and sprinkle it over their offerings, as a token of the blessing of the god of the Bayad weir. But holy water from the Bayad weir altar would have no interest or value for farmers on a different spur of the river.

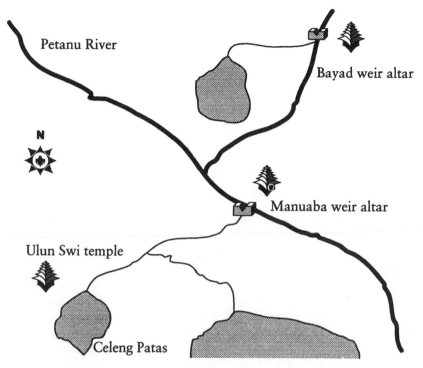

Figure 3.1. Holy Water for Celeng Patas Comes from Two Weir Altars: Bayad and Manuaba

Each temple has its own unique holy water, which signifies the temple, its god, and its congregation. In other words, each temple defines a social unit that is also signified by the holy water created in the temple. Holy water is thus like the temple's god but with the additional significance attached to the idea of upstream as origin. The most sacred variety of holy water, called *Bhatara Tirtha* ("Deified holy water"), is so imbued with the essence of the god that it is treated like a god and may represent the god who created it at rituals outside his temple. It should be emphasized that "holy water" does not signify society—or the sacred—in general but the specific social unit for which it is the upstream source.

Holy water thus provides a vehicle for symbolizing several types of social relationships. First, it establishes a means to define social groups by invoking their origins. The higher upstream one goes, the larger the social unit that may be drawn together by the waters. There is an origin for each level of an irrigation system, all the way up to Lake Batur and its Temple of the Crater Lake, the ultimate origin of everyone's water. Second, relationships between temples—and their congregations, the social units they represent—are symbolized by the seeking and joining of holy waters. It is customary to send delegations to request holy water from several temples for major rituals. The water is carried back in sacred vessels, each clearly identified with the name of the temple whose blessing it conveys. These waters are then poured into a common container, thereby combining the blessings of several temples and their gods into an elixir to sprinkle on the worshippers attending the festival.

Thus the *flow* of holy water from temple to temple establishes hierarchical relations between the temples and links them to a common origin. Perhaps the most dramatic illustration of this process occurs every year in the preparation of holy water for the farmer's fields for the "pregnancy of the rice" offerings at the end of the rainy season. The process begins at the Temple of the Crater Lake, the supreme water temple, on the rim of the volcano. In the early morning a few days before the beginning of the Ritual of the Tenth Month, a delegation of priests ascends the cone of the volcano to the summit, where steam issues from vents in the rock. While the delegation performs prayers and offerings to "request holy water" (*panuhur tirtha*), the senior priest collects droplets of water hanging from the rocks, which have condensed from the uprising steam. This water is then taken down to the temple, where it is mixed with holy water from the eleven springs around the lake. Later, during the Rituals of the Tenth Month, this holy water is distributed to delegations from over two hundred *subak*s. Each of the *subak*s brings a sacred vessel into which is poured about 1 liter of holy water. The *subak*s carry the water home and mix it with the waters of their regional water temples. Finally, it is taken to the *subak* temples and distributed to individual farmers, who sprinkle it at the upstream edge of their fields. In this way, each farmer and field is symbolically linked to the entire hierarchy of temples and water sources.

The concept of holy water is inseparably linked to hierarchy because holy water never flows upstream (the waters of lower-ranking temples are never sought for the rituals of temples higher up in the hierarchy). It is important to distinguish between the metaphors of hierarchy created by the *flow* of holy water and the hydro-logic of irrigation dependency created by the actual flow of irrigation water. This difference is clearly illustrated by the role of holy water in kinship temples, where hydro-logic plays no role. Kinship temples are not water temples, but, nonetheless, every temple has its own specific source of upstream water used to create the temple's holy water. Often, this is a well or spring. Similarly, each family maintains a domestic supply of holy water, usually obtained from a priest, which is used almost daily in small offerings at the household shrine. For more important ceremonies at the family ancestor shrine, it is preferable to augment this water with holy water from the local clan temple, if one exists.[7] In this way, the blessings of more distant ancestors are added to those of the household shrine. Similarly, for a major ritual at the clan temple, the temple's waters should be augmented by holy water from

the islandwide clan origin temple. For, like the drops of condensed volcanic steam from the Temple of the Crater Lake, the holy waters of a clan
origin temple evoke the sacred origins of the collective.

THE GODS

*These are the gods of Bali, written by Sang Mpu
Kuturan . . . first is the god who reigns in the
Ulun Swi temple, who cares for the life
in the rice terraces*

(Dewa Tattwa [History of the gods]
Ida Pedanda Made, Icaka 1865)[8]

Before proceeding further, we need to draw several threads of the argument together. Earlier, I suggested that water temple rituals articulate
links between temples in the watershed, so the ritual system encompasses
all the temples along a river. It was necessary to emphasize this point
because prior studies of Balinese rituals have generally assumed that the
symbolism of temple rituals is bounded by the temple walls. Instead, we
have seen that ritual symbolism is deeply concerned with relationships
between temples. We might, therefore, conclude that the proper level of
analysis is not the individual temple or *subak* but the system of temples
along a river.

From the standpoint of the role of temples in irrigation management, it
does make sense to think of a system of control that extends along the
entire watershed. It is also true that some temple rituals express this idea.
Thus the flow of holy water from the Temple of the Crater Lake through
the hierarchy of water temples or the annual offerings at the seaside Masceti temples convey an image of a water control system extending along
the length of the river. But there is a problem with proceeding at this level
of analysis, a problem that may appear to be merely a matter of emphasis
but in fact relates to the essential meaning of the ritual system. The point
is that regional water temples do not define themselves as local branches
of a wider system. Instead, each temple is at the center of its own microcosm. Surrounded by a different constellation of social institutions, each
temple honors its own specific collection of gods.

Offerings to these gods and libations of holy water define each water
temple's social identity and its place in the overall hierarchy. The symbolism is usually quite clear and explicit. Consider, for example, the Ulun
Swi ("Head of the terraces") temple Celeng Patas mentioned earlier as a
temple whose congregation seeks holy water from their upstream neighbors at the Bayad weir. But the holy water from the Bayad weir is only
one of several sources of holy water that are used to augment the holy

water of this Ulun Swi temple. The other sources of holy water for this
temple provide a more complete symbolic map of the temple's position in
the hierarchy of water temples. Celeng and Patas are both *subak*s, that
receive their irrigation water from one of two irrigation canals fed by the
Manuaba weir. The sister canal provides water for eight more *subak*s,
and all ten *subak*s constitute the congregation of a Masceti temple associated with the flow from the Manuaba weir. These relationships are
shown in figure 3.2.

The Celeng Patas Temple obtains its basic supply of upstream water to
make holy water from a spring near the Petanu River. To this is added
holy water from the following temples:

  1. the spring for the Masceti Temple
  2. the Bayad weir altar
  3. the village temples (*kahyangan-tiga*) of Manuaba

We have already noted the symbolism attached to the waters from the
Bayad weir shrine: the flow of waters to the Manuaba weir is directly

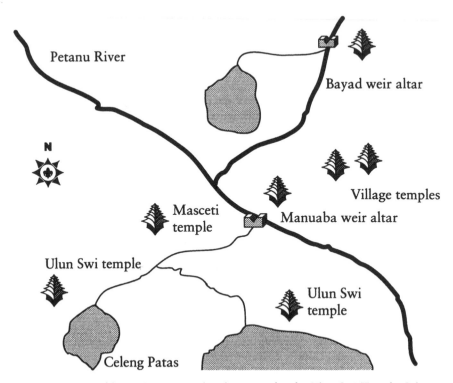

Figure 3.2. Additional Sources of Holy Water for the Ulun Swi Temple Celeng
Patas

affected by the regulation of the Bayad weir. The relationship to the Masceti Temple is equally clear: the Ulun Swi Temple forms part of its congregation. Finally, the practice of augmenting the holy water of local water temples with holy water from the village temples is quite common. In
this way, the interdependency of *subaks* and villages is expressed by min-
gling their waters. About once a generation, this relationship is given a
fuller exposition in a ritual called *ngusaba desa* in which the deities of
subak and village temples are jointly worshipped.

Holy water creates one set of symbolic connections; offerings to the
gods provide another. During the festival of the Ulun Swi Temple, the
following deities are specifically invited to receive offerings from the congregation:

1. God of the Ulun Swi Temple itself
2. God of the Masceti Temple of Manuaba
3. God of the Manuaba weir
4. Goddess of the Temple of the Crater Lake
5. Gods of the village temples of Manuaba
6. God of the origin temple for the Manuaba lineage of Brahmans, an
islandwide kinship origin temple
7. Lord Protector of the Earth (Ratu Ngurah)

The first four gods articulate the local hierarchy of water temples. The
fifth reaffirms the interdependency of *subaks* and villages. The sixth temple is very well known and important, as the origin temple for a senior
Brahmana descent group. It is located a few hundred meters downstream
from the Ulun Swi Temple, on a promontory overlooking the river and
the rice terraces watered by the Ulun Swi Temple. Legend links one of the
ancestors of the Brahmans to the creation of the Manuaba weir. The last
deity is Ratu Ngurah, the Lord Protector of the Earth, who may be in-
voked to guard the territory of the Ulun Swi Temple.[9]

Thus the symbolism of offerings establishes a temple congregation's
place in the local hierarchy of water temples and also links the temple lat-
erally to other nearby social institutions, such as village or kinship temples.

Offerings to the Gods

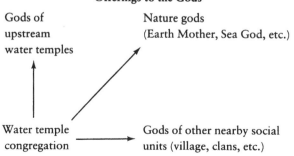

Similarly, holy water symbolizes lateral relationships between different types of temples, as well as hierarchical relationships between water temples.

Sources of Holy Water

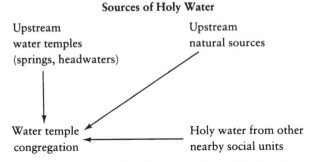

Offerings and holy water thus define the hierarchical relationships between water temples and the relationship of each temple to its local environment. Clear patterns emerge if we compare the symbolism of strictly regional temples to higher-level temples with larger and more inclusive congregations. For example, offerings to nature gods are seldom made at the smaller water temples but are reserved for the largest Masceti temples. Great gods are worshipped in great temples, lesser gods in local temples. This delineation appears to be in keeping with the general principle that the constellation of gods worshipped at each temple is related to that temple's social role, for the Sea God is not a local concern—he is a concern of the wider society represented by the higher-level temples.

To see the wider links established by water temples, we must move higher in the hierarchy, to the larger Masceti temples. Although these temples are also known as *Masceti*, they play a more universal role than those we have just considered and may be regarded as a different type. The two most important water temples along the Oos and Petanu are the Masceti temples of Pamos Apuh and Er Jeruk. They are, respectively, the farthest upstream and downstream Masceti temples along the Petanu and occupy a higher position in the water temple hierarchy than the other Masceti temples of this river. They differ from the other regional water temples of the Petanu in several important respects.

1. No offerings are made to the deities of the local village temples (*kahyangan-tiga*). Instead, offerings are made to several of the deities of the half-dozen supreme temples of the island. These temples, like Besakih and Batur, are often described as performing the same protective functions for the entire island that the kahyangan-tiga temples provide for a village. These temples are associated with the supreme gods and goddesses of the Balinese pantheon.

2. The offerings at temples like the Ulun Swi Celeng Patas are addressed

primarily to local deities. But at the major Masceti temples, offerings are also made to generalized nature gods, such as the Earth Mother and the Sea God.

3. In both of the major Masceti temples, the most elaborate offerings are given to the same three deities: the Deity of Mount Agung, the Goddess of Lake Batur, and the deity of the respective Masceti temple.

Both of these Masceti temples receive delegations from a much larger group than their immediate congregation of *subaks*. *Subaks* and water temples along the entire upper third reach of the Petanu offer *soewinih* contributions to the Masceti Pamos Apuh, which supplement the offerings of the fifteen *subaks* that form the temple's primary congregation. Similarly, the Masceti Er Jeruk is the proper site for offerings to placate the dangerous powers emanating from downstream (*kelod*), such as the Great Fanged Lord of the offshore islet Nusa Penida. The defense of the realm is the responsibility of kings, and so the deity of the Masceti Er Jeruk is a royal divinity, identified with the supreme gods of the island and attended by a divinized *sedahan* and scribe. Complete lists of deities receiving offerings at these two temples are as follows:

Both Temples

1. The Goddess of the Temple of the Crater Lake
2. The God of Mount Agung (and of the Temple of Besakih)
3. The deity of the Masceti temple itself

Masceti Temple Pamos Apuh

1. Tripurusa (the Hindu godhead, represented in abstract and generalized form)
2. The *sedahan* or major-domo for the deity of the Masceti temple, itself a god
3. The Grand Scribe, who like the *sedahan* assists the deity of the temple.
4. The Deity of Sakenan Temple (the most important seaside Masceti temple of Badung, who is associated with the control of malevolent powers emanating from downstream)
5. The Deity of the Head of the Ricefields (Ulun Swi) temples, which form the congregation of the Masceti temple
6. The Lord Protector of the Earth, a benevolent deity who protects the territory of the Masceti temple[10]

Masceti Temple Er Jeruk

1. The Earth Mother
2. The Sea God
3. The Deity of Ulu Watu, a seaside temple associated with the defense of the whole island against downstream demonic powers, similar to Sakenan Temple.

4. The deity of the *subak* ricefield temples, which form the congregation of this Masceti (there are no Ulun Swi temples in the cluster of temples associated with this Masceti).

5. The Great Fanged Lord, the demon-king of the offshore island of Nusa Penida, who is believed to send plagues, armies of demons, and ghostly soldiers to invade Bali, especially in the eighth month.[11]

The logic that dictates that wider conceptions of society are increasingly undifferentiated means that the highest-ranking Masceti temples inevitably transcend their roles as local water temples. As a regional water temple, the Masceti Er Jeruk sets irrigation schedules for its local congregation of *subak*s. But as guardian of the terraces and protector of the kingdom against malignant forces from the sea, the temple's potential congregation includes the whole of the realm. The ritual system is concerned not only with the temple's irrigation functions but with its wider role in the relationship between the social and natural worlds.

To define this wider role requires us to consider a further dimension of the ritual system: the symbolism of time. It has often been argued, most eloquently by Claude Lévi-Strauss, that time is the enemy of systems of symbolic classification such as those of the water temples.[12] According to Lévi-Strauss, ritual classification systems are always in danger of being washed away by the river of time. Time, in this sense, means change. But in the Balinese case, this argument does not hold, for time itself is thought to impose an order on the world. Balinese calendars define time not as a linear flow but as a structure composed of many interlocking cycles, based on the rhythms of growth of the natural and social worlds. The flow of time defines abstract patterns of order, which add a further dimension of meaning to the ritual system.

TEMPORAL CYCLES

The God of the Masceti temple, who controls the
rats, must be given offerings and the God of
Sakenan Temple, who controls grasshoppers,
should be given offerings. If there is a problem at
the weir, perform the balik sumpah ritual at the
Ulun Swi temple.

(*Dewa Tattwa* [History of the Gods]
Ida Pedanda Made, Icaka 1865)

For every Balinese farmer, the agricultural year includes a sequence of field rituals. Some are carried out in a little temporary shrine at the upstream corner of the farmer's fields; others involve offerings to various water temples. If we translate the names of these rituals, they appear to be keyed to the growth of the plants: "Water-opening"; "Transplanting"; "Flowering of the Plants"; "Harvest." The precise order of these rituals tends to vary slightly from village to village,[13] but a typical sequence goes like this:

Agricultural Rites in Linear Order

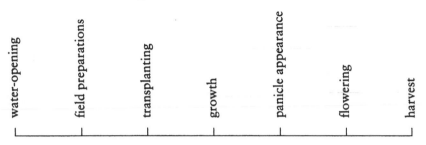

In any particular field, these rites appear to follow in a simple linear progression, marking the stages of growth of the rice plants. But in reality a single event, such as panicle appearance, may involve half a dozen water temples and two calendars. And "water-opening" ceremonies actually occur on several different calendrical cycles at different levels of the temple hierarchy. But because some "water-opening" ceremony inevitably precedes any field preparation, an observer watching the ritual sequence in a single field may erroneously conclude that one ritual simply follows the next, as "b" follows "a."

Of course, rice plants do grow linearly, and the panicle will infallibly appear at the end of the vegetative growth phase. But for panicle appearance to occur on schedule over hundreds of hectares of rice terraces, many water temples must coordinate their activities. By tracing the actual sequence of rituals, it becomes evident that the real subject of the ritual process is not the rice plants but the relationships between productive units in the water temple system. An example is provided by the Kedewatan irrigation system, which we first encountered in chapter 2.

This set of water temples begins a new productive cycle about once every ten years, with the "opening of the waters" (*mapag toyo*) ceremony at the Ulun Swi Temple. The date for this ritual is not predetermined. Instead, the process of setting the date and holding the ritual draws together all of the farmers who receive water from the same weir, a total of ten *subak*s that form the congregation of the Ulun Swi Temple.

The ceremony itself takes place at an altar that stands next to the weir, about 4 kilometers upstream from the rice terraces. This ritual activates the complete network of ten *subak*s, defines it as a productive and ritual

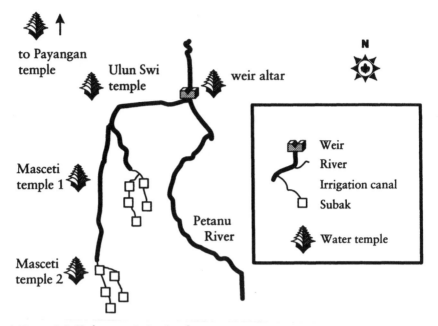

Figure 3.3. Kedewatan Irrigation System

unit, and establishes its relationship to the overall hierarchy of water temples and irrigation control. In the diagram, the main canal enters the terraces from the north. The Ulun Swi ("Head of the Ricefields") Temple is situated where the canal divides in two, just above the first set of terraces. On the chosen date, representatives from each *subak* bring their offerings to the Ulun Swi Temple. Using incense and prayers, the temple priest invites two deities to descend into the temple and join the god of the temple in accepting the feast that has been prepared for them. The two visiting deities are the Goddess of the Lake (Dewi Danu), the principal deity of the Temple of the Crater Lake, and the "Deity of the Masceti Temple of Payangan" (Ida Bhatara Masceti Payangan). The Masceti Temple of Payangan is the focal point for a regional cluster of *subak*s upstream from the Ulun Swi Temple, whose cropping patterns directly influence the water flow to the Ulun Swi Temple. Meanwhile, a small party made up of representatives of the ten *subak*s follow the main irrigation canal upstream to the altar that stands by the river weir and lay out more "deity offerings" for the god of the weir, the Goddess of the Lake, and the gods of the Masceti temples. At the climax of this rite, holy water from the Temple of the Crater Lake is poured directly into the entrance gate of the main canal. In this way, about once a decade, the ten *subak*s acknowledge their collective reliance on the weir, their neighbors upstream at the Payangan water temple, and the Temple of the Crater Lake by joining the symbolic flow of holy water with the flow of irrigation water at the weir.

The congregation of the Ulun Swi Temple consists of two Masceti temples, each of which sets the planting schedule for five *subak*s. The Masceti cycles begin with a ceremony called *muat emping*: offerings to the Earth Mother (Bhatari Pretiwi). *Muat emping* is performed when irrigation water reaches the fields, and the first annual rice planting is about to commence. The offerings to the Earth Mother are first dedicated at the Masceti temple at the beginning of the cultivation cycle and then distributed at the upstream corner of each farmer's fields.[14]

Field preparation is followed by *nuasen*, which marks the transplanting of rice seedlings into the fields. As *Mapag toyo* began the master cycle of the Ulun Swi Temple and *muat emping* initiated the Masceti cycles and the flooding of the terraces, *nuasen* begins the microcycles of individual *subak*s and farmers. In consultations at the Masceti temple, each of the five *subak*s sets a seven-day window for its members to perform *nuasen*, which must be coordinated with the flooding of the terraces. Each farmer must then determine the proper date on which to perform *nuasen* offerings at his field altar, which will set his own personal calendar for his field: it becomes "day one" for that particular rice crop, the beginning of a unique cycle. Months later, when he harvests the rice the farmer must perform the harvest ritual on the same date as *nuasen*. In effect, the growth cycle of a farmer's crop is timed to an accuracy of a single day. The cultivation cycle of the *subak* represents the aggregate of all of these individual cycles, which are tracked on a unique calendar called a *tika*. Plotted on the *tika*, the sum of all the individual cultivation cycles of the farmers equals the *subak* cycle. In a similar way, the aggregate of *subak* cycles equals the cycle of a Masceti, or an Ulun Swi. The structure of the temple hierarchy is embedded in these calendrical cycles, which equate longer cycles with larger and more comprehensive productive units.

This concept of large cycles encompassing many smaller ones has an interesting analogy in the composition of Balinese music. In a Balinese gamelan orchestra, small instruments play short, repetitive cyclical patterns. Larger instruments play at longer intervals, defining the beginnings and endings of melodies. All musical compositions are based on interlocking cyclical patterns, with long sections defined by the sounding of large gongs. In a similar way, high-ranking water temples are thought to encompass the activities of smaller ones, meshing many separate cycles into a single productive sequence.[15]

The *tika*, which defines time as composed of interlocking cycles, is one of two calendars used by the Balinese. The other is a luni-solar calendar, which enables the user to keep track of linear time—the progression of months and years. But the *tika* calendar is a different mathematical instrument used to keep track of many different intervals at once. Physically, a *tika* is a wooden or painted calendar that lays out a grid of thirty seven-day weeks. Each of the weeks is named, and any farmer can reel off the names of the weeks from memory.

But this is only the first and simplest classification of time portrayed by the *tika*. In addition to these thirty, seven-day weeks, the *tika* also keeps track of nine other weeks, with varying durations. Thus, there is also a three-day week, consisting of three named days: *Pasah*, *Beteng*, and *Kajeng*. The three-day week is concurrent with the seven-day week, so that if today is Sunday on the seven-day week, it is also *Pasah*, *Beteng*, or *Kajeng* on the three-day week. A symbolic notation (dots, lines, crosses,

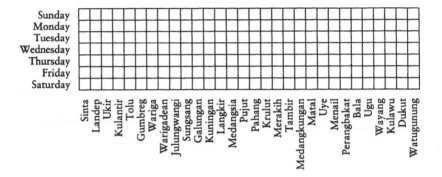

Uku (30 named 7-day weeks)

Figure 3.4. The Tika Calendar

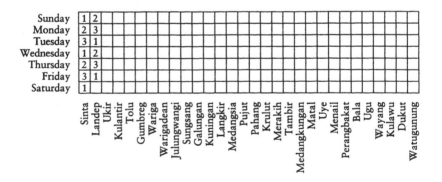

Day 1 = Pasah   Day 2 = Beteng   Day 3 = Kajeng

Figure 3.5. The Three-day Week Superimposed on the Tika

etc.) is used to superimpose the days of the three-day week on the grid of seven-day weeks displayed on the *tika*.

In addition to the seven-day week and the three-day week, there are also eight other weeks that vary in duration from one to ten days. For example, the one-day week consists of a single day, *Luang*, whereas the ten-day week consists of ten named days: *Pandita, Pati, Suka, Duka, Cri, Manuh, Manusa, Raja, Dewa, Raksasa*. The symbols inscribed on the *tika* enable the user to keep track of all ten concurrent weeks. Thus the first cell in the *tika* (Sunday in the week of *Landep*) is also the first day in the three-day week, the second day in the five-day week, the third day in the eight-day week, and so on.

If all these day-names were included on every cell, the calendar would become impossibly crowded. Instead, the symbolic notation permits a knowledgeable user to identify all ten day-names for any given date. For the farmers, however, the more important uses of the *tika* have to do with the timing of longer intervals. The symbols used to mark the days of the weeks emphasize the longer intervals defined by the intersections of cycles. For example, on the second day of the second week (*Landep*), the third day of the three-day week (*Kajeng*) falls on the fifth day of the five-day week (*Kliwon*). This conjunction of cycles occurs once every fifteen days, and is marked with a special symbol. Similarly, the conjunction of dates on the five- and seven-day weeks mark out thirty-five-day intervals, basic for the scheduling of many activities. Because the *tika* is independent of the seasons, it has no particular starting or stopping date. Starting from any given date, the *tika* helps mark out multiple intervals of any

1-day week:	vacant	
2-day week:	Menge	day 1
3-day week:	Pasah	day 1
4-day week:	Sri	day 1
5-day week:	Kliwon	day 2
6-day week:	Tungleh	day 1
7-day week:	Redite	day 1
8-day week:	Sri	day 1
9-day week:	Dangu	day 1
10-day week:	Sri	day 4
1-day week:	Luang	day 1
2-day week:	Pepet	day 2
3-day week:	Beteng	etc.

Figure 3.6. The First Day in the Tika Calendar

desired length up to 210 days, the growth duration of old Balinese rice (*padi del*).[16]

The principal practical use of the *tika* for the farmers is to synchronize concurrent production cycles, which may be of different lengths. Consider the complexity of timing water use and planting cycles for a productive system like the fifteen *subak*s of the Masceti temple Pamos Apuh. During the dry season, there is usually a need for rotational irrigation. A particular block of terraces may be flooded on a certain date for a specified number of weeks depending on the crop. Later, the flow may be reduced when the ground beneath the plow pan becomes saturated. Perhaps another block of terraces is scheduled to grow vegetables for a 105-day cycle and should receive irrigation water every third day of the five-day week during this 105-day interval. By using the *tika*, multiple concurrent cycles can be specified with ease and precision, with the assurance that they will mesh neatly together, synchronizing the labors of thousands of farmers.

The *tika* is a powerful instrument for calculating the orderly patterns of temporal succession. The social and natural worlds are defined as composed of many parts, all of which may be growing or changing at different rates. In the water temples, the uses of the *tika* extend beyond the synchronization of productive schedules, to structure the hierarchy of productive relationships. The personal growing cycles of individual farmers are aggregated into the cycles of the *subak*, weir, Ulun Swi and Masceti temples, and ultimately into the annual cycles of the Temple of the Crater Lake, which will be described in chapter 4. In this way, the productive process is defined as a hierarchical structure that emerges through the synchronization of the farmer's labors.

This wheels-within-wheels view of time assigns different ranks to different water temples, based on their role in the productive system. The highest rank belongs to major water temples, which control productive cycles for whole sections of rivers and blocks of terraces. Lesser temples control smaller cycles, involving smaller congregations of farmers. These differences in rank are symbolically marked by the architecture of temple shrines. All water temples include shrines called *meru*, named for the mythical Mount Meru, the sacred mountain at the center of the world. As Mount Meru is the home of the gods, so the *meru* shrines in temples are temporary homes for the gods during temple festivals. *Meru* are black wooden towers, with tiers of from one to eleven pagoda-like roofs (*tumpang*) rising above a central chamber. The higher the tower, the higher the rank of the god within. Whereas ordinary field shrines are usually single-storied, important Masceti temples may boast seven- or even nine-storied *meru* towers, signaling that they are of princely rank. For example, the god of the Masceti temple Pamos Apuh, controlling the productive cycles of dozens of lesser temples and thousands of farmers, is a five-storied god; whereas ordinary *subak* temples usually contain only three-storied *meru*. In general, the *meru* rank of a water temple depends on the scope of its productive role as defined by the hierarchy of productive cycles.

This ranking of temples by the height of their *meru* towers is not confined to the water temples but extends to all Balinese temples. We began this chapter with the observation that all Balinese social institutions build temples. Interestingly, there are no visible symbols that distinguish one type of temple from another. Instead, the symbolism of temple architecture has the opposite effect: the rank of all types of temples is expressed by the height of their *meru* towers.

If the hierarchical rank of water temples depends on their productive role, What determines the ranking of other types of temples? An example of another temple hierarchy, whose relevance to water temples will become apparent in a moment, is the set of temples that mark the rankings of descent groups in the Balinese version of the caste system. All Balinese are born into descent groups with caste rankings, which are proclaimed by the *meru* towers of household shrines to family ancestors. These household temples are found in the courtyard of every Balinese dwelling, instantly identifying the caste ranking of the inhabitants. Ancestor shrines for commoners may have from one to three *meru* roofs, high-caste aristocrats, five or more, with the highest rank of eleven roofs reserved for consecrated kings.[17] This symbolism of rank is especially important at the summit of the social hierarchy in the ancestor shrines of princes and kings. Because Balinese kingship was based on the principle of sacred descent, the *meru* towers of princes and kings defined their claims to power: a seven-storied princeling was outranked by a nine-storied rajah, both of whom were inferior in rank to an eleven-roof king. As Clifford Geertz observed in his study of Balinese kingship, the struggle of rival rajahs to achieve symbolic recognition as an "eleven-roof lord" defined the political arena of Balinese kingship; the dynastic struggles of the "theatre states": "The competition to be the center of centers, the axis of the world, was just that, a competition; and it was in the ability to stage productions of an eleven-roof scale, to mobilize the men, the resources, and, not least, the expertise, that made one an eleven-roof lord."[18]

In the context of the Balinese cult of divine kingship, the *meru* ranking of the shrine to the royal ancestors was a direct statement of a king's divine ancestry and, therefore, of his right to rule. The powers of kings were represented as a mandala of forces gathered around the royal shrine.

Thus the same image, an eleven-storied tower representing the cosmic mountain, served to represent the pinnacle of power for both the cult of divine kingship and the cult of water temples. But while kings base their claims to power on their divine ancestry, the powers of high-ranking water temples derive from their control of productive cycles. Despite these different origins, both types of power are represented on a single hierarchical scale: the nine-storied *meru* of a rajah is identical to the nine-storied *meru* of a major Masceti temple. The tension between these two sources of power reaches a climax at the apex of the water temple system, in the eleven-storied Temple of the Crater Lake, the subject of chapter 4.

CHAPTER FOUR

The Temple of the Crater Lake

FROM anywhere in central Bali, farmers need only glance up to the clouds around Mount Batur to be reminded of the ultimate origin of the water flowing into their fields. In the crater of the volcano, at an elevation high above the height at which rice may be grown, is an immense freshwater lake, stretching over 1,718 hectares.[1] This reservoir is regarded as the ultimate source of water for the rivers and springs that provide irrigation water for the whole of central Bali. Temple priests describe the mountain lake as a sacred mandala of waters, fed by springs lying at each of the wind directions, high above the irrigated lands. The steam from the caldera of Mount Batur represents the zenith of the mandala; the nadir is found in the depths of the lake. Each of the springs around the lake is regarded as the origin of waters for a particular hydrological region of central Bali. Thus, farmers from the district of Tejakula, in northern Bali, seek their most precious holy water from the northern spring of the lake, called Reijang Anyar; whereas the Unda river in the south is thought to originate from the spring called Bantah Anyut.

The entire mandala of the lake forms the center of a much larger mandala, consisting of the island of Bali and the seas that surround it. Priests describe the lake as a freshwater ocean, filled with life-giving water, which contrasts with the salt ocean that encircles it far below. The lake is the home of one of the two supreme deities of Bali, the "Goddess of the Lake," Dewi Danu. Her relationship to the farmers of central Bali is succinctly defined in a manuscript kept in her temple, "Because the Goddess makes the waters flow, those who do not follow her laws may not possess her rice terraces."[2]

According to legend, the goddess and her male counterpart, the God of Mount Agung, emerged from an erupting volcano in the Icaka year 310.[3] Together with other, lesser gods, they took possession of the land and waters of Bali. The goddess rules the lake and Mount Batur, the second-highest peak in Bali, whereas the god rules Mount Agung. As the male and female deities of the two highest mountains, they form a complementary pair, the supreme gods of the island. The male god of Mount Agung is worshipped at the temple of Besakih, high on Mount Agung, and is symbolically associated with the king of Klungkung, who claims supremacy over all other Balinese kings. But the Goddess of the Lake has no special relationship to any king or kingdom. Her principal congregation consists of several hundred *subaks*, which make annual pilgrimages to her mountaintop temple called Pura Ulun Danu Batur, the Temple of the Crater Lake.

From a religious standpoint, the Temple of the Crater Lake stands at the summit of the water temple system, and through its association with the Goddess of the Lake claims authority over the water in all of the irrigation systems of central Bali. But does this symbolic ownership of irrigation water translate into real control?

According to Balinese religious belief, the Goddess of the Lake and the God of Mount Agung share dominion over the island, a concept that is taken literally by the inhabitants of the mountains, who point to the side of the lake where the power of the goddess stops and the dominion of the god begins. In precolonial Bali, such beliefs were not a purely religious matter, but had important political implications, for the powers of kings were directly linked to those of temples and gods. In nineteenth-century Bali, before the Dutch conquest, the nominal king of Bali was the ruler of Klungkung. The claims of this king to supremacy over the other kings and princes of Bali were represented by his association with the God of Mount Agung, symbolized by the eleven-roofed *meru* tower in the royal palace. Indeed, in some contexts the king of Klungkung was actually identified with the god. His title, for example, was "Dewa Agung," meaning either "Great God" or "God of Agung." One of the principal functions of the Dewa Agung was the performance of rituals and sacrifices at the temple of Besakih, dedicated to the God of Mount Agung and his retinue.

As the home of the mountain goddess, the Temple of the Crater Lake ranks as the second most important temple on the island after the temple of Besakih. But unlike Besakih, the Temple of the Crater Lake is also the supreme water temple, with an enormous congregation of farmers. As a water temple, it is unique in several important respects, foremost among them its eleven-tiered *meru* for the goddess.[4] Unlike even the largest regional Masceti temples, which are left empty except during festivals, the Temple of the Crater Lake is kept perpetually open by a permanent staff of priests. A virgin priestess selects twenty-four priests of the temple, who are chosen in childhood as lifelong servants of the goddess. The priesthood is hierarchical, and at the summit of the hierarchy is a single high priest who is believed to be the earthly representative of the Goddess of the Lake. His association with one of the two supreme gods of the island gives him a status quite unlike that of any other temple priest and raises the question of his relationship to the other human being magically linked to a mountain god, the Dewa Agung or king of Bali.

THE GODDESS AND HER PRIESTS

The high priest of the Temple of the Crater Lake is called the Jero Gde. He is also called Sanglingan, "Lightning-struck," because he is selected in childhood by a virgin priestess[5] of the temple, after the death of his predecessor. The priestess goes into a trance to allow the Goddess of the Lake to possess her voice to name the boy who will become the new Jero Gde. From the moment of his selection until the day of his death, the Jero Gde is regarded as the earthly representative of the Goddess of the Lake. By day he offers sacrifices to her on behalf of the hundreds of *subak*s that make up the temple's principal congregation. By night, he may receive guidance from her in dreams. He is always dressed in white, the color of purity, and wears his hair long. Although he is of commoner caste, his permanent identification with the Goddess of the Lake sets him apart from all other Balinese priests.

It is true that during certain rituals some priests are believed to become possessed by a deity. For example, at the climax of the ritual for creating holy water, Brahmana high priests[6] are thought to incarnate the god Siwa. Similarly, trance mediums (*balian*) are regularly possessed by unseen spirits. But in every case, when the ritual or trance is finished, the link between priests and deities is broken. In contrast, the magical identification of the Jero Gde with the Goddess of the Lake continues for his lifetime. In the case of the current Jero Gde, it is said that signs of his special relationship with the goddess were detected even before he was chosen. As he explained to me: "Before I was chosen, I had a feeling—a strangeness in myself. I mean, often when I went home, I was given a name alluding to the presence of a god."

Once, I asked him what it was like for an eleven-year-old boy to suddenly take on the responsibilities of a Jero Gde. His answer stressed the guiding role of the goddess: "The Deity chose me through the trance of the Virgin Priestess. Then I immediately went through the ceremonies of 'installation'—I was purified to become the Jero Gde. At that time I was still eleven years old. . . . But because I was selected by an imperial deity (Ida Sasuunan), there were no problems. I simply went along, just as I do now. I had become the Jero Gde, even if I was still a child."[7]

Although ordinary priests are not identified in this way with deities, kings are. In particular, the king of Klungkung, acknowledged even by rival princes as the highest-ranking Balinese king, was symbolically identified with the male god of Mount Agung and Besakih temple in the rituals of the royal cult. But whereas the powers of the Dewa Agung derive from his descent, those of the Jero Gde originate in the logic of the water temple system. Unlike the king of Klungkung, who claims symbolic dominion over the whole of Bali, the authority of the Jero Gde is strictly limited. As the earthly representative of the Goddess of the Lake, his powers extend to the Temple of the Crater Lake and the waters believed to originate from the lake. Essentially, he is a temple priest, but his relationship to the Goddess of the Lake gives him a special authority over irrigation water. As he himself remarked: "It is only the Goddess of the Lake who can properly give water. She already embodies, incarnates water, which she gives to her *subak*s, from the lake."[8]

Does the symbolic identification of the Jero Gde with his goddess endow him with control over water rights? One afternoon I put this question to a *subak* head who is also the elected leader of the fifteen *subak*s of the Masceti temple Pamos Apuh. This was his response.

> SUBAK HEAD: It's like this. Everything that concerns the *subak*s is interconnected. The word is, *anugraha* ["grant" or "gift"]. So that—as with the fifteen *subak*s located at our Masceti temple— the flow from the spring has been calculated. It produces enough for so many hectares. Now if, for example, there was a request for more water, obviously the Jero Gde must lower his hand, give a decision. So it won't happen that those who have received the 'grant'—from the Masceti temple and the Batur temple—don't get enough water. Because they have the right from earlier times. Because these things are usually written in the records at the Temple of the Crater Lake.

This answer appeared to affirm the authority of the Jero Gde over the allocation of water rights. But I wondered whether the priest merely gave his blessing to whatever decision had been taken by the farmers. Had he ever refused a request for irrigation water?

> SUBAK HEAD: Earlier, there was a request to open new terraces here—a request that went straight to the Temple of the Crater Lake. But, well, maybe because the Jero Gde was concerned about the people of my village, anyway he didn't give permission. If he had, there would have been a lot of twists and turns! So it was dropped—up 'till now, it hasn't happened. The water can't be taken.
>
> We, too, once had a desire to open new lands, convert some dry fields to rice terraces. We asked permission from the Temple of the Crater Lake, so that our water would be sufficient for the new terraces. But the Jero Gde declined.
>
> LANSING: Where?
>
> SUBAK HEAD: Just upstream from the Bayad weir, we wanted to use that water. There is a spring there, we wanted to use it. We weren't

going to build a new weir on the river, just use that spring. But if we did, the Bayad weir would have been affected [i.e., there would be a reduction in the flow reaching the Bayad weir]. So we had to abandon the idea.[9] [See chaps. 2 and 3 for maps of the Bayad irrigation system.]

LANSING: Where does the authority of the Jero Gde come from?

SUBAK HEAD: Belief ... overflowing belief. Concerning Batur temple—really that is the center, the origin of waters, you see. At this moment, the Jero Gde holds all this in his hands. At the Temple of Lake Batur.

This answer was in accord with the image of the role of the Jero Gde and the mandala of waters described by the temple priests. Evidently, the *subaks* belonging to this Masceti acknowledged the right of the Jero Gde to decide upon water allocations in the name of the goddess. But to truly resolve the question of the extent of the temple's authority, I sought out disputes over water rights that were still in progress. One of the most interesting cases involved the destruction of a weir.

A Quarrel between Subaks

The village of Pengalu lies at high elevation and began growing rice on irrigated terraces only ten years ago. Formerly, they relied on rainfall to grow dry rice and vegetable crops. In 1986, the village sent a messenger to urgently request a visit from the Jero Gde. In response, the Jero Gde sent a temple messenger to inquire into the case. I spoke to the messenger, who described the problem as follows:

TEMPLE MESSENGER: It had to do with water. The source was a little to the north of the village of Pengalu, to the northwest. The water was taken by Pengalu and brought down. Earlier, there was enough. But now in the dry season, there wasn't enough for Penginyahan [the village immediately downstream from Pengalu]. So this became a problem. The water for Pengalu—the new *subak*—was taken back by Penginyahan.

On the appointed date, I drove with the Jero Gde to the village. By observing what he said and did, I hoped to be able to gauge the extent of his real powers over irrigation. We were accompanied by two temple messengers, who are responsible for this region of central Bali, and two of the regular priests of the Temple of the Crater Lake.

When we arrived at the village of Pengalu, the entire *subak* was seated in their village meeting hall, awaiting our arrival. We were led to seats on

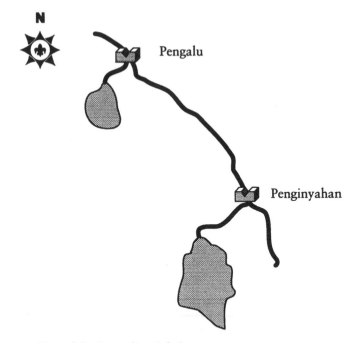

Figure 4.1. Map of the Quarreling *Subaks*

an elevated platform, where four village leaders joined us facing the *subak*. I requested permission to tape the meeting, and the Jero Gde nodded his acknowledgment. Rather nervously, the village leaders agreed. After brief welcoming remarks, the head of the *subak* explained the problem.[10]

> SUBAK HEAD: So we built a weir on the Telaga Genteg stream. The weir was built by the whole community. The idea was to raise the waters to irrigate terraces for the hamlets of Kerta and Mawang. . . . A little while ago, if I'm not mistaken on the 21st and 22d of January, our *subak* was demolished by *subak* Penginyahan. Why the people of Penginyahan wrecked our weir,[11] we don't know. So since the 22d of January 1986 we of *subak* Pengalu haven't had water. No water at all enters *subak* Pengalu. There were about 200 people from Penginyahan, led by the heads of their *subak* and village. The government—the police, kabupaten and kecamatan[12]—have taken this in hand, but nothing has been done. So that you may know, Jero Gde, that this is how things are for *subak* Pengalu. Our *subak* is ten years old; we have harvested rice for ten years; and we have joined the congregation of the Temple of Batur. Now Penginyahan has engaged in destruction. So *subak* Pengalu up to now hasn't planted rice. Our fields are empty.

JERO GDE: In these things, if we find a path the way we do in Bali, there is only one [way], which is the direction upstream, to the origins. Isn't it so? Who is the owner of these waters? In truth, when matters develop into a big confrontation, everyone's wishes are bad, then everything turns bad. And the effect is, the water is not used. Water that is needed. So it is. So this new problem, first I must take it up to the regent [*bupati*]. Such things, every aspect must be taken up or they can't be concluded. Now apparently this forest area is only producing about a hundred liters of water, right?[13] If things don't work out, that water is definitely wasted. Lost, useless. My concern is, I don't promise, but let us together make strenuous efforts, force things into the very best path, then perhaps we can obtain the opportunity to fix this situation of ours, our dam at Pengalu. May the village easily receive this path, which is my decree, so that the path you've begun with the bupati can be followed to the end. Together!

After these remarks, the Jero Gde asked to visit the site of the damaged weir. The entire structure had been washed away, and the river was flowing freely in the direction of Penginyahan, a few kilometers downstream. After looking the situation over, the Jero Gde asked the *subak* to gather around him, and addressed them.

JERO GDE: I am ready to add to my former words. As I asked earlier, who owns these waters? Clearly it is only the deities who prevent this spring from drying up, is it not so? What about downstream? Now you of Pengalu already have the right to use some of this water. And for those below [i.e., the Penginyahan irrigation system] there was no shortage, formerly? For Pengalu here, just how many hectares were in use before the dam was destroyed?

SUBAK HEAD: About 30 hectares.

JERO GDE: So now, my wishes are, remember the goddess! Things are not good now, so the medicine must be applied quickly. As for me, I feel very sad. Together, then, let's begin.

Legally, disputes about irrigation fall under the jurisdiction of the government office of the *sedahan*. In modern Bali, the office of the *sedahan* continues to perform the same tax-collecting functions that it carried out under Dutch rule. And, just as in the time of the Dutch, the *sedahan* is supposed to decide questions of water rights. The degree to which this legal arrangement is the basis of actual practice may perhaps be judged by the fact that the office of the *sedahan* in the regency in which these events took place does not possess a map of any irrigation system. Instead, the *sedahan*'s staff maintain records of land ownership that are used to calculate taxes.

Within this governmental structure of irrigation control, the Jero Gde has no role. Indeed, from an administrative standpoint he does not exist. But government offices are staffed by Balinese, who live in a world of water temples. In this case, the bupati (head of the regency) became involved because the struggle between the two *subaks* had become a police matter.

Soon after viewing the damaged weir, the Jero Gde paid a formal call upon the bupati, urging him to provide technical assistance while the Jero Gde would try to facilitate a compromise between the quarreling *subaks*. The Jero learned that the government had already developed plans for the construction of a new concrete weir at Pengalu. These plans, however, could not go forward unless the quarrel between the *subaks* could be settled. The Jero Gde sent temple messengers to the two *subaks*, who agreed to a provisional compromise concerning water rights, by which the Pengalu *subaks* were to receive one-third and the Penginyahan *subaks* downstream would receive the remainder. If, however, the two-thirds share of the Penginyahan *subaks* proved to be inadequate, they reserved the right to reopen the question of water shares. Construction of the new weir commenced soon after the Jero's meeting with the bupati, and within a year a new concrete structure was standing on the ruins of the old temporary weir.

CREATION OF A NEW SUBAK

One day in the summer of 1983, a small delegation of farmers arrived at the temple and were ushered into the kitchen to be given refreshments and a chance to informally state their request. They came from a small village in northern Gianyar and represented a group of thirty-six families who wished to create a new *subak*. They had discovered a spring high in the mountains, about 3.4 kilometers from their village, and wished to use the water to create rice terraces on their land. They had many questions: Could they use the water? What would be required for them to create a *subak*? And, most importantly, were the chances of success good enough for them to invest the necessary labor and funds? The village was quite poor and to build the necessary irrigation system would involve many months of labor and stretch their resources to the limit.

After listening to their request, the temple staff guided them in presenting their offerings at the shrine of the Goddess of the Lake. When they had received their blessing of holy water, a temple messenger[14] accompanied them back to their land to inspect the site of the proposed new *subak.* The spring appeared to be producing approximately 30 liters of water per second. Although it seemed likely that the water from the spring must eventually flow into the Ayung River, the location was so remote that it proved to be impossible to determine where this occurred, and therefore, which weir was next downstream. Thus there was no need to obtain permission from neighbors downstream to share the water. The new *subak* of Gateh could have all of it, if they could get it to their fields. The question was whether the spring was large enough and permanent enough to be worth the trouble and expense of digging terraces, tunnels, and canals. After inspecting the spring and the proposed route of the irrigation canal, the temple priests advised them to proceed.

A few months later, I was invited by the temple priests to accompany them on a trip in which they hoped to constitute formally the new *subak.* On the appointed morning, representatives of every family in Gateh appeared at the temple in two large trucks, bearing offerings. The offerings were laid out beside the main shrine to the Goddess of the Lake, and *mapiuning* (request) prayers were offered to inform the goddess of the desire of the village to create a *subak.* Temple priests prepared the holy water vessel called Bhatara Tirtha, which represents the presence of the goddess herself.

In this guise, the goddess joined us as we boarded the trucks and drove to the vicinity of the spring. With the priests bearing Bhatara Tirtha at the front of the procession, we descended a steep ravine and followed the stream at its bottom to the spring. The priests selected a spot just above the spring for the new shrine to the goddess and gave instructions for its construction to the *subak* leaders. Then a makeshift temporary shrine was constructed around Bhatara Tirtha, and the *subak* seated themselves facing the shrine and the spring, while the priests led them in prayers to the goddess. In this way, the new shrine was dedicated as a place where the *subak* could address the goddess and acknowledge her gift of water.

This concluded the ceremonies at the spring. Because the terrain was very rugged, we returned to the trucks and drove to the village, near the site of the proposed new terraces. Rough terraces had already been prepared, and work had begun on the main canal system. The temple priests walked over the whole area, accompanied by the priests and *subak* leaders, and suggested that work on the canal be postponed at this end because the location of the canal would ultimately depend on the configuration of the tunnel and canal upstream. It was clear that an irrigation tunnel at least several hundred meters long would have to be constructed near the spring. The priests suggested that the *subak* seek advice from a team of professional tunnel builders.

Finally, the priests chose a location for a new Ulun Swi (Head of the rice terraces) Temple: atop the highest terraced hillside, near the presumed entry point for the planned irrigation canal. Several priests measured out the floor plan for the temple and explained the placement of shrines. There were no prayers or offerings because the Ulun Swi Temple would not be dedicated until the water was actually flowing into the terraces.

Two years later, I returned to the village in the company of the Jero Gde. The irrigation system was functioning, and the first crop of rice had been planted in about half of the terraces. The water supply was not sufficient to irrigate the remaining terraces, which was something of a disappointment to the *subak*. However, they looked forward to bringing offerings from their first rice crop to the Temple of the Crater Lake for the Tenth Month ceremonies, at which time they would request more water from the goddess.

THE POWERS OF THE JERO GDE

We have seen that the Jero Gde exercises considerable authority over water rights. His power in the visible world (*sekala*) ultimately stems from his relationship to the Goddess of the Lake, in the realm of the immaterial (*niskala*). This relationship is symbolized through his identification with the principal shrine of the goddess at the temple.

As the plan of the temple shows (see app. 1), the highest *meru* tower at Batur is the eleven-storied shrine to the Goddess of the Lake (fig. A.1., #24), which is also identified with the Jero Gde. To indicate the strength of this association, the temple staff point out that when he dies, the Jero Gde will be cremated in an eleven-storied bier similar to the *meru* shrine. The number of stories on a cremation bier (*wadah*) in Bali is an index of caste rank. Commoners are cremated in biers with from one to three stories, depending upon the supposed rank of their lineage. Twice-born aristocrats of noble caste are cremated in taller biers, with eleven stories being reserved for the highest-ranking consecrated kings. The eleven-storied cremation bier of the Jero Gde thus sets him apart from all other Balinese of commoner caste, indicating that he is not merely a servant of the goddess but is identified with her in a much more fundamental way.

Further proofs of his relationship to the goddess and the lake-mandala were said to have occurred when he was chosen to become the new Jero Gde. He was not present at the temple when the Virgin Priestess went into a trance. Instead, a delegation from the temple came to find him. He was then eleven years old, a number that is magically significant not only because of the eleven-storied shrine to the goddess but also because of the eleven sources of holy water and the eleven springs around the lake.

LANSING: It is said that when you were chosen to be Jero Gde there were certain signs?

JERO GDE: Yes, there were signs. . . . The first thing I experienced was a dream. I dreamt that I ascended into the main shrine, with eleven stories. I asked my parents, What does it mean? They answered, "Ah, there is no doubt, you will be chosen Jero Gde." I was amazed! What, me become the Jero Gde? What's this? I didn't believe it.

Then I went with my friends, in search of a spring to bathe in. And we found eleven! Eleven bathing springs! In one day! We children didn't realize at first; we didn't ask, it was the parents who urged us to search. We were just thinking about bathing! Why this happened—maybe the deity inspired one of the adults to set us on this. But the effect was, I was cleansed.[15]

The next day, a delegation from Batur arrived. Then suddenly the light became very clear. When the Batur delegation approached, the wind came up from nowhere, Ba-ba-bah! Thunder, BAH! And rain, heavy rain! Then we set out, and the rain stopped; it was strange. I was escorted directly to the temple. I felt that all of these were signs from the goddess.[16]

A few moments later, while we were still talking about his experiences, the Jero Gde suggested a parallel between his own installation and the ceremony of royal consecration for the last king of Klungkung, organized by the Dutch in 1929.

JERO GDE: Perhaps there was some inspiration at [the palace of] Klungkung—I don't know. . . . The signs were the same—the sudden appearance of a great wind.

This parallel between the position of the Jero Gde and that of the king of Klungkung, was repeatedly brought to my attention. The issue crystallized when I was told by several of the elders that they were encouraging the Jero Gde to undergo the ceremony of royal consecration for a king, *abiseka ratu*.[17] According to the elders, the performance of *abiseka ratu* at the temple would entitle the Jero Gde to the title Dalem Sanglingan. Dalem is a royal title for the Klungkung royal dynasty, thus "Dalem Sanglingan" would mean something like "divinely chosen ruler." When I spoke to the Jero Gde, he said that he did indeed expect to undergo the *abiseka ratu* ritual someday. But he emphasized that he would never be a king in the usual sense, that his powers extended only to the temple itself and the *pepasyan:* the forty-five *subaks* that form the principal congregation of the temple. But what might these powers be, assuming that the *abiseka ratu* ceremony were ever to be performed?

According to tradition, the *abiseka ratu* ceremony for the consecration of a king must be performed by Brahmana high priests attached to a royal court. It seemed to me doubtful that the high priests of a realm such as Klungkung would recognize the legitimacy of the *abiseka ratu* ritual for the Jero Gde, who was after all born a commoner. For although the last Dewa Agung was killed by the Dutch in 1908, some members of the royal family survived and have continued to carry out religious ceremonies at the temple of Besakih. A few years ago, the *abiseka ratu* ritual was performed by the court priests of Klungkung for one of the members of the royal family, who received the title Ratu Dalem. The title connotes kingly status but is inferior to the title Dewa Agung.

As soon as possible, I went to Klungkung and interviewed one of the high priests of Klungkung. Another Brahman joined our discussion to assist me in putting my questions: Should the *abiseka ratu* ceremony be performed for the Jero Gde? How does his role compare with that of a consecrated king?

BRAHMAN PRIEST: Those are the rules in the mountains, at Batur: after he has become the Jero Gde, he has the right to receive everything that goes into or out of the Batur Temple. He must divide—Who is to receive what? The cost of his installation is borne by the people. Since he became the Jero Gde, everything is guaranteed by the people. At the temple, he has authority.

BRAHMANA: That means he doesn't undergo *abhiseka ratu*, right?

BRAHMAN PRIEST: No.

LANSING: Or—not yet? They say that when he is older, he may undergo the *abiseka* ritual?

BRAHMAN PRIEST: Now, let's say he proceeds with *abiseka ratu*, What further title would he gain? He is already Jero Gde. His livelihood—riches really—are guaranteed by the people. When he dies the people will, ah, . . . he is already rich. The fruits of these labors mean, he is rich! But when he dies, the choice of a child [to succeed him], the "awakening," can't be his son. [In other words, unlike kingship, the position of Jero Gde is not hereditary.]

LANSING: Have you ever participated in the installation of another such priest, or only at Batur?

BRAHMAN PRIEST: No, only there at Batur temple. At Besakih temple this doesn't exist. It's different for the temple priests at Besakih. But at Batur, the Jero Gde is empowered—he alone owns the temple. . . . When they choose the Jero Gde there, it is not a royal Highness who decides. It is a deity's inspiration.

LANSING: And that is why he has the title of *Sanglingan*?

BRAHMAN PRIEST: Yes. Chosen from Above. Otherwise, it could not be. It means, indicated by a burst of lightning. *Sanglingan*, if you seek its meaning, means cleansed.

LANSING: Outside of this priest at Batur, are there any others?

BRAHMAN PRIEST: No.

LANSING: One only in Bali?

BRAHMAN PRIEST: Yes.[18]

The priest's remarks seemed to confirm the special status of the Jero Gde but left the question of the ceremony of royal consecration still in doubt. I immediately returned to the temple, and sought out one of the elders to ask about the precise sequence of rituals planned for the *abiseka ratu* of the Jero Gde. This list bore virtually no resemblance to the *abiseka ratu* ceremony described in Balinese and Dutch texts.[19] Instead, the Jero Gde himself makes offerings at the major shrines (fig. A.1, #19, #24, #22, #23) and the shrines to the deities Pertiwi (the Earth Mother), Dalem Baturenggong, and I Ratu Gde Mekolem. Then, according to the elder:

ELDER: He bathes eleven times in one day and changes his clothing eleven times. Then he has finished *abiseka ratu*.

LANSING: That's all?

ELDER: As of now, it hasn't been performed. I've admonished him three times. He didn't want to. Because he still wants to work, to acquire wealth. When he is ready, we're prepared. This can't be done by a *pedanda* [Brahmana high priest].

LANSING: But doesn't it require a Brahman priest to perform *abiseka ratu*?

ELDER: That's different. That is *abiseka ratu* for a king. For a kingdom. Like Bangli, Klungkung, or Gianyar. It's for a kingdom! This is *abiseka ratu* for the title as Jero Gde.

LANSING: But for the kingdoms of Gianyar, Klungkung, and so forth, it is permitted to perform *abiseka ratu* with a Brahman priest?

ELDER: The king's high priest [Bhagawanta] or another Brahman priest [*pedanda*]. But here it is not possible.

LANSING: Why not?

ELDER: Because here, his control extends only to the powers of the temple. The affairs of Batur Temple. His control extends down the lines of *pepasyan* [member *subaks*] that follow Batur Temple. It is they who honor him! They who bring the offerings, you see.

LANSING: I've heard that the ceremony is like a death.[20]

ELDER: That which dies is only feelings, desires. Removing the anchors. That is why it takes eleven times. So that pollution is banished! Up to the very second, that is the requirement for the ritual bathing. So that mind and spirit are elevated.

LANSING: Bathed—in holy water!

ELDER: Holy water! Holy water from the eleven sources of the lake, the eleven origins. From the lake! Because the lake has eleven sources, eleven springs. One goes this way, another that way and so forth. From each we take an essence [*sari*] to cleanse the Jero Gde.[21]

The symbolism of this ritual seemed to focus on the identification of the Jero Gde with the eleven-pointed mandala of the lake and with the goddess. Later, I spoke to other Brahman priests, who did not question the unique relationship of the Jero Gde to the Goddess of the Lake and confirmed that this relationship parallels the identification of the king of Klungkung with the God of Mount Agung. But the ritual that the priests of the Temple of the Crater Lake insisted on calling *abiseka ratu* bore no resemblance to the ritual for the consecration of kings. Moreover, both Brahmans and temple priests agreed that even with the title of Dalem Sanglingan, the powers of the Jero Gde would still be confined to the temple and the waters of the lake.

While I was struggling to make sense of this, the temple scribe, who is himself symbolically identified with a shrine at the temple (fig. A.1, #20–#21), drew my attention to an aspect of the identity of the Jero Gde to which I had paid little attention: his line of descent. Upon the death of his predecessor, each new Jero Gde must be chosen from a descent group called the Paseks of the Black Wood.[22] Because this is a commoner lineage found only in the mountains, I assumed that it had no bearing on the relationship of the Jero Gde to the king of Bali. But the temple scribe suggested that I read the history of the Paseks of the Black Wood, which is related in a chronicle similar to the dynastic chronicles of Balinese kingdoms.

I learned from the chronicle that the ancestors of the Jero Gde trace their beginnings to a time before the age of kings, in the distant past. Their story begins with the emergence of the Goddess of Mount Batur and the God of Mount Agung from the erupting volcano and the creation of the first human beings. Soon after the gods take possession of Bali, they are visited by the great priest-god Mahameru, who decides to bathe in the waters of the crater lake. As he explains to the other gods:

After bathing I continued my journey to Besakih, but suddenly I saw a statue of black wood which looked very like a human. My heart was very attracted and I wished to bring the statue to life, so I performed yoga semadhi and requested Hyang Kawi (the Creator) to permit the statue to become a person. My prayer was answered, the statue became alive, and I heard words from the Ether instructing me to teach him the sacred knowledge, so that shortly there would be priests in Bali.[23]

The descendants of the living statue became the Paseks of the Black Wood from whom the Jero Gde is chosen. The chronicle is thus a myth of origins connecting the Jero Gde with the arrival of the gods on the mountaintops of Batur and Agung and the origins of human society. The site at which the black wood came to life is now marked by the origin temple of this descent group, which is symbolically associated with the Temple of the Crater Lake. The Paseks of the Black Wood believe themselves to be the most ancient of Balinese lineages, and at the festivals of their origin temple, they seek to renew their contact with the prehuman sources of power in the mountains and the lake.

But how, I wondered, were these powers related to the question of kingship? The temple scribe drew my attention to the relationship between the Jero Gde and the second-ranking priest in the temple hierarchy, called the Lesser Jero Gde (Jero Gde Alitan). As the Greater Jero Gde is identified with the eleven-storied shrine to the Goddess, the Lesser Jero Gde is identified with two nine-storied *meru* towers for the God of Mount Agung, which stand alongside the shrines to the goddess. Their nine stories indicate that the God of Mount Agung ranks second to the goddess in her own temple on her mountaintop. And, as with the Greater Jero Gde, the lineage history of the Lesser Jero Gde provides an explanation for the sources of his power. The Lesser Jero Gde is chosen from the descent group called Pasek Gelgel, whose legend is told in their chronicle, the *Babad Pasek Gelgel*. Gelgel was the first Balinese royal dynasty, the first possessors of the temple of Besakih on Mount Agung, whose descendants became the kings of Klungkung. According to their chronicle, the Pasek Gelgel were a commoner lineage who became the most loyal servants of the Gelgel kings. Some of them were sent into the mountains to establish the royal power of Gelgel in these remote regions. However, the mountain people were never completely subjugated by Gelgel, and the contest between the power of the courts and the more ancient powers that dwell in the mountains has never ended.

Thus the two priests draw their power from different sources. In the festivals of their origin temple, the Pasek Gelgel derive their power from the royal court of Gelgel, the first and greatest Balinese kings. Through Gelgel, they are linked to the God of Mount Agung, Besakih Temple, and the royal dynasty of Klungkung. The Paseks of the Black Wood, by contrast, trace their power further back in time, to a line of priests created from the Black Wood beside the lake. Symbolically, the Greater Jero Gde represents a divine power more ancient than the king of Bali.

As interpreted by the temple scribe and the elders, the two chronicles provided a coherent explanation of the relationship between the temples, shrines, and gods.

Goddess of the Lake	God of Mount Agung
Temple of the Crater Lake	Temple of Besakih
Water	Fire
Jero Gde	King of Bali

Within the temple, these contrasts are replicated:

Greater Jero Gde	Lesser Jero Gde
11-storied *meru*	9-storied *meru*
Paseks of the Black Wood	Paseks of Gelgel

But I wondered whether the princes and Brahmans would accept this relationship. Had the temple priests constructed a sort of counterideology to the claims of the king of Klungkung? Although the temple was clearly preoccupied with the question of its relationship to the temple of Besakih and the royal dynasty of Klungkung, I wondered if the interest were reciprocated by the princes of Klungkung and their priests.

Meanwhile, in the late summer of 1987 the Jero Gde decided to organize the largest ceremony in the ritual cycle of the temple, called Panca Wali Krama. The water level in Lake Batur was low, and the *subaks* were pressing the Jero Gde to carry out Panca Wali Krama, the most potent of the temple's rituals, to end the drought. The Jero Gde sent notification to the king of Klungkung, his court priests and other princes of his intention to perform Panca Wali Krama. Their response to this invitation promised to provide some answers to my question. I had already interviewed many priests without fully understanding their responses. But if the king of Klungkung and his priests actually attended the Panca Wali Krama, the nature of their participation would presumably signal their relationship to the temple and the Jero Gde.

PANCA WALI KRAMA

On October 22, 1987, (the Dark Moon of the Ninth Month) Panca Wali Krama was performed at the temple, for the first time in the lifetime of the current Jero Gde. I arrived five days earlier, when preparations were already well under way.

The central courtyard of the temple is a large open space surrounded by stone walls and towering gates. During the regular annual cycle of rituals, it is used as the performance space, where the temple dancers and orchestras play for large crowds.[24] For Panca Wali Krama, eleven temporary shrines were laid out in the shape of an eleven-pointed *nawa-*

sangha mandala in the center of the courtyard, symbolically identifying the summit of Mount Batur with the cosmic center. At the climax of the rituals, twenty-two Brahmana high priests would be seated in pairs facing each of the points of the mandala, where they would sanctify holy water and then use this water for a ritual of purification and renewal.

Requests for the vast quantities of offerings needed for these rituals had been sent to the *subaks* and princely houses of central Bali. The princes of Bangli, Gianyar, and Ubud and the royal family of Klungkung responded by sending *jajan bumi*, grand cosmological symbols made of edible materials, which are the most extravagant of all Balinese offerings. Over a period of several weeks, millions of rupiah and several tons of offerings were donated by the *subaks*. Meanwhile, delegations of priests from the temple were dispatched on journeys to seek holy water from crater lakes in the mountains of the neighboring islands of Lombok (Mount Renjani) and Java (Mount Bromo), as well as the supreme (*sadkahyangan*) temples of Bali. While the holy water and offerings were gradually accumulating at the temple, the Greater Jero Gde himself set off on two journeys. The first was an expedition to the home of a priest high above Besakih temple, in search of the most sacred bell in Bali, the Genta Kentel Bumi. The bell is kept in a temple that was partially destroyed by lava in the 1963 eruption of Mount Agung and ordinarily never leaves Mount Agung.

Once the bell had been secured, the Jero Gde proceeded on his next quest: holy water from the sea floor, below the seaside temple of Batu Bolong in Badung. On this occasion, he was accompanied by all the remaining temple priests and orchestras and more than two hundred vehicles, mostly trucks, filled with *subak* members. The procession stopped twice on the way from Batur to the sea, outside the palaces of Bangli and Gianyar. Temporary platforms had been constructed for offerings from local farmers in the open courtyards outside each palace. Thousands of farmers waited as the Batur priests unloaded the images of the temple's deities from the trucks to the accompaniment of music from the temple's sacred orchestra. The gates to the palaces swung open and gamelan orchestras marched out as the offerings were readied. Court priests from the palaces presented the offerings of each realm to the goddess, and the Batur priests sprinkled the worshippers with holy water.

It was near nightfall when the procession reached the sea at Batu Bolong. Toward midnight, as the crowd thinned out, the Jero Gde led a procession of temple priests to climb the black lava rocks exposed by the receding tide. Standing beneath the royal umbrellas and grasping the sacred black whips that are the emblems of his power, the Jero Gde asked the Sea God to draw back, so that he could collect sweet water bubbling up from artesian wells in the sea floor. At low tide, frightened young priests raced out to collect the freshest water they could find to be used in the preparation of holy water at the temple.

The following morning, the procession began to climb back up Mount Batur. At noon, surprised tourists were told to climb out of their vehicles and wait patiently, for "The goddess has descended into the Masceti temple of Ubud," and all traffic must cease. After receiving the homage of the *subaks* and the princes of Ubud, the procession returned to the temple, and at noon on the following day the ritual reached its climax. At each of the eleven shrines, high priests gathered all the sacred waters that had been collected from the sea floor, the caldera of Mount Batur, the eleven sources of Lake Batur, the supreme temples of Bali, and the crater lakes of neighboring islands. Seated in the Bale Gajah (fig. A.1, #8) of the middle courtyard, the king (Ratu Dalem) of Klungkung added his prayers to those of the priests of his court. At each of the eleven directions of the mandala, pairs of priests were presented with vials containing a few ounces of each of the different varieties of holy water that had been collected. As noon approached, the Brahman priests performed rituals to bless and augment the sacred powers of the waters.[25] Afterwards, this water was sprinkled on the offerings at each of the points of the mandala, symbolically effecting the purification of the realm.

After each priest completed his rituals, the waters were poured into a single container at the center of the mandala and given a further blessing. Precisely at noon, the Greater Jero Gde was summoned to the center of the mandala by the senior Brahmana priest, who placed the sacred vessel containing all of the combined holy waters on the head of the Jero Gde. As he emerged from the ceremonial enclosure, the Jero Gde was met by the other priests of the temple, who poured the holy water into more containers filled with the temple's own holy water. Such mixtures are thought to retain the potency of the original vials of water actually used in the rituals. Then, led by the Jero Gde, the entire team of twenty-four temple priests began to sprinkle this water over the waiting crowds.

In the afternoon, sacred dances[26] were held in the inner courtyard of the temple (fig. A.1, #27), while the senior court priest of Klungkung led a team of four Brahmana priests in the dedication of additional offerings to the deities of the temple (fig. A.1, #28a). For once, tourists were strictly excluded. The images and emblems of the deities (*arca*) were carried out of their normal resting place in the *peparuman agung* (fig. A.1, #14), and borne in a ceremonial procession three times around the shrines of the inner sanctum by the temple priests and one of the princes of Ubud. The Greater Jero Gde personally carried the black whips and then positioned himself to receive each of the *arca*, which he placed in a temporary shrine (fig. A.1, #28) where they might receive the offerings dedicated by the

Brahmana priests. As night fell, the prayers concluded, and the images of the gods were carried reverently back to the *peparuman agung* shrine.

Analysis of the Ritual

We can distinguish six principal stages in the sequence of rituals.

1. *The collection of holy water.* Ordinarily, the holy water for the temple is acquired from the eleven springs of the lake-mandala. For Panca Wali Krama, additional holy water was collected from the crater lakes of adjacent mountains, as far away as the neighboring islands of Java and Lombok, and the sea floor. These locations represent the distant sources of sacred power in the mandala of which Batur is the center.

2. *The sanctification of holy water.* The whole of Panca Wali Krama focused on the symbolism of holy water with respect to the powers of the temple. The holy water that had been collected was mixed into a single essence and then redistributed in containers within the sacred enclosure of the nawa-sangha mandala. Here, on the climactic day of the ritual sequence, the Brahmanic rituals for the sanctification of holy water were performed by the highest-ranking Brahman court priests.

3. *The purification of the realm.* After the final preparation of holy water, teams of Brahman priests used this water to sanctify the offerings laid out in shrines before them to purify the realm. The realm in this case extends to the region from which the holy water was originally sought. The many social units participating in the ceremony made their principal contributions here in the form of offerings to the gods summoned to the ritual. In addition, the king of Klungkung and a prince of Ubud participated in these rites not merely as witnesses but by performing the sequence of prayers appropriate to their caste status (*rsi*). They were seated, however, outside the sacred enclosure, and their prayers were said to play an auxiliary role, enhancing the power of the ceremony. The Jero Gde did not participate in these rites but waited outside the mandala until the process of purification was finished.

4. *The presentation of holy water to the Jero Gde.* After the purification, the Jero Gde was summoned into the center of the mandala, where the Brahman's assistants collected vials of holy water from all eleven pairs of Brahmana priests. These waters were poured into a single container, which the senior Brahmana placed on the head of the Jero Gde.

5. *The distribution of holy water.* After the initial holy water blessings for the waiting crowds, the ritual arena shifted to the inner sanctum. Here, more Brahman priests presented offerings to the deities of the temple, which were also sprinkled with holy water. Meanwhile, the *subaks* filed in to pray and to fill their *sujung* containers with holy water to take home for field offerings.

6. *Offerings to the deities.* After the purification of the temple and the realm, the Jero Gde led the temple priests in bringing out the emblems of the temple deities from the inner sanctum, and the court priest of Klungkung led a team of Brahman priests in the presentation of offerings to the temple gods.

Panca Wali Krama—a grand purification of the realm, organized by the Jero Gde, conducted by Brahmans, and attended by princes—was virtually a paradigmatic royal ritual. Is the Jero Gde, therefore, a kind of king? Students of kingship, from Frazer to Hocart, Dumezil and Heesterman have argued that kings represent a universalistic concept of society, one which defines a relationship between two kinds of power: temporal and sacred/religious. Like the Brahmans, the Jero Gde is a kind of priest, who makes no claim to the temporal powers of a king. Nonetheless, his role in the conduct of Panca Wali krama resembled that of a king. For unlike the Brahmans, the Jero Gde did not participate in the rituals of purification within the sacred enclosure. It was only after the purification had been completed that he entered the nawa-sangha to receive the holy water. Nor did he join the Ratu Dalem of Klungkung—a prince who *has* undergone the rituals of royal installation, including *abiseka ratu*—in the performance of auxiliary prayers. His role was rather that of recipient of the holy water (phase 4), after the purification rituals were complete. In phase 5, he used the freshly charged holy water for the rites of renewal: the offerings to the temple's deities and the distribution of holy water to the *subaks* and princes. His role was to effect the purification of the realm, using the holy water that had been prepared for him, and later to make offerings to the goddess and her retinue on behalf of the *subaks* and the realm.

The sacred authority of the Jero Gde derives from two distinct sources, the first of which is appropriate to a king, whereas the second is not. The first is his relationship to the Goddess of the Lake. As a divinely chosen *sanglingan* priest, the Jero Gde is identified with the Goddess of the Lake. He is, therefore, not a "technician of the sacred," like the Brahman priests. Instead, he is himself an icon of divinity. It is as the chosen representative of the goddess that he receives the holy water from the Brahmans at the center of the mandala.

But his identity does not derive solely on his iconic relationship to the goddess. The Temple of the Crater Lake—the pinnacle of the irrigation systems of central Bali—is also his. His authority over the temple is unique, quite unlike that of ordinary temple priests. Within the framework of the "Rajapurana Ulun Danu Batur" (the mythical charter of the temple), he has complete authority over all the temple's affairs. His identification with the temple invests him with a particular symbolism, which diverges in an interesting way from that of a king.

In chapter 3, we investigated the logic of holy water and the symbolism of water temple rituals. A single clear principle emerged: holy water from each water temple stands for that temple as a social unit. The holy water of the Temple of the Crater Lake signifies the origin waters for all of the *subak*s and temples that acknowledge the lake-mandala as the ultimate source of their livelihood. The temple is a real water temple, with a multisubak congregation like that of a Masceti or Ulun Swi temple. But because the congregation of the temple consists of hundreds of *subak*s, it represents the most universal concept of society articulated by the rituals of the water temples. Just as the holy water of a *subak* temple signifies the *subak*, the holy water of Panca Wali Krama signifies the totality of *subak*s dependent upon Lake Batur—a concept almost indistinguishable from that of society itself.

Mythically, the idea of Batur as origin is replicated in the chronicles, which trace the creation of human society on Bali to the arrival of the gods at the mountaintops of Batur and Besakih. The myth of origins is also recast, in slightly different form, in the chronicle of the Paseks of the Black Wood, which identifies the Jero Gde with the first human created from the Black Wood atop Mount Batur and gifted by the gods. Thus both the chronicles and the ritual symbolism of holy water identify the Jero Gde with the origins of society, the essential mystery of the transformation of nature into humanity. The sources of his power derive from the era before the age of kings.

The Jero Gde is, therefore, neither fully divine nor fully human. It is significant that he does not merely represent the idea of the unity of the temple's congregation as a distinct social unit: the mystery of his identity explains that unity by providing a compelling mythical account for the origins of society. The Jero Gde is not only the First Human. He is also an icon of the temple itself, the social world that continues to originate from the ever-flowing waters of the lake.

It is now possible to draw some conclusions concerning the issue of kingship. It is significant that when Balinese talk about the Jero Gde, the fact that his powers extend only to the temple, the rivers, and *subak* congregations is sure to be noted. Hydraulic solidarity between water temples, from a farmer's field altar to the temple itself, is ultimately based on the hydro-logic of irrigation dependency. The system is, therefore, strictly bounded—the temple makes no claims on *subak*s lying outside its hydrological domain. Even the universalistic claims of Panca Wali Krama involve a clearly defined hydrological region, bounded by the crater lakes of Bromo to the west and Renjani to the east. The symbolic systems that invest the Jero Gde with authority originate in the internal logic of the water temple system. Wider claims to temporal and sacred power—true kingship—would not be extensions of this logic but claims of a different order. The ritual described as *abiseka ratu* for the Jero Gde bears no re-semblance—other than the name—to the conventional *abiseka ratu* cer-emony for the installation of kings, for it makes no claims to universal power. Instead, like all of the rituals of the temple, it is essentially a rite of purification involving the waters of the lake. The Jero Gde is not an unfinished king, for his identity does not depend upon totalizing claims to power. Instead, his identification with the goddess, the temple, and the mandala of the lake place him at the summit of the water temple system of central Bali.

CHAPTER FIVE

Chance Observations and the Metaphysics of Taxation

.

WE ARE NOW in a position to—as it were—enter the library of the Temple of the Crater Lake and read the manuscripts relating the history of its relationships with the *subak*s. The concept of Lake Batur as a mandala of waters gives meaning to the cryptic lists of specific obligations owed to the temple by the *subak*s. As we shall see in this chapter, a formal structure underlies the relationship of *subak*s to the temple, which is ultimately based on the hydro-logic of irrigation dependency. The many manuscripts dealing with ritual obligations may be interpreted as attempts to translate the temple's cosmological role into a legalistic framework of claims and obligations, which ultimately defines the scope of the temple's powers.

An exploration of the temple's recent history inevitably leads us back to the colonial archives on irrigation because both are concerned with essentially the same phenomena, but from such alien perspectives that neither acknowledges the other's existence. As we saw in chapter 1, water temples do not appear in the colonial discourse on irrigation and the state. But now that we know what to look for, it is possible to reexamine the colonial literature for traces of the temple system. Our concern is no longer with Dutch theories about irrigation, but with the chance observations of travelers or colonial officials that may shed some light on the extent of the temple's actual authority over irrigation, in the days when the Dutch thought they were in control.

This chapter begins with a reinterpretation of European observations of the temple, and proceeds to an analysis of the temple's own claims to power.

CHANCE OBSERVATIONS

In 1830, a missionary traveler was sent to Bali by the Singapore Christian Union to explore the prospects for "extending the benefits of Education and the knowledge of Christianity" to the Balinese. At that time—sixteen years before the first Dutch invasion—very little was known about Balinese culture. The missionary's report begins with a brief list of the principal Balinese courts, after which he turns his attention to the "riches of Bali."

> Bali has several inland lakes or reservoirs of water situated near the tops of high mountains, several thousand feet above the level of the sea. These lakes all contain fresh water, whose rise and fall corresponds to the sea. Their depths are great, but irregular: in some parts bottom has been found at forty or fifty fathoms and in other parts it is said no bottom can be got at the depth of several hundred fathoms. Some of them are long, and others round, the largest about four miles across, and twelve in circumference; at any rate, they contain water enough to irrigate the inhabited parts of the island with little trouble and expense; and however much water is taken from them, they never seem to decrease. These lakes form the riches of Bali; in a country where there are no great rivers, and where the inhabitants have to depend for subsistence entirely on the irrigation of their rice fields, these lakes are indispensable, and without them it appears evident that so great a population could not be maintained. The scarcity of waters elsewhere is so great, and all the rivers so insignificant, that persons travelling in the dry season are obliged to carry water with them, but by means of these lakes the diligent husbandman is enabled to obtain water enough for all his wants, and consequently two crops of rice are taken annually.[1]

In this case, the facts (which are wrong) confirm the myth. The lakes do not have tides, nor do they have river outlets. But in the context of temple rituals the crater lake is described as an ocean,[2] a metaphysical idea that the missionary evidently took literally. It is also part of the mythology of the temple that the lakes are connected to the rivers by underground tunnels. The water in the lakes is thought to pour out continuously through these tunnels, yet "however much water is taken from them, they never seem to decrease." This belief in underground tunnels from the crater lakes as the source of irrigation waters is also mentioned in Liefrinck's 1887 report: "There are temples by the shore of every lake in Bali, for it is believed that the streams are fed from the lakes by underground tributaries. Yearly pilgrimages must be made to these sanctuaries."[3]

But what of the temple itself? In 1918, an architect named P. A. J. Moojen was employed by the governor general of the Netherlands Indies to undertake the first survey of major temples in the newly conquered principalities of south Bali. Moojen was also asked to assist in the repair of temples and palaces damaged by a major earthquake in 1917. One of the temples that had been severely damaged was Batur. In his first report to the governor general, Moojen observed that

There are six temples which are superior to the many village temples, which are most sacred to the Balinese and are honored outside the borders of the little kingdoms in which they are situated. Several authors on Bali give various names for these six, and Frederich mentions that in the *Oesana Bali* itself there are different temples mentioned. However, it is certain that the Temple of Besakih is the most holy, followed by the Temple of Batur, also called Temple of Mount Lebah. Further information given to me by knowledgeable sources also points to this, and I even received a written request to start quickly on the repairs to the Batur temple.[4]

Thus in 1919, Besakih and Batur were (in Moojen's estimation) the two most important temples in Bali, whose authority transcended the borders of the kingdoms in which they were located. By good fortune, the actual letter that he refers to in this passage, urging the immediate repair of Batur, is preserved among Moojen's papers in the archives of the Royal Institute for Anthropology and Linguistics in Leiden. The letter itself is perhaps the single most important historical document of the colonial period concerning Batur. It was written by the sedahan agung of Klungkung on November 27, 1918, addressed to Their Excellencies the Paduka Kangding Soewan and the Dutch controleur of Klungkung. The letter is written in Malay and reflects the struggles of the sedahan agung in trying to convey the role of the temple to representatives of an alien administration. The letter itself is not very long, and the basic point is clear enough, but the full meaning requires a little unpacking. Here is a verbatim translation.

To Their Excellencies Kangding Soewan and Controleur Kade at Klungkung,
    With this letter your servant wishes to inform His Lordship Kangding Soewan, with no other purpose than to cleanse my heart by assisting with the task of the Court (the peace of the Realm) according to the customs of Bali, that is the Buddhist religion or the religion of holy water; the important matter I wish respectfully to bring to your Lordship's attention since your Lordship Kangding Soewan holds authority over the lands of Bangli, [is that] I hope that you will advise the [Dutch] Regent in Bangli, so that he will assist with the temple at Batur at the Ulun Danu, the home of the Deity called the Goddess of the Lake who has the power of control over water, the male has power over fire, this is very important according to Balinese religious custom, because the Deities of Mount Batur and Mount Agung are the children of the Deity of Mahameru who were given power over Bali, for example as your Lordship Kangding Soewan and other rulers of Bali derive your powers from Bogor [the Javanese mountain nearest the Dutch capital of Batavia], so it is exactly according to your servant's beliefs in Bali, in accordance with the literature of *sesana kawi*, because there are many visible signs which your

servant can use which are only slightly different, for it is not necessary for human beings to see the gods, for example it is like a tree which is shaking, it is certain that the tree is shaken by the wind even though human beings cannot see the form of the wind itself.

Furthermore, if your servant plants rice and does not diligently perform worship it is certain that the rice will be meager and the harvest greatly lacking, much of it will die, therefore concerning that which is called of greatest importance, which has the power to rule both night and day, the creator of that which is seen and that which is unseen, *rwa bineda*, there are temple priests [*mangku*] who are seen therefore it is certain that earlier there was the unseen, for example because that which is visible exists it is certain that it comes forth from a Divinity, therefore it is extremely important that the two aspects of this, Mount Batur and Mount Agung, receive worship, as your servant advised earlier in Badung, and because it is easy to make things right at Batur if the people at Batur are assisted by their father.

Therefore your servant hopes that your Lordship Kangding Soewan will fully accept your servant's advice.

There are an illegible signature and the imprint of an inked stamp with the words "Sedahan Agoeng van Kloengkoeng." As we know, the author of the letter occupied an official position under the Dutch administration, with responsibilities for tax collection and irrigation.

The first point that the sedahan agung was trying to clarify to the Dutch was the significance of the Batur temple—a significance based on its role as the home of the deity called the Goddess of the Lake, who has the "power of control over water" (*jang berkuasa mamegang aer*), as the male God of Mount Agung has power over fire. There is an interesting parallel between this description and that of the 1830 missionary report, which stated, "They acknowledge Brahma as the Supreme God, whom they speak of with high respect, and whom they suppose to be the God of fire; next to him they rank Vishnu, who is said to preside over the rivers of waters."[5]

But to continue with the sedahan's request, he points out that the God of Mount Agung and the Goddess of Batur were given authority over Bali by the Deity of Mount Mahameru, the ruler of the cosmic mountain at the center of the Indian cosmos. In other words, says the sedahan, the God of Mount Agung and the Goddess of Mount Batur derive their power from a greater deity who rules Mahameru, just as the Dutch rulers of Bali derive their power from Batavia. Actually, the center of Dutch power is not traced to the city of Batavia but Bogor, the mountain closest to Batavia. Evidently the sedahan conceives of the power of the Dutch as emanating from a mountaintop rather than a city.

The sedahan uses a striking image to illustrate the reality of the power of the Goddess of the Lake: when a tree is shaken, even though one cannot see the wind itself, one can see the proof of its power. So if he were to plant rice without performing the proper rites, it is certain that the harvest would be very poor.

The last passage is enigmatic, but one possible reading would go like this: The rwa bineda doctrine of cosmic dualism that he quotes tells us that the visible and invisible worlds are indivisible. If one can see that there are temple priests (*mangku*) in daylight, it is sure that they (or the power that animates them) originated in the invisible world.[6] This interpretation suggests that the sedahan is trying to explain the importance of the sanglingan priesthood, chosen by the Goddess of the Lake via the trance mediums. The temple is, therefore, the home of the goddess and also of her chosen priests, who provide the means to communicate with her and provide the necessary sacrifices. Finally, the sedahan concludes by urging that the repair of the temples is extremely urgent, as he had already suggested on a previous occasion.

The sedahan agung's request ultimately reached Moojen, who studied the temple extensively and drew up careful architectural plans for its restoration. The temple was then located within the caldera itself, alongside the shore of the lake, as is illustrated in the accompanying plans and photographs.

Moojen wrote enthusiastically that "The fame of holiness, coming from this temple, has risen after the last eruption of Batoer in 1905 even more by the miraculous way by which it was then saved from total destruction. The glowing lava stream was stopped just at the main entrance in an inexplicable way!"[7]

This description is confirmed by the sketches of Nieuwenhuis, who visited the temple shortly after the eruption. Moojen estimated the cost of restoration of the Batur temple at Fl 30,000, a small fortune in 1919. This included a sizable budget for labor. Batur was the only temple for which Moojen requested funding for labor, for a very interesting reason. As he explained in his report, "Wages for labor are not budgeted [for other temples] since among the people it is the custom and tradition to supply this. But for one budget I have made an exception and that is for the temple of Batoer. . . . [Like Besakih], Batoer is of importance to the population of the whole of Bali, and from almost all parts of the island smaller or larger shrines have been built there, or the people have paid a share in their construction."[8]

Thus according to Moojen's report, the importance of Batur transcended the boundaries of the former principalities. Unlike other temples, support for Batur came not only from nearby villages but from the whole island.

Moojen's interest in the temple was primarily architectural, and he

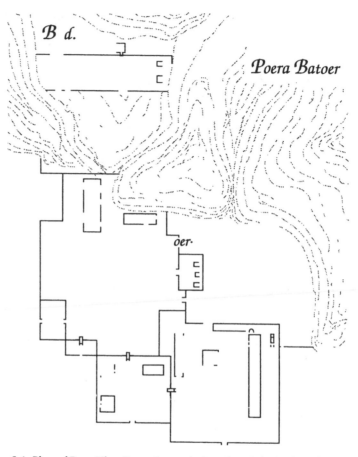

Figure 5.1. Plan of Pura Ulun Danu Batoer before the 1917 Earthquake (from the papers of P. A. J. Moojen)

wrote very little about its cosmological role. But the importance of the temple to the *subaks* is confirmed by other reports. For example, the final report (*memorie van overgave*) of G. A. W. Ch. de Haze Winkelman, Resident of Bali and Lombok, dated April 1937, contains the following remarks:

> In several areas the custom exists that the inhabitants of a watershed by sending deputations participate in the worship in the sanctuaries dedicated to the goddesses of the mountain lakes (Batoer, Bratan, Boejan, and Tamblingan). Holy water is obtained during temple feasts by the representatives of the subaks. The subak members meet the delegations and ceremoniously share out the holy water, and the subak members then sprinkle their fields with it. In

Figure 5.2. Baris Gde Dancers in front of the Temple of the Crater Lake (Pura Ulun Danu Batur) before the 1917 Earthquake (from the archives of the KITLV, Leiden)

this way, they can participate in the blessing that the goddess of the lake—as keeper of the irrigation waters—shares with the farmers.

Let it also be mentioned that the festival calendar of the subak has no (or at the most only an incidental) relation to the organization of the religious ceremonies that are in the charge of the village community.[9]

Here we have in so many words "the lake goddess as the keeper of irrigation waters." In fact, most of the pieces of the irrigation puzzle are here: the separate calendar of the *subaks*, the pilgrimages to the lakes to obtain holy water to sprinkle on their fields, the temple festivals, and the goddess not merely as mistress of lakes or holy water but "irrigation water" (*bevloeiingswater*) itself. One can find similar references in other documents of the colonial era. For example, V. E. Korn observed that "From several village regulations from Karangasem, this opinion appears without doubt, that the water of the central Balinese lakes—Bratan, Batur, Buyung and Tamblingan—is in the hands of the gods, on whose good will it depends if the rivers will receive enough water through underground canals (a widespread belief)."[10]

Why were these pieces not assembled into a comprehensive picture of the water temple system? In chapter 1, I suggested that it was not in the interests of the colonial government to do so. As long as water temples were regarded as a purely religious phenomenon, their practical or managerial activities were not seen as posing a challenge to the authority of the government. The decapitation of the Balinese kingdoms did not create a crisis in irrigation management because irrigation was managed by the temples. Essentially, as long as the temples continued to function, there was no reason for the Dutch to inquire very deeply into the structure of intersubak coordination. Even in cases involving the construction of new irrigation systems or settling disputes over water rights, presumably only quite unusual circumstances would bring these matters to the attention of the Dutch. As we saw in chapter 4, such questions are generally settled today without recourse to the government.

The major practical impact of the Dutch administration was the construction of permanent weirs and the lining of some irrigation canals. In most cases, these structures were built as replacements for existing earth-and-log weirs and so did not drastically affect the existing pattern of water rights. When the Dutch organized the construction of entirely new systems, presumably the temple system would have functioned to redefine water rights and cropping patterns.

On one important issue, however, the water temples and the bureaucracy advanced apparently contradictory claims: both claimed the right to the *soewinih* or "water tax." Indeed, for different reasons, both the government and the temple priests regarded the *soewinih* as the key to power.

THE METAPHYSICS OF TAXATION

One could argue that the most fundamental issues in the Dutch interpretation of irrigation rights centered on the question of the *soewinih*. In chapter 1, we saw that colonial officials chose to interpret the *soewinih* as a royal water tax, which had gradually lapsed into the control of lesser princes, thus weakening the sovereign. This interpretation provided a rationale for "restoring" a centralized system of taxation as a means of strengthening both irrigation and the state. The "revived" *soewinih* royal irrigation tax could be used to fund improvements in the irrigation system, as it had originally been intended to do. Management of the *soewinih* was entrusted to the sedahans, who would in this way regain control over irrigation.

But as we saw in chapter 1, the Dutch themselves recognized that there were problems with this interpretation of the *soewinih*. The Temple of the Crater Lake is located in the former mountain kingdom of Bangli, which never went to war with the Dutch. In Bangli, as Van der Heijden noted, the sedahan had "nothing to do with the irrigation system, nor with the getting of the soewinih."[11]

Moreover, in Bangli, according to Van der Heijden, "recognition of the water use, the 'soewinih,' was formerly not to the king or his lords [poenggawas], but to the foremost subak temples."[12]

Even in Badung, where part of the *soewinih* was collected by the princes, much of it was used for ceremonies at water temples such as Sakenan. In general, Dutch observations of the actual uses of the *soewinih* conflicted with the tax policy, which treated the *soewinih* as a royal irrigation tax. Nonetheless, the government proceeded to enforce its claims to *soewinih* as both a source of revenue and a proof of legitimacy.

Meanwhile, however, the farmers continued to offer *soewinih* to the water temples. How could these conflicting claims be reconciled by the officials actually engaged in collecting taxes for the government? The answer is to be found in the accounts kept by the sedahans, whose job it was to collect agricultural taxes. In these records there is no mention of *soewinih*. Instead, the tax records of the colonial period indicate that farmers paid annual taxes (*pajeg*), assessed not on the basis of water rights but on agricultural land. Evidently, then, although the Dutch defined the taxes paid by farmers as *soewinih*, as far as the farmers themselves were concerned they were paying *pajeg*, a simple tax on agricultural land. The difference between these two kinds of tax is purely metaphysical: an ordinary land tax, although an excellent source of revenue, lacked the intangible essence the Dutch had sought to validate their claims to power.

Like the Dutch, but for different reasons, the Balinese also attached great symbolic value to the *soewinih*. Lacking the means and, perhaps, the desire to coerce *soewinih* contributions, the Temple of the Crater Lake nonetheless received a steady flow of *soewinih* from the *subak*s. The basis of this system is outlined in a passage from one of the manuscripts in the temple's library, which describes the obligations of *subak*s to the temple and the goddess. (Additional text and a brief exegesis by the lesser temple scribe are included in the notes.)

Babad Patisora: Reminder of the Deity's Entitlements

Leaf 28.a.1. //O// Reminder that the sacred ruler at Batur [Dewi Danu, the Goddess of the Lake] possesses a congregation of 45 villages. The village of Batur is reminded of what is owed from the possessions held by these villages. They are also reminded

> 2. of the specific taxes owed to the sacred ruler. They risk the curse of the Deity if they neglect these obligations. And the rice terraces belonging to the sacred ruler, [are] held in trust by the village
> 3. of Batur. And if they [Batur] do not offer up the rice taxes to the sacred ruler for each yearly temple festival and offer the contributions to the Deity at Tampurhyang, the people who hold the rice terraces belonging to the sacred ruler
> 4. will be cursed by the Deity. May this curse never occur. If the people of the Deity of Batur do not follow the instructions of the Deity,

Leaf 28.b.1. and provide the contributions specified, their crops will fail and they will be cursed by the sacred ruler at Batur. And the people of central Bali, if they forget the holy places

> 2. at Batur, they will instantly suffer disasters, their works will fail, all that they plant will die, because the Deity is entitled to the essence of the work of the people of central Bali. This essence is named sasalaranta. Because the Deity
> 3. makes the waters flow, those who do not obey her rules may not possess her rice terraces. At Sawana Batu 25 tenah of ricefields, and the village of Talepud
> 4. is reminded that the Deity possesses 10 tenah.

(This formula is repeated for numerous villages. One tenah of unhulled rice is approximately 25 kilograms.) (From *Rajapurana Ulun Danu Batur*)[13]

The "Rajapurana" defines clear differences between types of congregations and their obligations to the temple, which may be summarized as follows:

1. *Pepasyan* (the inner mandala)

These are the forty-five villages of central Bali specifically mentioned in the "Rajapurana," which hold in trust the "possessions of the Goddess." Each year, they are required to bring to the temple the specified contributions. The number of *pepasyan*—45 villages—is highly significant. The total number of deities worshipped at Batur is also forty-five, and the staff of the temple consists of 45 priests and elders. At the temple, each day begins at dawn when a slit drum (*kulkul*) is struck 45 times. The forty-five villages of the *pepasyan* are conceived as a ring encircling the summit of Mount Batur. In other words, in the "Rajapurana" the forty-five *pepasyan* define the region known as "central Bali," which surrounds the summit of Mount Batur and the lake-mandala.

2. *Subak*s offering *soewinih* (the mandala of waters)

The motivation for *soewinih* offerings is the concept of irrigation water as possessing an essence (*sari*) that has the power to bring forth life. It is within the sacred mandala of the lake that water is imbued with this essence. The lake is defined as an ocean (*segara*), the dwelling place of the goddess who is the female incarnation of Wisnu. Her life-giving waters pour out continuously through underground tunnels, yet somehow never diminish the level of the lake.

*Subak*s whose lands lie within the area believed to receive water from Lake Batur, therefore, owe *soewinih* (a portion of their harvest) to the goddess. *Subak*s located in more distant regions, to the east of the Unda River, for example, are not obliged to bring *soewinih*. Similarly, *subak*s in most of western Bali make their *soewinih* contributions to the lake temples of Bratan, Buyan, and Tamblingan. These lakes, however, are thought to be connected to Lake Batur by an underground tunnel, so that an especially diligent *subak* from Tabanan might occasionally wish to make additional offerings to the temple at Batur. According to the books kept by the greater scribe, at present, 207 *subak*s or *ulun swi* congregations (which may include more than one *subak*) regularly offer *soewinih* to the Batur Temple.

3. *Pejati* offerings to the goddess (the human world)

Any *subak*—or, for that matter, any person or group—may request holy water from the temple for blessings and purifications. For example, *subak*s having trouble with rice pests or a water shortage often seek holy water from the temple. In return for the holy water, it is customary to make *pejati* offerings.

To keep track of these offerings and contributions, the greater scribe keeps several records and accounts books. The first is simply a list of the *subak*s that have voluntarily joined the temple's congregation by agreeing to offer *soewinih* every year for the rituals of the Tenth Month. If we visualize the forty-five villages of the *pepasyan* as forming the first circle of the temple's congregation, then the 207 *subak*s that offer *soewinih* may be regarded as the second circle. The outer circle consists of all other *su-baks*, which may lie beyond the river boundaries of the temple but may, nonetheless, make occasional pilgrimages to the temple. Delegations from other institutions, such as villages or kinship groups, often visit the temple to request holy water for their major rituals.

The scribe records all of these visits in a separate daily ledger, while in a third ledger he keeps track of the storerooms and expenses of the temple. Most of the materials received in the storerooms are used almost immediately to feed the temple's visitors. On a busy day, the temple will feed hundreds of worshippers. Priests and elders are also entitled to obtain their meals from the temple kitchens during their three-day shifts and may take home small quantities of food for their families each week. Surplus food is eventually sold, the proceeds going to the temple treasury.

Thus the *soewinih* has a well-defined role in the context of the temple's relationships with the *subaks*. It is, in fact, the basis for the temple's claims for broad support, from *subaks* not specifically mentioned as *pepasyan* in the "Rajapurana Ulun Danu Batur." *Soewinih* is sometimes also presented to regional water temples, such as the Masceti Pamos Apuh, which receives token *soewinih* contributions from many downstream *subaks*. The Masceti in turn dedicates these offerings to the goddess. In a sense, the right to collect *soewinih* is the foundation of a temple's temporal power.

COSMOLOGICAL RIVALRIES

From a purely metaphysical point of view, the Temple of the Crater Lake is a place of interchange between the visible and invisible worlds. But it is also a major redistributive center. Tons of *soewinih* offerings are brought to the temple each year, providing the raw materials for the grand rituals and feasts that validate the temple's cosmological role. It is in this context that what might be termed the politics of *soewinih* comes into play. We concluded the previous chapter with an account of the Panca Wali Krama rituals of 1987, the grandest of all the "major works" (*karya agung*) at Batur, which rivaled in its splendor the enormous ceremonial displays of nineteenth-century Balinese courts. Through an unusual combination of circumstances, I was given an unexpected insight into the importance of *soewinih* to this ceremony.

In 1985, rainfall was reduced over much of Bali, and the drought continued in 1986. Consequently, to the dismay of the *subaks* the level of water in the lake began to fall. On the shore of the lake at the opposite end of the crater from Batur, a small temple bears the same name as the Temple of the Crater Lake: Ulun Danu Batur. Literally, the name means

"Head of Lake Batur"—a description of the temple's physical location. But in the summer of 1986, the head of the village in whose territory this temple is located gave a newspaper interview in which he suggested that this little temple was the true home of the Goddess of the Lake and that if the *subak*s would bring *soewinih* to him perhaps the drought would end.

This announcement created a sensation at the Temple of the Crater Lake. It was said that the rival village was really only motivated by the desire to obtain the *soewinih* offerings of the *subak*s. But the level of the lake was falling, and some of the elders candidly admitted that a continuing drought might provide a pretext for a serious challenge to the authority of their temple. The major argument advanced in support of the rival temple was its location beside the lake. The present Temple of the Crater Lake is situated on the rim above the caldera, far from the lakeside. It was said to have been moved to this location in 1927 after a volcanic eruption destroyed its predecessor. But the partisans of the rival temple claimed that the history of these events had gone up in the smoke of the volcanic fires. The true Ulun Danu Batur temple must surely be located close to the lake.

While this argument was going on, I happened to go to Holland to research the history of the temple in the colonial archives. On my return to Bali in the summer of 1987, I brought copies of all the documents, plans, and photographs of the temple I had found in Holland to contribute to the temple's archives. Among them was the following account, from the memoirs of a controleur stationed in Bali in 1926.[14]

> The village of Batur was situated before August 1926 at the foot of the volcano Batur. It was a neat, well-kept village, which could be seen clearly from the crater.[15]
>
> On the 3d of August 1926, at 1 A.M., Mount Batur began to erupt. Along the northwestern slope a long crevice appeared with a lot of noise and thunder, from which fires and many lava fountains spewed forth. I was informed of this and went to Kintamani, and descended to the village of Batur. It was impossible to get an overview of the situation: the inhabitants were not worried and trusted in the power and will of the gods and in the temple, which already once before had stopped the lava-stream. From above you could see that the lava-stream was not moving towards the village. However, it seemed to me that the continuous eruptions would eventually fill the hollow in which the village was nestled. In the afternoon of the first day a new source of lava came into being at about 1,200 meters distance from the village. With the sound of a diesel engine, it regularly emitted large waves of blood-red glowing lava. A lava stream started to move towards the village.[16]
>
> Above all this, the sky was blood-red, dyed by twenty-one lava fountains,

glowering and spouting lava. Very heavy explosions made the surroundings resound; the echo went on and on against the rim of the crater.[17]

The report goes on to describe the abandonment of the village and the temple, which were soon buried under tons of lava, and the relocation of the temple to the rim of the crater. When I presented this account and the other documents I had brought to the scribe at Batur, I was not aware of the challenge from the partisans of the rival temple. To my surprise, the scribe did not quietly place these papers in the archive but brought them triumphantly before the Jero Gde as documentary proof of the temple's claims to be *the* Temple of the Goddess. Late that night, I was summoned to join the Jero Gde and the other priests at a shrine beside the lake, where they were already deep in a discussion of the significance of the fortuitous appearance of these historical documents. Among the other papers I had brought were Moojen's plans and papers, including the letter from the *sedahan agung* pleading for assistance with the rebuilding of the temple in 1918. Moojen's papers also included architectural plans with sketches of the major shrines, including the principal shrine to the goddess. After I translated the relevant passages for the priests, there was a general discussion of their significance. The challenge from the rival temple was based on its claim to be a more appropriate vehicle for *soewinih* contributions to the goddess. But these documents appeared to provide proof of the temple's authenticity. Moreover, their appearance at precisely this moment of crisis could be interpreted as more than coincidental. After prayers and meditation, the Jero Gde announced his decision to set in motion the Panca Wali Krama purification ritual.

In the end, according to the elders, the very grandeur of the Panca Wali Krama constituted an effective response to the challenge from the rival temple. The vast outpouring of *soewinih* offerings from the *subak*s simultaneously proved their loyalty and provided the wherewithal for a convincing display of the temple's cosmological function.[18] The *subak*s' support for Panca Wali Krama might, indeed, be likened to the massive effort to rebuild the temple in the aftermath of the 1927 eruption. Among the papers I brought to the temple was a report by Controleur Haar, who described the mobilization of funds and labor for the reconstruction of the temple:

At this moment the members of the new village of Batoer are busy preparing the terrain for a new temple. A request to have the whole of Bali participate in this new construction by means of handing over contributions was already made, but will later be prepared more closely by the Anak Agoeng of Bangli and proposed again. It was thought to request a contribution of 5 cents per family head. If you count the number of people at around 1 million (in 1920 the census says that most families consist of 5 people), then approximately 200,000 people would bring in an amount of 10,000 guilders.[19]

Within a few years of the disaster, a new temple was in place on the rim of the crater, overlooking the black lava marking the ashes of its predecessors. I found no records in the Dutch archives to indicate whether the government assisted with the rebuilding, but the elders say that everything was done by the *subaks* and the people of Batur.

The rivalry between temples that raised the stakes for Panca Wali Krama in 1987 brings to mind the endless quest for power that is the main theme of Balinese dynastic chronicles. It is interesting that princes as well as temples could act as intermediaries in the conveyance of *soewinih*, a fact noted in the 1930s by Korn.[20] Competition to be the most effective channel for *soewinih* offerings seems to have flourished among both temples and princes. Proof of the efficacy of *soewinih* offerings was always to be found in next year's harvests. Bad harvests might demand more offerings next time, but they might also mean that the wrong channels were being used for the offerings. A temple or a prince who could not amass the material and labor needed to perform the necessary rituals on an impressive scale was in danger of losing the mandate of heaven.

POWERS OF THE TEMPLES

The Temple of the Crater Lake that Liefrinck admired was shaken to pieces in an earthquake, and its successor, which Moojen sketched, now lies buried under tons of volcanic rock. Ironically, it was the destruction of the temple that brought it to the attention of the Dutch in 1917 and again in 1926. Under ordinary circumstances, the comings and goings of *subaks* and temple priests attracted little attention from colonial officials. But after each disaster, the massive outpouring of assistance for rebuilding impressed Dutch officials with the temple's importance for the whole of Balinese society.

Although colonial officials did not pursue the question of the temple's role with regard to irrigation and water rights, scattered references in the colonial archives shed some light on this question. As we have seen, nineteenth-century European visitors to Bali noted that all irrigation water was believed to originate in the crater lakes. Underground tunnels originating at Lake Batur were thought to connect all the lakes and ultimately ensure the flow of water into the rivers and springs that fed the irrigation works. Europeans also identified the role of the Goddess of the Lake as the mistress of irrigation waters and observed the annual pilgrimages of the *subaks* to the lake temples. Altogether, such observations would appear to confirm the historical continuity of the temple's role with respect to irrigation.

If we turn to Balinese manuscripts dating from the colonial era, a more detailed picture of the water temple system becomes available. Interpreting the meaning of these texts, however, depends upon a prior understanding of the belief systems that are the foundation of the temple rituals. A single brief example should make this point clear. Consider the following passage from the *Dewa Tattwa* (History of the gods), a well-known religious text.[21] The passage begins with a list of calendrical offerings that should be made at any Ulun Swi (Head of the Ricefields) temple. After the list comes the following warning:

> If these ceremonies are not performed at the Ulun Swi temple, and the Masceti temple, and to Rambut Sedana, the rice terraces will not be productive, nothing will be sufficient, there will be short measures, not enough to eat or drink, because the essences will be taken back by the deities of Gunung Agung and Batur, so the realm will be consumed by drought, there will be plagues and epidemics, humans will be distressed, by the god who reigns in the Ulun Swi temple.

If a colonial officer happened to read this passage, he would surely have interpreted it as nothing more than an injunction to make a series of religious offerings. But from another perspective, the entire water temple system is implicit in these few lines. Rambut Sedana is a deity of prosperity associated with the Rice Goddess. Thus the text says that if offerings are not made to her and to the local water temples, there will be plagues, droughts, and epidemics, resulting in the failure of the rice crop. To neglect the offerings at these local water temples—the Ulun Swi and Masceti—is to risk offending the Goddess of Batur and the God of Mount Agung, which would precipitate a general social catastrophe.

This passage echoes the warning from the "Rajapurana Ulun Danu Batur," that neglect of the water temples will lead to the spread of pests and diseases and the loss of the water needed to make the crops grow. With the advent of the Green Revolution in Bali, these words became prophetic.

CHAPTER SIX

Massive Guidance

THE COLONIAL ERA ended in Bali in 1947 with the birth of the nation of Indonesia. But the end of colonialism did not mean a return to traditional society, to the world as it had been before the arrival of the Dutch. The instruments of government created by the Dutch were not dismantled but carried over into the postcolonial era. In Bali, as elsewhere in Indonesia, the period from independence to the fall of Sukarno in 1965 was an era in which local government bureaucracies, lacking funding, were largely inactive. But this was soon to change. During the 1950s, Indonesia was forced to import nearly one million tons of rice each year. After the fall of Sukarno in 1965, the new government made self-sufficiency in rice a major goal for national development. Coincidentally, the late 1960s also marked the beginnings of the "Green Revolution" in Asia, the spread of new rice-growing technologies that promised to dramatically increase rice production. The Indonesian government became an early and enthusiastic supporter of the Green Revolution, which it adopted as the cornerstone of a policy of agricultural modernization to be spearheaded by regional and local bureaucracies. With its financial position greatly strengthened by revenues from offshore oil, in the late 1960s the Jakarta government began to invest billions of rupiah in the rehabilitation of bureaucracies, at the provincial, regency, and district levels.[1]

As one of the major rice-producing regions of Indonesia, Bali was one of the first targets of the Green Revolution. In its fundamental aims, the new campaign to modernize agriculture resembled the programs launched by the Dutch after the conquest of South Bali in 1908. In both cases, the major purpose was to boost total rice production, converting rice from a subsistence to a cash crop. But there were important differences between the policies of the Dutch early in the century and those of the Green Revolution. The engineers of the colonial age had little to offer in new technology and were, in any case, poorly funded. In contrast, the Green Revolution offered a comprehensive and highly successful new agricultural technology, backed by new bureaucracies flush with cash and in search of a mission.

If the powers of the water temples were rather hazy for the Dutch, they were entirely invisible to the planners involved in promoting the Green Revolution, who regarded agriculture as a purely technical process. The only question about the traditional social system was how much resistance it might offer to the spread of the new technologies. In the early 1970s, a series of new agricultural policies encouraged continuous cropping of Green Revolution rice and a shift to bureaucratic management of irrigation and cropping patterns. As a result, the water temples lost control of cropping patterns over most of Bali.

There have been many studies of the effects of the Green Revolution in different parts of Asia.[2] Most have focused on socioeconomic issues, such as changes in the distribution of farm incomes. In Bali, however, the changes introduced by the Green Revolution went beyond the distribution of income to affect the basic structure of the productive system. As we have seen in earlier chapters, before the Green Revolution, irrigation management was largely controlled by the water temples. By removing them from power, the Green Revolution set in motion a social experiment, a practical test of the importance of water temples in rice production. The experiment is not yet finished, but there is enough evidence to permit a preliminary evaluation of the results.

This chapter begins with a historical overview of the Green Revolution in Bali and then proceeds to an analysis of its effects on the productive system.

THE GREEN REVOLUTION

The Green Revolution in Asia began at the International Rice Research Institute (IRRI) in the Philippines. In 1962, IRRI agronomists developed a new high-yielding variety of rice called IR-8, which matured in 125 days and produced 5,800 pounds of grain per acre on test plots. In the late 1960s, IR-8 and its successors reached Indonesia. Because the IRRI rice was designed to be responsive to chemical fertilizers, it was necessary to provide farmers with access to fertilizers and pesticides as well as the new seed stocks. In 1967, the Indonesian government invited a Swiss company, CIBA, to develop a system for furnishing these necessities to farmers. The new program was called BIMAS (*Bimbingan Massal*), or Massive Guidance. Despite initial failures of the BIMAS program to increase rice production, the government decided to invest heavily in a national program to achieve self-sufficiency in rice. This program was based on two components: government subsidies to reduce the cost of fertilizers and pesticides to the farmers and extension of BIMAS (which the government took over in 1971) to all major rice-growing regions of Indonesia. To ensure that farmers would have access to the fertilizers and pesticides required to grow the new "miracle rice," a government banking system (the People's Bank) was empowered to provide credit to small farmers for the specific purpose of purchasing agrochemicals and farm machinery. Massive Guidance brought rapid results: by 1974, 48 percent of the terraces of south-central Bali were planted with the new rice; three years later, the proportion had climbed to 70 percent.[3]

Within a few years of the beginning of the Green Revolution, the government took two further steps that had a profound impact on the water temple system in Bali. The first was a shift in cropping patterns. IR-8 proved to be highly susceptible to an insect called the brown planthopper, which is estimated to have destroyed two million tons of rice in Indonesia in 1977. Rice scientists at IRRI came up with a new variety of rice, IR-36, which was resistant to the planthoppers and had the further advantage of maturing very quickly.[4] In Bali, the use of IR-36 was strongly encouraged. Balinese farmers were forbidden to plant native varieties, which take much longer to mature, are less responsive to fertilizers, and produce less grain. Instead, double-cropping or triple-cropping of IR-36 (or other high-yielding rice varieties) was legally mandated. Farmers were instructed to abandon the traditional cropping patterns and to plant high-yielding varieties as often as possible.[5]

The second step was taken as a result of a series of studies by foreign consultants on ways to improve the performance of Balinese irrigation systems. These studies culminated in the Bali Irrigation Project (BIP), a major engineering project launched in 1979 by the Asian Development Bank. The aims of the project were succinctly defined in their feasibility study:[6]

> The Bali Irrigation Project (B.I.P.) is the first large scale attempt in Bali island to improve the irrigation systems. Past interventions by the Department of Public Works have been limited to isolated improvements, with negligible external consequences. In contrast, the B.I.P. will intervene in 130 subaks (about 10 percent of the total Bali subaks), many sharing the water from the same river. The impact of the main improvements will concern:
>
> –River water sharing and subak coordination
> –New Operating & Maintenance rules
> –Programmed cropping patterns
> –Use of measurement systems
> –Changes in cropping techniques
> –Yield monitoring systems
> –Taxes and water charges
>
> In consequence the Subak may lose some of its traditional facets, especially part of its autonomy.

The principal emphasis of the project was the reconstruction of thirty-six weirs and associated irrigation works at an estimated cost of about forty million dollars.[7] Because in most cases these "*subak* improvement schemes" were not designed to bring new land into cultivation, economic justification for the project was largely based on a mandated change to continuous rice cropping for as many *subak*s as possible. In the long run, according to project officials, this would generate a minimum of 80,000 tons of additional rice production each year, which could be sold for export and thus provide the $1,300,000 per annum needed to repay the project loan to the Asian Development Bank.[8] All of these estimates were later revised upward as the project added sixteen *subak* improvement schemes to the original plan.

As a later evaluation report on the project noted, "The introduction of the Project coincided with the government's push for self-sufficiency in rice and the encouragement given to farmers to extend the substitution of short rotation varieties [of rice] for the traditional long duration varieties. . . . These factors temporarily led to the abandonment of the Balinese cropping calendar, traditionally the key to overall watershed and irrigation scheme management."[9] By the late 1970s, the mandated change to continuous rice cropping began to remove the temples from control of irrigation and cropping patterns. In the upper reaches of the rivers, where coordination of irrigation was essential during the dry season, farmers often refused to abandon the temple schedules. But further downstream, the threat of legal penalties against anyone failing to grow the new rice led to continuous cropping of Green Revolution rice. Religious rituals continued in the temples, but field rituals no longer matched the actual stages of rice growth. As soon as one crop was harvested, another was planted, and cropping cycles began to drift apart. During the rainy season, no one was likely to run out of water. But during the dry season, the supply of irrigation water became unpredictable. Soon, district agricultural offices began to report "chaos in the water scheduling" and "explosions of pest populations," as in this 1985 report by the Department of Public Works of the regency of Tabanan.

I. Background

Concerning the explosion of pests and diseases which recently attacked the rice crops, such as brown planthoppers, rodents, tungro virus, and other insects, in the Tabanan regency; and also with regard to the frequent problems which began to arise at about the same time concerning water sharing during the dry season, various groups are now urgently working to get on top of the problem. The result has been acknowledgment of the following factors which caused the explosion of pests and diseases:

1. In areas with sufficient irrigation water, farmers are now planting continuously throughout the year.

2. In areas with insufficient water, farmers are planting without a coordinated schedule.

In other words, the farmers/subaks have ceased to follow the centuries-old cyclical cropping patterns.[10]

A similar report for the neighboring regency of Gianyar tells the same tale, beginning with the massive damage to crops caused by the brown planthopper in the late 1970s. As elsewhere in Bali, farmers in Gianyar were encouraged to plant the planthopper-resistant rice IR-36. But IR-36, although unpopular with planthoppers, fell an easy victim to a viral disease called tungro. As a result, the planthopper plague was quickly followed by an "explosion of the tungro virus."

The Explosion of the Tungro Virus

Tungro began to be a problem in Gianyar in 1980, and steadily increased until the explosion in 1983/84, destroying 421.15 hectares of rice completely, predominantly the variety IR 36. . . . A temporary remedy was found in the new rice variety PB 50. In one cropping season, tungro was reduced, but immediately afterward the new rice was afflicted by *Helminthosporium oryzae*.[11]

Following a by now familiar pattern, the new PB 50 rice proved vulnerable to two new diseases, as described in the Gianyar report:

The Explosion of Helminthosporium and Rice Blast

Problems with *Helminthosporium oryzae* actually began in 1977/78 when five hectares were reported to be damaged. The explosion began in 1982/83 when 6007.95 hectares of paddy were afflicted.[12]

Thus by the mid-1980s, Balinese farmers had become locked into a struggle to stay one step ahead of the next rice pest by planting the latest resistant variety of Green Revolution rice. Despite the cash profits from the new rice, many farmers were pressing for a return to irrigation scheduling by the water temples to bring down the pest populations. But to foreign consultants at the Bali Irrigation Project, the proposal to return control of irrigation to water temples was interpreted as religious conservatism and resistance to change. The answer to pests was pesticide, not the prayers of priests. Or as one frustrated American irrigation engineer said to me, "These people don't need a high priest, they need a hydrologist!"

THE CRISIS

Doubtless because the idea of religion playing an important role in agriculture was inconceivable to development planners, it was not until well into the 1980s that development agencies like the Asian Development Bank began to become aware of the practical role of water temples in irrigation management. The first internal evaluations of the Bali Irrigation Project simply reported that various problems had arisen with pest infestations and water shortages that kept rice production from meeting the project's goals. Unsurprisingly, these reports made no mention of water temples, except to note the existence of a Balinese "rice cult."[13] But as reports from field-level officials about the water temples accumulated, eventually the temples came to the attention of senior bank officials. At first, there was little reaction. In the words of a bank evaluation report, the replacement of the water temples by bureaucratic systems of control was seen "as an almost inevitable result of technical progress."[14] Citing Clifford Geertz's analysis of agricultural rituals as a template for cultivation cycles, planners argued that the need to increase rice production made the old schedule of agricultural rituals obsolete. To sustain high levels of rice production, farmers would have to maintain continuous cultivation of high-yielding, short-duration Green Revolution rice. The old ritual calendar, based on the growing cycle of native Balinese rice, might have played a useful role in the past before the advent of chemical fertilizers and pesticides. But the Green Revolution had made the old agrarian calendar irrelevant. The water temples might continue to exist as religious institutions but their practical role in water management would inevitably disappear.[15]

However, by the mid-1980s pressure was mounting on local officials in Bali to return control of irrigation systems to the water temples. A team of agronomists from the agricultural faculty of Bali's Udayana University was commissioned by the Department of Public Works to investigate and reported that "the farmers were pushed to plant rice at the highest possible frequency each year, which gave rise to disorganization in water use."[16] The report urged the government to take note of "the negative effects experienced as a result of the policy of continuous uncoordinated rice planting" and emphasized "the connections between the hierarchy of subak temples and cropping patterns."[17]

At about this time, I also began to try to communicate the role of the water temples to the officials at the Asian Development Bank who controlled the Bali Irrigation Project. In several written reports, I tried to show that the rituals of the water temples were not a template for an outmoded cultivation system but a system of ecological management with deep historical roots in Balinese culture. Agriculture was a social as well as a technical process, dependent on the "hydraulic solidarity" achieved by the temple system. Continuous rice cropping threatened both the ecology of the terraces and the social infrastructure of production. But these arguments failed to make much impression on the bank officials.

ECOLOGICAL MODELING

In the spring of 1987, I began a new phase of research on the ecological role of the water temples in collaboration with a systems ecologist, Dr. James Kremer. My investigations had convinced me that the primary role of water temples was in the maintenance of social relationships between productive units. The question that Kremer and I wished to address was, Did these systems of social coordination have measurable effects on rice production? The Green Revolution approach assumed that agriculture was a purely technical process and that production would be optimized if everyone planted high-yielding varieties of rice as often as they could. In contrast, Balinese temple priests and farmers argued that the water temples were necessary to coordinate cropping patterns so that there would be enough irrigation water for everyone and to reduce pests by coordinating fallow periods. Kremer suggested that these alternatives could be formally evaluated in an ecological simulation analysis. Furthermore, such an analysis might yield deeper insights into the reasons for regional differences in the organization of water temple networks.

Our first idea was to investigate cases in which water temples had been removed from irrigation management. But we quickly concluded that it would be impossible to learn very much from such a study because it would be difficult to directly associate events such as pest infestations with the absence of temple control. Moreover, a temple-by-temple comparison would not reveal the effects of higher-level systems of coordination between temples. The water resources available to any single temple are affected to some degree by the irrigation schedules of their neighbors upstream, and we hoped to be able to evaluate the importance of such cooperative arrangements in water management. One of the key features of the temple system, from an ecological point of view, is the difference in the scale of social coordination from one region to another. The pattern of temple organization differs substantially in the mountains, where streams and irrigated areas are small, as compared to the seacoast, where the rivers are much larger. To evaluate the importance of these differences in the productive system, we decided to model all of the irrigation systems that lie between two rivers in south-central Bali, the Oos and the Petanu.

Based on my earlier fieldwork, we knew that water temples make decisions about cropping patterns by taking into consideration the trade-off between two constraints: water sharing and pest control. As previously noted, if everyone plants at the same time, all will also harvest at the same time, and a widespread fallow period can reduce pest populations by depriving them of food and/or habitat. On the other hand, if everyone plants the same rice variety at the same time to coordinate their harvests and fallow periods, then irrigation demand cannot be staggered. Striking an optimal balance between these two constraints is not a simple matter because the choices made by upstream farmers have implications for their downstream neighbors, and constraints such as the amount of water available for irrigation vary by location and by season.

The simulation model we constructed was specifically designed to evaluate the effects of different levels of social coordination on irrigation demand and pest control. A technical report on the model is included as an appendix to this book; here we will consider only the logic of the model and its most significant results. We began by dividing the watershed of the two rivers into 12 subsections, specifying the catchment basins for each of the weirs for which hydrological data were available. For each of the 172 *subak*s located in these basins, we specify the name, area, the basin in which they reside, the weir from which they receive irrigation water, and the weir to which any excess is returned. We also specify the real spatial mosaic connecting these *subak*s. Thus, for each one we note the neighboring *subak* on all four sides or another kind of boundary, like a river, road, or village.

With this geographical setting, the simulation model computes the growth and ultimate harvest of rice for all 172 *subak*s based on the assumptions contained in three submodels. These submodels define the physical hydrology of the rivers and irrigation systems, the growth of rice and other crops, and the population dynamics of pests. Based on historical data on rainfall by season and elevation, runoff to the rivers is calculated. Irrigation demand for each of the *subak*s is computed from the cropping pattern specified in the model. Growth of rice depends upon the variety being grown and the available water supply, and the harvest is reduced if the supply from the rivers is insufficient to meet the demand. The level of pests in each *subak* depends on immigration from adjacent cropland plus growth in place if rice is being grown.

Seven choices of management scenarios are supplied that span the range of coordination among the 172 *subak*s, from all following the same cropping pattern to 172 different schedules. These choices assume that the *subak*s plant and harvest together in groups that parallel to various degrees the subdivisions of the temple hierarchy. Of these choices, only two have actually occurred (as far as we know): the first, in which each

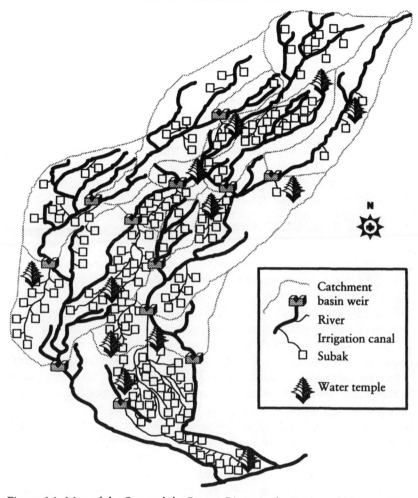

Figure 6.1. Map of the Oos and the Petanu Rivers in the Region of Gianyar. The catchment basins, irrigation system, and *subak*s are shown in relation to major water temples. Map is not to scale.

subak acts as an independent unit setting its own cropping pattern; and the fourth, in which each water temple sets a cropping pattern for its *subak* congregations. But by including a range of five other hypothetical options, it is possible to evaluate a range of possibilities in the social co-ordination of production while holding the biological and physical factors constant. The model is used to compare the results of many simulation runs, so as to reveal the effects of changing specific assumptions, such as daily rainfall, river flow, irrigation demand, or the rate of pest diffusion.

Because one goal of the modeling is to compare irrigation systems and water temples at different points along the rivers, the computer keeps track of results for each of the twelve catchment basins. In the upper reaches of the rivers, irrigation systems originating at several weirs are generally organized into a single Masceti temple unit with carefully staggered planting intervals designed to maximize water sharing. At these high elevations, the amount of water in the rivers is comparatively small. In contrast, at lower elevations there is much more water in the rivers, so the cropping patterns of upstream irrigation systems have little effect on the amount of water available for downstream neighbors. On the other hand, at lower elevations, the potential damage from rice pests is greater because the rice terraces extend over large areas, and it is possible for pest populations to build up more quickly than in the narrow upstream valleys. The results of a series of simulations that show these results are displayed in time series plots for four catchment basins. In this simulation, all farmers are assumed to be planting three crops of Green Revolution rice. Rainfall, river flow, and pest damage rates are all normal (based on historical data for 1985–1986). Notice that pest levels are higher when each *subak* sets its own cropping patterns, because pests immigrate from adjacent *subak*s. In contrast, when cropping patterns are set by water temples, pest levels are reduced by coordinated fallow periods. Pest damage is also higher in the lowlands for the reasons described.

Along with pest damage, the model also permits a detailed analysis of the likelihood of water stress at various levels of social coordination. The model calculates water stress whenever a *subak* does not have enough water to meet the requirements of the cropping pattern that has been selected. These numbers are based on monthly flow rates for each catchment basin and irrigation demand for each cropping pattern (see the Appendix for details). The model expresses water stress as the percentage of *subak*s that experience a reduced rice harvest owing to water shortages. The graph below shows the results of running identical simulations at each of the seven possible levels of irrigation management. At one extreme, each individual *subak* sets its own cropping pattern, resulting in 172 uncoordinated cropping patterns for the whole watershed. At the other extreme, the entire watershed follows a single cropping pattern, which results in major water shortages. As the graph indicates, the least amount of water stress occurs when water temples set the cropping patterns.

Because water sharing and pest control represent opposing constraints

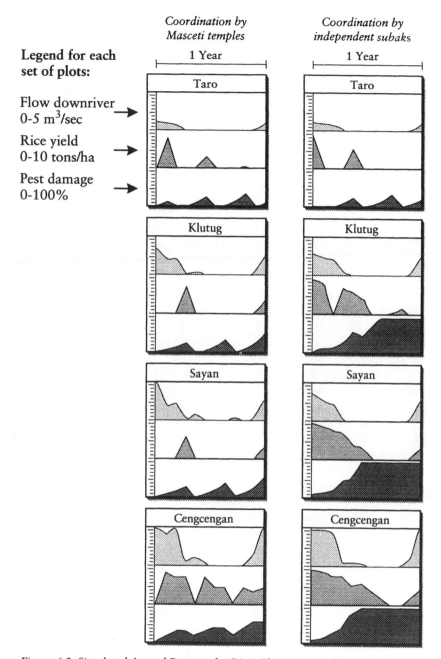

Figure 6.2. Simulated Annual Patterns for River Flow, Rice Yield, and Pest Damage. Compares two runs of the model differing only by the scale of coordination among the *subaks*. Each panel of three plots shows average results for the catchment basins. Note the increased levels of pest damage (up to 100 percent loss of crop) that result when all *subaks* plant and harvest independently. This results in a reduction in rice yield per crop. The downstream river flow is Taro → Klutug → Sayan → Cengcengan.

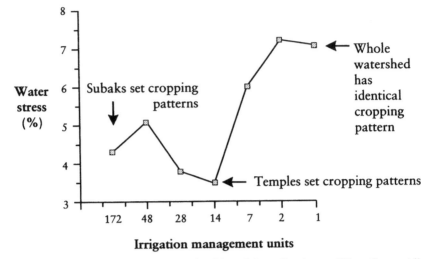

Figure 6.3. Effects of Different Levels of Social Coordination on Water Stress. All farmers are double cropping Green Revolution rice.

on water management, a key question is which level of social coordination strikes the optimal balance between them. For a cropping pattern in which all *subaks* are planting two crops of high-yielding rice, the results are displayed in table 6.4.

In this case, damage from pests is highest at the *subak* scale of coordination. Most *subaks* are too small to reduce pest levels by fallow periods because the pests can easily migrate to neighboring ricefields. On the other hand, pest levels are very low if the entire watershed follows a single cropping pattern because the fallow period extends over thousands of hectares. But pest levels are also minimized if cropping patterns are set by water temples. The water temples strike an optimum balance between pest control and water sharing (fig. 6.4).

A similar pattern emerges if the cropping pattern is changed from two to three crops of Green Revolution rice. Pest damage is highest if the *subaks* act as autonomous units.

Water stress is low at the *subak* scale and high at the watershed scale. But the optimum scale of social coordination remains the water temples.

As in the previous case, this result is owing to the effect of the temples in simultaneously minimizing water stress and damage from pests.

Multiple runs of the model with different cropping patterns (including traditional Balinese rice) and different physical and biological constants confirm this basic pattern: regardless of the rice variety and cropping pattern selected, coordination of cropping patterns by Masceti temples produces the highest yields by striking an optimal balance between water

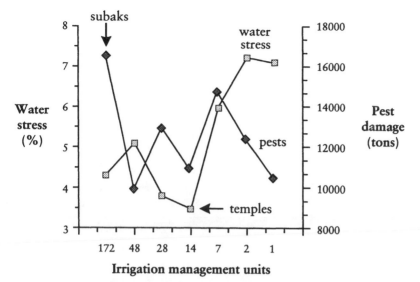

Figure 6.4. Effects of Different Levels of Social Coordination on Pest Damage and Water Stress. All farmers are double cropping Green Revolution rice.

stress and pest damage. This level of coordination in the model corresponds most closely to the actual pattern of water temples along these rivers.

The model shows strong hydrological connectivity between irrigation systems in the upper and middle sections of the rivers. Near the sea, even in the dry season, so much water is in the rivers that cropping decisions by upstream *subaks* appear to have a minimal effect on downstream *subaks*, assuming a normal year for rainfall. However, low rainfall increases the interdependency of *subaks* even in the lower portions of the rivers. With respect to the second constraint, the model predicts that pest damage will occur more rapidly in the lowlands, where there are fewer natural barriers to pest diffusion. Altogether, the water-sharing constraint is most significant for upstream Masceti temples, whereas pest control is more critical downstream. But overall, the model supports the conclusion that the social organization of cropping patterns plays an important role in the management of terrace ecology. The real productive significance of the ritual system is not in the imposition of fixed cropping patterns but in the ability to synchronize the productive activities of large numbers of farmers. The water temples are a social system that manages production, not a ritual clockwork. For these reasons, the ecological model suggests that removing the temples from the control of production ultimately threatens the entire productive system.

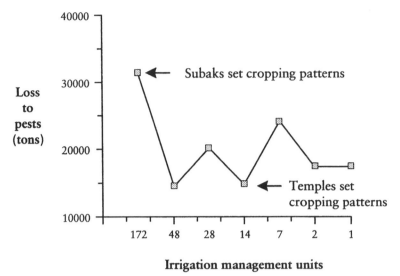

Figure 6.5. Pest Damage at Different Levels of Social Coordination. All farmers are triple cropping Green Revolution rice.

REEVALUATION

We reported these results to the Asian Development Bank in 1988 and received a sympathetic audience. The final evaluation report for the Bali Irrigation Project reversed the bank's earlier skepticism towards water temples, noting that

> The substitution of the "high technology and bureaucratic" solution in the event proved counter-productive, and was the major factor behind the yield and cropped areas declines experienced between 1982 and 1985. ... The cost of the lack of appreciation of the merits of the traditional regime has been high. Project experience highlights the fact that the irrigated rice terraces of Bali form a complex artificial ecosystem which has been recognized locally over centuries.[18]

The report noted that erosion of the strength of the traditional vertical integration among water temples threatens "the long term sustainability of the irrigation systems."[19] The report concluded with the observation that "no post-evaluated project of the Bank exhibits self-sustained and high performance comparable to Bali."[20]

But perhaps the most satisfying result was the visit of the Project Evaluation Mission to the Temple of the Crater Lake, which was described in this way in the final evaluation report:

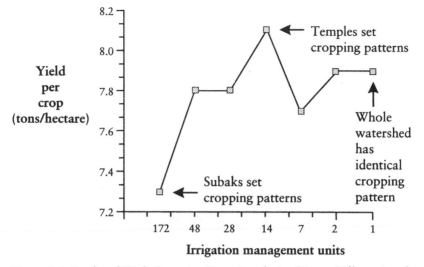

Figure 6.6. Results of Triple Cropping Green Revolution Rice at Different Levels of Social Coordination

The Project Evaluation Mission interviewed leaders of the high Water User Group at Batur who have been instrumental in the proper establishment of some 45 new subaks during the last ten years. Apart from providing the required spiritual background, they often provided technical advice, for example on spring development, canal and tunnel siting and building, and clarifying water allocation issues. In light of the minimal success of the Project Office to develop new irrigation areas, it is suggested that there would be benefit from seeking advice from them. At the least, it is considered that this exercise would be of assistance in bringing the two parallel water development and management institutions into closer contact and could have more far-reaching impacts.[21]

At the time of this writing, official policy towards irrigation and water temples in Bali is in a state of flux. The need to sustain high levels of rice production and to divert some flows formerly used for irrigation to urban uses continues. Nonetheless, for the first time, the water temples have achieved recognition by state irrigation bureaucracies, and today the temples have regained informal control of cropping patterns in most of Bali.

Sociogenesis

IT IS SOBERING, in retrospect, to consider the apparent ease with which the history of Balinese irrigation was rewritten into a story of feudal kingdoms. Water temples, the Goddess of the Lake, the *tika* calendar, the *soewinih*, and the opium monopoly—all were very nearly submerged beneath a manufactured history of *subak*s, sedahans, and reconstituted kings. For the colonial authorities, irrigation was inextricably tied to sensitive issues of sovereignty, taxation, and the legitimacy of colonial rule. The Dutch established bureaucratic systems to "control" the various aspects of irrigation. These bureaucracies collected taxes, built irrigation works, performed land surveys, and issued reports testifying to the success of colonial rule. Meanwhile, the water temples continued to function. Because the Dutch model of irrigation vastly underestimated the complexity of the sociobiophysical systems involved in rice production, water temples and bureaucracies coexisted without creating technical problems in irrigation control. Most Balinese rice terraces continued to produce two crops per year, as they had before the arrival of the Dutch. Because the two institutional systems were so unlike as to be unrecognizable to one another, coexistence was possible.

The advent of the Green Revolution in the 1970s altered this situation. By then, the Dutch were gone, but the institutional systems they had created persisted, now staffed by Western-educated Balinese and other Indonesians. For these officials, irrigation was understood to be controlled by bureaucracies: rational, anonymous instruments of the state. The failures of the Green Revolution revealed for the first time that this bureaucratic model of irrigation control was hopelessly oversimplified. The state's claims to control irrigation—or at any rate, to manage terrace ecology—were hollow. In reality, *subak*s were not autonomous units; terrace ecology could not be sustained by continuous rice cropping; and water temples played a major role in hydrological and biological management. But the managerial role of the water temples was not easily translated into the language of bureaucratic control.

To discover the kinds of controls exerted by water temples, we searched for the actual mechanisms at work in particular irrigation systems. In the case of the two rivers we studied, a major social response to the problem of sustaining the rice terraces as productive ecosystems is summed up in the concept of "hydraulic solidarity." The physical facts of hydrological interconnectivity and the need to create coordinated fallow periods for pest control place a premium on cooperation. All farmers who share water from the same weir must cooperate in construction, maintenance, water allocation, and the management of disputes. They are also likely to face the necessity of coordinating cropping patterns with upstream, downstream, and lateral neighbors. In the absence of such coordination, there is the danger of "chaos in water distribution" and an "explosion of pest populations," as occurred in the aftermath of the Green Revolution. Hydraulic solidarity is sustained by the need for tight continuous cooperation from one block of terraces to the next.

With regard to the temples, the most basic question is the relationship between their instrumental role in managing the flow of waters and the symbolic systems that define their social and cosmological roles. I have argued that there is a consistent logic to the complex ritual practices involving water temples. Essentially, water temples establish symbolic connections between productive groups and the components of the natural landscape that they seek to control. The natural world surrounding each village is not a wilderness but an engineered landscape of rice terraces, gardens, and aqueducts created by the coordinated labor of generations of predecessors. Anthropomorphic deities evoke this residual human presence in an engineered landscape, which Marx has called a "humanized nature." Each weir is the origin of an irrigation system, which has both physical and social components. The concept of a "deity of the weir" evokes the collective social presence at the weir, where free-flowing river water becomes controlled irrigation water.

On a larger scale, chains of water temples articulate the hydro-logic of each irrigation system. All water temples are physically located at the upstream edge of whatever water system they purport to control. Temples link the physical features of the irrigation systems to social units according to a logic of production: the congregation of a water temple consists of the farmers who obtain water from the irrigation component "controlled" by the temple's god. Within each temple, along with the shrine to the temple's principal deity are additional shrines for other gods. Offerings to these gods provide a way for the temple congregation to acknowledge their relationships to other temples and the social and physical units they represent. Each temple creates its own unique holy water from "upstream" sources, which evokes the sacred origins of the collective and represents the blessing of the temple's god. Relationships between related water temples and their congregations are symbolized by the joining of holy waters. The "flow" of holy water from temple to temple establishes hierarchical relations between temples. Thus water temples define the institutional structure—the hierarchy of productive units—that manages the rice terraces as a productive system.

HUMANIZED NATURE

The water temples must, therefore, be understood, not only as a system of irrigation management but in terms of their role in the process of sociogenesis. It is tempting to see the rituals of the temples as part of the superstructure, in the Marxist sense; a religious commentary on the economic realities of managing rice production. But to do so is to mistake the relationship between society and the "humanized nature" of the rice terraces. In reality, the flow of holy water is as much a part of the irrigation system as the flow of rivers and springs. Farmers can count on the delivery of water to their fields for a particular span of time, just so long as they can rely on the system of social relationships that makes that flow possible. How are these social relations sustained?

We have already drawn upon Marx's argument, which explains the origins of the concept of society in light of the concept of "humanized nature." According to Marx, each succeeding generation acquires a concept of society through an awareness of historical process, by observing the physical evidence of the labors of their predecessors. Every society transforms the wilderness that surrounds it into a civilized landscape. "Humanized nature" is thus the countryside of a civilization at a given epoch. But Marx went on to argue that "humanized nature" ultimately confronts mankind as "an alien and hostile world standing over against him."[1] Marx did not pursue the question of how the particular characteristics of different man-made environments are related to specific social formations. Instead, he immediately turned his attention to the issue of alienation and the "object-bondage" of labor.[2]

Thus from a strict Marxist perspective, there is no distinction between a weir in a river and a bridge or a house: they are all evidence of society's historical presence. And indeed, a weir in a river is not necessarily a symbol of anything in particular. What is missing from Marx's concept of humanized nature is an appreciation of the constituting role of the symbolic system. My argument is that the ritual system of water temples defines the symbolic meaning of productive relationships. A weir is just a weir, but the concept of holy water from a weir shrine transforms the weir into the symbol of a specific social unit. It is through this symbolism that farmers acquire concepts for social units more abstract than the immediate face-to-face community of neighbors. The Bayad weir is merely a small dam in a stream, but a few drops of water from the Bayad weir shrine, poured into the entrance gate of the Manuaba weir downstream, defines a definite social relationship between the *subak*s of Bayad and Manuaba. This relationship is more abstract than the relationship between farmers in a *subak*, because its only concrete symbol is a vial of holy water, but it is no less vital to the productive system. The ritual system is not merely a gloss on productive relationships, for in the long run it is the social relationships constructed by water temples, not the mechanics of water flow, that create and sustain the terrace ecosystem.

POWER

"Power," says Michel Foucault, "is not an institution, and not a structure; neither is it a certain strength we are endowed with; it is the name that one attributes to a complex strategical relationship in a particular society."[3] The Temple of the Crater Lake sits high on its crater rim, above the elevation where the rivers and streams have their headwaters, miles from any actual irrigation works. If a king or a modern bureaucrat were to seize control of the temple, he would not thereby gain control of a single irrigation system, for there are no engineering control points near the temple or the lake. The flow of water from the lake into the groundwater system is not under human control. Where does power lie in such a system?

We have seen that the water temple system is based on a hierarchy of productive relationships. Each social unit is defined by placing it in a structure of relationships that unfold in time and link it to the creation of a "humanized nature." But the entire system of water temples is only one component of Balinese society. There are other temple networks and other hierarchies that are not based on the logic of productive relationships. Indeed, most water temples contain shrines to deities that represent other social units, from villages to kings. These relationships ultimately define the boundaries of the powers of the water temples in the Balinese social universe.

An example of a ritual in which the water temples are defined as a component of a larger whole is the decennial ngusaba desa festival, in which the gods of village temples and water temples are mingled to express the complementarity of villages and rice terraces. At this level, the question of the rank of the temples does not arise, for the congregations of villages and local water temples are identical. But at higher levels in the temple hierarchy, the powers of water temples come into conflict with the imagery of power based on caste. The powers of water temples derive from the principle that the rank of a temple depends on the size of its congregation and its productive role. On the other hand, the religious cult of Balinese kingship places farmers, no matter how numerous, at the bottom rank of the social hierarchy. The affairs of village temples were no concern of kings, and one might imagine that the same would be true of all water temples. But the functions of important regional water temples, such as the larger Masceti temples, overlapped with those of kings because both were concerned with the prosperity of the realm. Indeed, so similar were their functions that princes sometimes competed with water temples for the right to collect *soewinih* offerings.

A common solution to this problem was for a prince to lay claim to the local Masceti temple as one of the state temples of his realm. Responsibility for the support of the temple would then be divided between the prince and the *subak*s. By this means, the prince could secure control not of the mechanics of irrigation, but of the flow of offerings. These offerings would be dedicated to the gods in the name of the prince and his realm as well as that of the local *subak*s. Thus the Masceti Er Jeruk was supported by both its local *subak* congregation and the royal house of Sukawati. Similar arrangements existed between the Masceti Payangan and the rajah of Tegallalang, and the Masceti Gunung Sari and the rajah of Ubud. In this way, the water temple cult (if so we may call it) was subsumed within the cult of kingship.

But at the summit of the water temple hierarchy, this solution was not possible. No single king was in a position to claim the Temple of the Crater Lake. Although the ritual system expressed a complementary relationship between the temple and the king of Bali (identified with the royal dynasty of Klungkung), in fact Klungkung was too weak to mount an effective claim to this title. The temple is located not in the kingdom of Klungkung but in the territory of the tiny mountain kingdom of Bangli, a frequent military rival of Klungkung.

In fact, one interpretation of the symbolism of temple shrines suggests the opposite relationship: an attempt to subsume the cult of kingship within the cult of water temples. Within the temple, the main shrine to the goddess is flanked by smaller shrines to several royal dynasties: Mengwi, the most powerful kingdom of the last century (fig. A.1, #18); Tejakula to the north (#17); Blahbatuh to the south (#23); Klungkung, which still lays claim to supremacy over other kings (#22); and the pavilion of the kingdom of Badung (#12). Thus we have the main shrine to the Goddess of the Lake surrounded by a constellation of royal dynastic shrines, suggesting an image of the temple as the symbolic center of a mandala of kingdoms descending from the lake. This image becomes actualized in rituals like Panca Wali Krama, when many kings and princes bring their offerings and prayers to the temple.

This image is further strengthened by two other complexes of shrines at the temple, which represent sources of power that are also not directly involved with rice production. One is the Chinese temple to the Great Lord Harbormaster (fig. A.1, #16/16A), which is tended by the Chinese community. In the precolonial era, each king had a harbormaster or trading master, usually Chinese, whose powers derived from his connections to the world of trade that lay outside the borders of Balinese kingdoms.

Another set of shrines is connected with the ancient lineage of metal-smiths and their special gods of iron and fire and sharp weapons (#38–#43). Although they seem unlikely candidates for shrines in a water temple, Chinese merchants and Balinese smiths share one significant characteristic: both wield formidable powers, whose sources lie outside the cults of kingship and water temples. Their inclusion within the temple incorporates additional sources of power into the mandala of forces that are gathered inside the Temple of the Crater Lake.

But this symbolism inevitably conflicts with the imaging of power in the royal cult. The conflict is most clearly evident in the position of the Jero Gde. Born into the commoner lineage of the Paseks of the Black Wood, the Jero Gde is magically identified with the lake mandala, the goddess and the Temple. As the representative of tens of thousands of farmers and dozens of regional water temples, the Jero Gde represents the *subak*s, sacrificing on their behalf to the supreme gods of the Balinese pantheon. As the earthly representative of the goddess, he is entitled to the highest rank, symbolized by his eleven-storied shrine. But from the perspective of the royal cult of kingship, eleven-storied rank is reserved for consecrated kings, and the Paseks of the Black Wood are merely one of many commoner lineages.

We do not know how this conflict was resolved in earlier periods of Balinese history. My point, however, is not to insist upon a particular interpretation of the relations between princes and the water temples, but only to note that a contradiction exists between the powers of the temple, based on the logic of *erga*, and the powers of kingship. This conflict has its origins in the contrasting logic of these two symbolic systems, not in any material constraints. For unlike the Masceti temples, the Temple of the Crater Lake has no control over a specific irrigation system; there is no question of a material logic of hydrology dictating the scope of its powers. Nor does it possess coercive powers like those of a sedahan or a Dutch officer. Yet it exercises the power to create new irrigation systems, to decide where irrigation water will flow, and to resolve disputes over water rights. The sources of this power lie in the logic of the symbolic system, in the concepts of holy water and productive cycles. Ultimately, it is the flow of holy water that generates the flow of water through the irrigation canals.

SOCIOGENESIS

"The greatness of Hegel's Phenomenology," according to Marx, is this, "that Hegel grasps the self-generation of man as a process." Marx hoped to retain this essential insight, while transposing Hegel's analysis from idealist philosophy to history. The arguments developed in this book suggest the need to perform a similar critique of Marx himself, retaining his insights into the relationship between nature, society, and history, while transposing the level of analysis.

Marx described "humanized nature" as a mirror reflecting society's historical development. Like his contemporaries, what Marx saw in nature was evolution: a continuous linear process of growth. For Marx, the evolutionary progress of society was a scientific reality, which could be read from the social landscape just as Lyell could read geological history from the stratigraphy of Scotland.[4] But we are inclined today to see nineteenth-century concepts of social evolution as metaphysical, as ideas that are read into, not out of, the landscape.

The images of society that the Balinese see in their terraced landscape do not reflect the progressive linear order that Marx and Hegel understood as "history." Instead, for the Balinese nonlinear patterns of temporal order emerge from the regular progression of natural cycles, the seasons of growth and change. When Balinese society sees itself reflected in a humanized nature, a natural world transformed by the efforts of previous generations, it sees a pattern of interlocking cycles that mimic these cycles of nature. Whereas Marx regarded nature in terms of linear evolutionary progress, a Balinese farmer may be reminded instead of the intricate patterns of the *tika* calendar, or the interlocking cyclical melodies of the gamelan orchestras.

AFTERWORD

VALERIO VALERI

"A BIG BOOK," somebody has written, "is a big evil." As a yet unredeemed sinner, I am envious of Steve Lansing for his remarkable achievement: he has written a book that is as short as it is pithy and as clear as it is elegant. Although I was greatly honored by his request that I write a foreword to it, I must confess that I did not find the task an easy one. A foreword, I understand, may be valuable for either (and ideally both) of two reasons: because it brings out more clearly and in a briefer compass the argument of a book and because of the authority of the person who writes it. On neither count could I hope to write a useful foreword. The book is so clearly and economically written that a summary in my own words would only retard (and perhaps even impede) the reader's progress through it; and as for authority, I am afraid that Lansing surpasses me in that too. Thus my only hope to contribute something that the author has not already done much better himself lays in writing an afterword, that is, in sharing with the reader some of the effects that the book has had on my own thinking. It is inevitable that by following my own train of thought I will be led to suggest a few expansions, some geographical, some theoretical, to Lansing's arguments. But my purpose is not to superimpose my thinking on his: it is to pay homage to his study by giving a practical illustration, through my own experience, of its fertility and the extent of its possible ramifications.

Bali has often been used in the controversies on "Oriental despotism" to illustrate two diametrically opposed views: according to some (Marx and Wittfogel included) it exemplified the managerial control by the king of the main means of agricultural production, irrigation water; according to others (from Liefrinck to Geertz), on the contrary, it demonstrated the degree to which egalitarian associations of producers (the *subaks*) could prosper by developing and organizing irrigation in almost complete autonomy relative to the state. So battles between "the free enterprise system" and "state capitalism" were waged on Bali too, but by Western scholars. Although ethnographical and historical evidence was for the most part on the side of those who asserted the farmers' autonomy, their thesis was weakened by their inability to account, as their opponents seemed to be able to, for coordination above the lower level of the irrigation system. One partial exception was Geertz's rendering of this system in his book *Negara*.[1]

Geertz argued that agricultural ritual provided the framework for rice cultivation and, thus, for the distribution of water. Wet-rice growing requires water in decreasing quantities: maximum at the beginning, none at the end. If all *subaks* planted rice at the same time, there would not be enough water for all. Hence, although all *subaks* follow the same cycle as constituted by the same set of rites, they do so in a staggered way. Each lower-level cycle is thus inscribed in a high-level cycle, which covers a whole hydrogeological area from the mountain to the sea. This high-level cycle is started at a calendrically determined time by a "water-opening" rite performed in the highest (both in status and physical elevation) temple of the area. Because Geertz claimed that the ritual cycle taking place in this temple was "state-legitimized,"[2] it seems that he recognized a role for the state in the irrigation system at the highest level. But, in agreement with the general structure of his description of the Balinese state, he viewed this role as purely ceremonial and disconnected from management. Kingship anchored the system ritually, but the actual politics of irrigation were largely independent from it, and the system's baricenter was at a much lower level, that of *subak* or immediate intersubak relations.

Lansing's study vindicates Geertz's basic point that the system is constituted by the framework of agricultural ritual and associated temples or shrines but departs from it in some crucial aspects. First, he does away with Geertz's contrast between "mostly ceremonial" at the top and "mostly politics and technology" at the bottom.[3] He shows that the system is homogeneous at all levels, that ritual is constitutive in the same way from top to bottom. Second, he does away with a related Geertzian contrast between greater royal involvement at the top (which, in terms of power and management, means no intervention because at the top there is *only* ritual) and lesser (or no) royal involvement at the bottom. Lansing shows that the system is equally autonomous at all levels because the water rites at the highest temple are in the hands of a commoner high priest, independent of any king; the high priest's jurisdiction, in fact, cuts across the territorial boundaries of kingdoms.

Third, Lansing reverses Geertz's view that the center of gravity of the system sat very low: on the contrary, he appears to be arguing that it sat, and still sits, very high because in his own analysis the irrigation system requires a much greater and more precise coordination than is recognized by Geertz. One reason for this heightened requirement was not seen by any previous student: rice agriculture demands not only optimum distribution of water but also pest control. As Lansing brilliantly shows, the two requirements work against each other: optimal water allocation requires staggered distribution timing (as in Geertz's model), but pest control requires that all fields in a large area be planted and harvested at the same time. The balancing of the two requirements to achieve optimal scheduling determines the agricultural calendar in that area. Decisions are taken in the water temples on which the irrigation area depends and assume a ritual form that emphasizes the hierarchical interdependence of all levels of the system.

The revolutionary aspect of Lansing's work, then, lies in having transcended the terms of the debate on Balinese irrigation by providing a new point of view that incorporates insights from both sides. Like Marx and Wittfogel, he argues that irrigation requires a high level of coordination and an ultimate center; but contrary to them, and going much further than Geertz in this respect, he shows that this *centered* (rather than *centralized*) system of coordination is independent from the state and, in fact, somewhat in conflict with it. The autonomy of the irrigation system in Central Bali is embodied by the Jero Gde, the high priest of the Temple of Lake Batur, from which all streams in the area are believed to flow. Although, as Lansing emphasizes, this priest's direct or indirect involvement in irrigation matters extends only over Central Bali, he is in a sense the high priest of the water cult for the whole island. Several facts indicate this status: the belief that his lake is connected, through underground tunnels, to all others and thus to all irrigation channels in Bali; the occasional offerings given him, in exchange for holy water, by *subaks* lying outside his direct jurisdiction; the fact that there is no priest like him in the temples attached to the other lakes. Even more significant, in my opinion, is that the Jero Gde is symbolically paired with the Dewa Agung of Klungkung, the most important ruler of Bali and in theory its "king of kings."[4]

This pairing does not simply provide additional evidence that the authority of the Jero Gde, as that of the Dewa Agung, extends in certain aspects to the entire island. It also constitutes an extraordinarily interesting fact of its own. Indeed, I would like to argue that the Jero Gde and the Dewa Agung form together an hitherto unrecognized diarchic structure and that considering each of the two authorities as part of it helps to clarify their identity. Moreover, this Balinese structure appears to have some striking points of similarity with the diarchies found elsewhere in the Indonesian archipelago, particularly in its eastern part. I must add, though, that these similarities become apparent only after a certain amount of reinterpretation and redefinition of both Lansing's presentation and of current views of dual authority in Indonesia. I can scarcely do this in full here, but let me give some of the facts as I see them.

One can find in Lansing's book much evidence for ideas of symbolic complementarity between the Jero Gde and the Dewa Agung, particularly, but not exclusively, as seen from the Jero Gde's point of view. As the Dewa Agung is an embodiment of the God of Mount Agung, the highest mountain in Bali and an active volcano, associated with maleness, fire, and Brahma, so the Jero Gde is the embodiment of a female manifestation of Vishnu, the Goddess of Mount Batur who is associated with water and the lake. Furthermore, at least according to his own family chronicle, the Jero Gde, who is of commoner status, is the autochthonous authority because he descends from a statue of black wood that was animated by an ascetic and thus became the first human in Bali. In contrast, the Dewa Agung descends from a later immigrant who combined in his person the identities of a Brahman priest and a warrior and thus embodied, one may suggest, the generative nucleus of the caste system. Although Lansing mentions these facts, he does not make them the cornerstone of his analysis, which focuses on the Jero Gde and says little about the Dewa Agung and more generally about Balinese kingship. But to anyone familiar with the literature on dual authority in Eastern Indonesia and the Pacific, the attributes by which the two figures are opposed are extremely suggestive.

The contrast between an autochthonous, popular authority connected with the fertility of the soil, the rhythms of nature and agricultural production, and *female* like those rhythms and the earth itself, on the one hand, and an immigrant, noble, and *male* authority on the other hand, is one that can be recognized in many societies of those areas. It reflects, in my opinion, a deeper contrast: that between the most fundamental, most unquestionable grounds for social existence (relative to which all are ultimately equal) and the *noble* values (wealth, military force, ability to attract, generative potency, etc.), which are unequally distributed and which allow those who have them most[5] to weave and reweave around their persons hierarchical networks defined by relationships of clientship, alliance, descent, debt, or even servitude.[6] In the ethnographic literature, the opposition is usually represented as one between *spiritual* and *secular* authority; but this characterization is highly misleading because both sets of qualities involve relations with the world of spirits, who are believed to be their common source, and because both have symbolic and material aspects.

Of course, this basic polarity is realized in many different ways in different societies and even in different historical periods in the same societies. Furthermore, the ideal of complementarity with which it is usually associated often masks rather badly the ambiguities, tensions, overlappings, and appropriations with which the relationship is fraught. Both points are illustrated by the societies of Sumba, an island east of Bali. In the district of Kodi, in the western part of the island, the calendrical rhythms that regulate the agricultural and ritual cycles and thus constitute the basic productive and moral framework for the entire community are determined by the Rato Nale, the "priest of the sea worms."[7] The name of this priest points to his connection with a natural event that occurs each year at a time that he is able to predict: the swarming of sea worms that brings the fertility of a female goddess to the rice plants growing in the fields. Because this event is beyond human agency, the social and productive sphere anchored to it is rendered undefeasible and free from the encroachments of the various "men of prowess" who exist in Kodi. Their client networks and their authority are established against this taken-for-granted background and cannot encompass it and modify it to satisfy their projects. Farther east, however, the relationship between the two poles of authority changes considerably.

In all the Kambera-speaking areas of East Sumba one man of prowess (*maramba*) has become dominant, and as a result, the priestly representative of the community (*ratu*) has seen his autonomy reduced or eliminated. This loss of autonomy of the symbolically female ratu is linked to the loss of autonomy of the productive process and his agents, now predominantly controlled by the ruler (both symbolically and empirically male). The outcomes of a complicated dialectic are, of course, very varied and cannot be discussed here. Suffice to say that in Umalulu the ratu has preserved a fair amount of his prerogatives but has become so vulnerable that the king may kill him and substitute one of his slaves for him; in Kapunduku he has maintained a connection with the agricultural calendar, but he has been reduced to the status of "royal priest," in fact, royal slave, while some of his prerogatives (including the right to trace descent from the original ratu) have been usurped by the king himself; in Rindi, he has disappeared altogether, and his functions have been appropriated by the royal lineage.[8] Variations comparable to those in Sumba can be found in the neighboring islands of Sawu, Roti, and Timor.[9] On the whole, they seem to indicate that the development of a strong kingly power tends to undermine the autonomy of the priestly authority as I have defined it.

But the Balinese case as described by Lansing seems to defy this generalization precisely where we would have expected it least, that is, where kingship is reported to have been strong. For there the priestly authority presiding over the basic productive process, rice cultivation, its calendrical rhythms and its religious correlates—the whole complex that Lansing felicitously calls "hydraulic solidarity"—has been able to preserve its autonomy to a large extent. The Jero Gde has even been allowed to claim, through the mandalalike structure of the Temple of the Lake, a hierarchical superordination to kingship *in the context of the productive process*. One can find in Lansing's study a fair amount of evidence for counterclaims of superiority from the kingly side and for ambiguities, conflicts, and overlappings in the relationship between Jero Gde and king. More fundamentally, similar tensions are evident in the relationship between the cult of irrigation water and the cult of the king (what in Old France used to be called "la religion royale"). I think that more attention should be paid to these tensions and particularly to their most recent manifestations, such as the Jero Gde's appropriation of the name of a royal ritual—*abiseka ratu*, the anointment of the king—for one of his own purification-divinization rituals. Many of the facts that Lansing himself reports indicate that kings have often attempted to encroach on the water cult, for instance by becoming intermediaries in the transfer of *soewinih* offerings. Nevertheless, I think that Lansing is basically right in claiming that the ritual organization of irrigation and its ultimate reference, the Jero Gde, have successfully avoided encompassment by kingship.

How can this fact be explained? By the inability of any Balinese ruler since the fall of the unified kingdom of Gelgel (in the second half of the seventeenth century) to achieve supremacy on the island? Lansing demolishes this thesis, dear to the heart of Dutch colonial administrators. There is no evidence, he claims, that the irrigation system was controlled by Balinese kingship before its fragmentation.[10] By the persistence of an Indonesian, pre-Indic ideological substratum? But we have seen that in Eastern Indonesia the autonomy of the priests connected with the regulation of production tends to disappear with the reinforcement of royal authority.

The puzzle remains to be solved. Or, perhaps, the puzzle exists because we do not understand a political ideology that discourages the indefinite expansion of kingly power, especially in the direction of the basic grounds of its existence. One such ground has long been recognized because it is what is most Indic in Indic Bali: it is the universe of moral axioms and their ritual expressions embodied by the Brahman priest.[11] But a second ground, no less fundamental, must be added after Lansing's study: it is constituted by the regulated flow of water, the basic framework of rice production and, thus, of the productive base of the kingdom. I suggest that Balinese kings recognize the relative autonomy of this basic framework for the same reason that they recognize the relative autonomy of the Brahmans—because they both embody fundamental conditions of the possibility of kingship itself. Kingship is, therefore, ultimately dependent on them. If this is so, we are faced with a very interesting paradox: something that looks like an Indonesian, pre-Indic structure has been preserved or, perhaps, even developed through the extension of an Indic argument. But we are also faced, more importantly, with the necessity of looking again into the Balinese conception of kingly power. Whatever the ultimate result, we must be grateful to Lansing for having made a discovery that sets the rather stagnant waters of Indonesian political anthropology in motion and thus will irrigate new fields in the scholarly landscape.

One of the most brilliant aspects of *Priests and Programmers* is its use of some Marxian ideas to make sense of the basic facts about Balinese agriculture by irrigation: it is neither a merely technical nor a merely political process but a symbolic, in fact, religious process as well. Briefly, this religious character is a consequence of the fact that human labor humanizes nature not only because it transforms nature into something useful for man but also because in doing this it impresses itself on nature. Thus, transformed nature appears to human consciousness as objectified labor. It symbolizes the power and value of labor together with the social relations that mobilize it and make it possible, in externalized form. Such symbolic aspects of objectified labor, of "humanized nature," are elaborated and reproduced by ritual. As Lansing points out, they are not "a mere gloss on productive relationships" but necessary to the existence of those relations. This is another way of saying that there can be no form of production without a form of consciousness, that consciousness is always consubstantial with labor. It is in this sense that rice cultivation in Bali is ritually constituted.

Lansing's analysis of the place of holy water in Balinese irrigation rituals illustrates this Marxian point.[12] The holy water that is the main ingredient of the rituals performed in the irrigation temples concentrates in itself, and thereby makes more evident, the symbolic value that permeates in diffuse form all the irrigation water. This symbolic value refers to the hierarchy of social relations that makes it possible—through labor—for water to flow through the rice terraces. That holy water signifies this hierarchy explains why it is ritually used to connect higher level water temples to lower level ones. Although empirical water does not, or does not necessarily, flow throughout an entire irrigation system, holy water does because the holy water used in subordinated temples combines the holy waters taken from hierarchically superordinated temples, all the way up to the supreme temple (in Central Bali, the Temple of Lake Batur). In this way, holy water as used in water temple ritual signifies two things: that each segment of an irrigation network presupposes the whole system; and that the circulation of water as a means of agricultural production presupposes the circulation of water as a means of social reproduction. Empirical water is included in holy water just as irrigation as a technical process is included in irrigation as a social process.

This brilliant explanation of holy water in agricultural ritual falls short of being Marxian in one crucial aspect, however. Why is it that the symbolic value of holy water—human labor in the particular social form it takes in Balinese wet-rice cultivation—is fetishized? That is, Why is it that human labor is not simply externalized, objectified in water, but *alienated* in it? Why is it, in other words, that Balinese labor does not recognize its own power in the water? Why does it view water as an external and alien power on which it depends? In the final pages of his book, Lansing denies that Marx's vision of an alienated "humanized nature" applies to Bali, but this denial is a bit too hasty. It renders the religious character taken by the social relations of production and by the holy water that symbolizes them, quite incomprehensible, at least from the Marxian point of view. I suspect that Lansing refuses to take this last, but crucial, Marxian step because he finds that the argument that sustains it is inapplicable to Balinese relations of production, particularly as he has depicted them. Indeed, as is well known, Marx argues that laborers do not recognize themselves in their own products when they do not have control of the means of production. But if this argument does not apply to Balinese water (and land), what explains the fetishized character of labor's symbols in Bali? Lansing does not tell us. Moreover, the Marxian approach to "humanized nature" runs into an even more troubling difficulty in Bali.

This approach, with its emphasis on labor as the fundamental relation between human activity and nature, works well in domains like irrigation where an instrumental relation between human activity and nature predominates. It works much less well in domains where communication is more important than labor and where, therefore, nature is appropriated for symbolic purposes independently of instrumental ones.[13] Of course, as Lansing's analysis shows, the instrumental relation between human labor and nature cannot be separated from a symbolic one, inasmuch as labor only exists in the context of particular social relations and, thus, in a particular communicative form. Thus holy water does not signify only the instrumental relation between the principal means of production and human labor but also, and more importantly, the form of the social relations of production. Nevertheless, what is specifically Marxian in this argument is that the choice of water as a symbol is motivated by the fact that it is the principal means of production. In the theoretical framework adopted by Marx, homo faber is ultimately more explanatory than homo loquens. But in the Balinese context, this ontological presupposition creates very serious difficulties, for holy water is used extensively outside the domain of irrigation ritual. Indeed it is such a generalized ritual medium that Balinese religion has been called a "religion of the holy water."

It seems impossible to view this generalized use of holy water as an extension of its use in irrigation ritual. Hence a Marxian interpretation of holy water in irrigation ritual furnishes some additional reasons for the use of that medium in a particular domain but is unable to give us a truly general theory of it. On the contrary, it presupposes such theory as is made evident, I think, by the fact that the basic value of holy water in irrigation—namely its ability to signify hierarchical relations and their effects—is also its basic value in most other ritual contexts. A truly general theory of holy water must account for why hierarchical values have become attached to this medium independently of instrumental relations with it. I do not presume to suggest what this theory is or even what it should be. But it seems to me that if my premises are correct, such theory will have to presuppose some intellectual operations at work: the apprehension of certain physical properties of water (it flows from above to below, it circulates and regenerates, it cleanses and gives life, etc.) that make it "good to think," uniquely able, among the objects of nature, to become the embodiment of certain social and logical properties and thus to become "humanized"—an object transacted in the communicative world created by man.

These physical properties, of course, are only potentials for meaning. They have to be used socially to be actualized and regularized as meaningful. In fact, their specific cultural meanings can only exist because water is subjected to social operations. The process of conceptualization of nature, therefore, goes hand in hand with the process of its practical appropriation. But this practical appropriation is not just instrumental and does not occur just in labor. Water has to be appropriated in many forms, some communicative, some instrumental, to be apprehended in a particular mental form. But reciprocally, it must be apprehended in some mental form to be symbolically and instrumentally appropriated. This is precisely why I have claimed elsewhere that a theory of symbolism cannot do without a theory of concept formation—and reciprocally.[14]

The important point is that although Marx is right in rejecting the idealist reduction of the synthesis of object and subject to a mere intellectual act, he is wrong in not recognizing that this synthesis does not occur in mere labor either. Human activity consists of interrelating practices of various kinds—intellectual, instrumental, communicative, and so on. To separate one of these practices in order to make it the transcendental, or even ontological, foundation for all others it to distort both what is separated and what is left of the whole after the separation. The relations that define human activity are without foundation or, what amounts to the same thing, provide at each moment all the foundation that is needed. Translated into the Balinese context, this theoretical point amounts to saying that holy water cannot be explained, Marxistically, by labor alone or, Durkheimianly, by the requirement of solidarity alone, or, idealistically, by the workings of intellect or sentiment unaided by all the rest.

Let me stop my musings here. They suffice, I hope, to show some of the reasons why I consider Lansing's book theoretically, and not just ethnographically important. He has brilliantly renewed Marx's theory of humanized nature and has forced us to see its strengths and limitations; and in the course of doing this he has shown, to paraphrase Kant, that production without ritual is blind and ritual without production is empty. Moreover, he has allowed us to situate Balinese social relations in a wider geographical context. In has often been claimed that under Bali's Indic veneer beats an Eastern Indonesian (and even Austronesian) heart. But the pulsations of this heart were not always very audible, to the ear of a student of Eastern Indonesia at least, in the evidence usually presented to support the claim. Lansing has now provided what I believe is cogent evidence for some Balinese ideas and practices that really do bear comparison with what is found in societies farther east. It is not the least contribution of this brief but remarkably stimulating book.

Plan of the Temple of the Crater Lake

1. Anantabogha
    Shrine for the World Serpent
2. Bale Kulkul
    Tower for drum
3. Bale Kulkul
    Tower for drum
4. Bale Pekajah
    Here one requests purification by holy water before entering the inner courtyards
5. Bale Gong Gde
    Orchestra pavilion for the 50-piece gong gde orchestra
6. Kertamasa
    Shrine for offerings keyed to Icaka months
7. Bale Pengeraosan
    "Speech Pavilion," where guests are welcomed
8. Bale Gajah
    Pavilion for priests and elders
9. Pesepilan
    "Secrets" shrine
10. Bale Angklung
    Pavilion for angklung orchestra
11. Dapur Suci
    Temple kitchens and storerooms
12. Bale Badung
    General purpose pavilion named for the kingdom of Badung
    Here the scribe receives delegations; priests and guests rest; offerings are readied for presentation at the main shrines; anthropologists take notes.
13. Bale Pemujan
    Pavilion for worship, similar to #12
14. Peparuman Agung
    Sacred storehouse for images of the gods and temple heirlooms

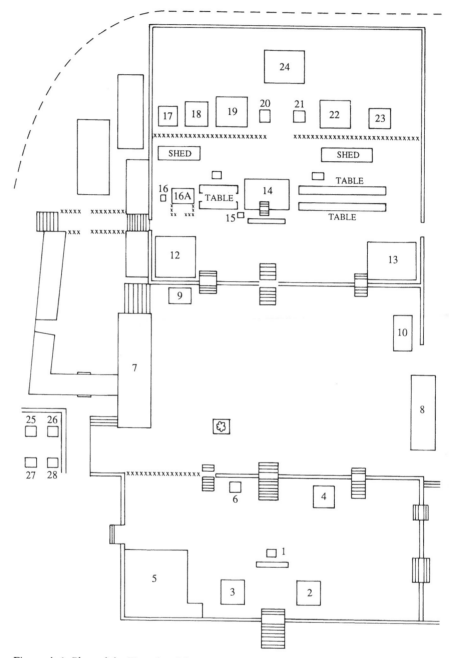

Figure A.1. Plan of the Temple of the Crater Lake

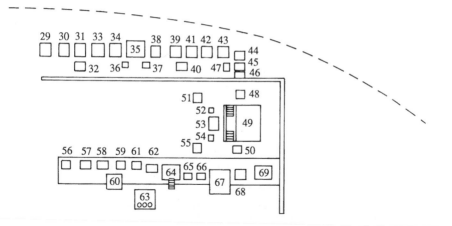

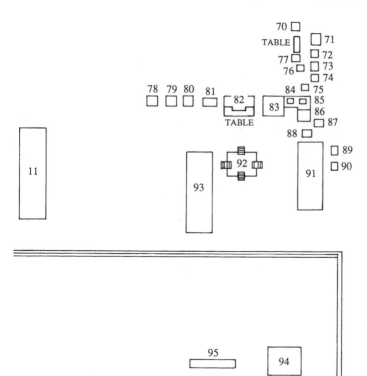

15. Jajan Gumi
    Pedestal for the offering called Jajan Bumi, a cosmological symbol made of edible ingredients

Tables: These permanent tables were recently installed to replace the temporary tables made of bamboo and to provide a place for offerings to the deities. Beneath the innermost row of tables, the priests store containers for holy water and rest during the long rituals.

16. Pelinggih I Ratu Gde Subandar
    Shrine for the Great Lord Harbormaster, provisioner to the supreme gods. This shrine and 16A are supported and maintained by Balinese of Chinese descent.

16A. Peparuman Ratu Gde Subandar
    Sacred storehouse for the Great Lord Harbormaster, a god of money

17. Meru Tumpang 3
    Three-storied *meru* shrine associated with a deity of the district of Tejakula in North Bali

18. Meru Tumpang 5
    Five-storied *meru* shrine for Bhatari Sakti Manik Astagina, a goddess associated with the ancestry of the former kingdom of Mengwi in south-central Bali

19. Meru Tumpang 9
    Nine-storied *meru* shrine for Ratu Gde Meduwe Gumi (Great Lord who owns the Realm) associated with the temple of Lempuyang

20. Pelinggih Penyarikan
    Shrine for the scribe (*penyarikan*). The ambiguity of this name is intentional, for the shrine refers both to a divinized scribe who is the servant of the greater gods and the human scribe of the temple.

21. Pelinggih Penyarikan
    The hierarchy of temple priests includes two scribes, the greater and lesser. Perhaps for this reason, there are also two of these shrines.

22. Meru Tumpang 9
    Nine-storied *meru* shrine for Bhatara Gde Gunung Agung, the supreme deity of Mount Agung and of Besakih Temple

23. Meru Tumpang 5
    Five-storied *meru* shrine for the deity of the former princedom of Blahbatuh

24. Meru Tumpang 11
    The supreme shrine of the temple, with eleven stories, which is the maximum. This shrine is identified in two ways: either as the shrine of Dewi Danu, the Goddess of the Lake, or as the shrine for Bhatara Kalih Putranjaya. Bhatara Kalih Putranjaya means "the Two Gods of Putranjaya," or "the Dual God Putranjaya," the Goddess of the Lake and the God of Mount Agung. However, the goddess is supreme in this shrine, even when she is symbolically linked to the god.

25. Bebali Courtyard
    Middle courtyard of the main temple, usually used for performances by the Baris Gde and Rejang dancers, the Gong Gde orchestra, Topeng dancers, and other bebalian performances

26. Nawa-sangha
    During the Panca Wali Krama ceremonies of 1987, the *nawa-sangha* temporary offerings enclosure was situated here.

27. Wali
    The innermost courtyard of the main temple

28. Temporary Bale for Panca Wali Krama
    Here the emblems and images (*arca*) of the deities were placed for blessings by Brahmana priests (*pedanda*) at the conclusion of Panca Wali Krama.

28A. Temporary Platforms for Brahmana priests
    During the final phases of Panca Wali Krama, four *pedanda*s conducted their prayers (*dewa yajna*) from temporary bamboo and wood platforms situated here.

29–34. These six shrines form a group. The names of the deities worshipped in them are as follows:

29. Ratu Ayu Pecatu
30. Ratu Ayu Pinget
31. Ratu Ayu Kling
32. Ratu Ayu Shri Penpen
33. Ratu Ayu Kebek Sai
34. Ratu Ayu Teka Sai
    The meaning of this collection of shrines is suggested by the names of the deities. Ratu is a royal title, and Ayu means attractive and has a feminine connotation. The meanings of the names of the goddesses are as follows: Pecatu is a measure of rice; Pingit means sacred and is described as the sibling of Pecatu; Shri means the Rice Goddess; Penpen means to keep or save; Kling means utterance or command; Kebek sai means always full, always present, and Teka sai means always comes or comes every day.

The relationships among these deities are described in terms of a process. "After the command of Ratu Kling, the Rice Goddess retains the rice. The rice is saved in sacred (*pinget*) measures (*pecatu*), it always comes and the *pecatu* is always full (*kebek sai*)."

35–37. Shrine 35 is a three-storied *meru* shrine for the deity of the Pasek clans. All of the priests of the temple belong to one of the Pasek clans. The Greater Jero Gde belongs to the Paseks of the Black Wood (Kayu Selem), whereas the Lesser Jero Gde is a Pasek of Gelgel, the legendary southern kingdom. See the text for interpretation.

35. I Ratu Gde Pasek (or Kepasekan)
36. Pepelik (offering shrine for #35)
37. Pepelik (offering shrine for #35)

38–43. The next set of shrines also form a group. The identities of the deities worshipped in the shrines are as follows:

38. Ratu Gde Manik Blabur
39. Ratu Gde Manik Melele
40. Pepelik (offering shrine for #39 and #41)
41. Ratu Gde Manik Senjata
42. Ratu Gde Manik Malegadan
43. Ratu Ngurah Runcing

These shrines are often used by the metalsmiths (Pande clans). Melele means sharp; Malegadan means burnished or gleaming; Senjata means edged weapon, and Runcing means sharp. Blabur means rain. Some informants suggest a link between rain and the cooling of metal after it has been forged; others insist that this shrine is not connected with the smith shrines directly. Rather, they say, it is a shrine where one may ask for rain.

44–47. No longer exist

48. Ratu Gde Perahu

The deity of boats. One informant suggested that this deity is a messenger who travels along waterways.

49. Meru Tumpang 3

Three-storied shrine for Ratu Mpu Dwijendra/Ratu Pura Jati. Shrine to the divinized priest Mpu Dwijendra, linked to the origin of the lineage of the Greater Jero Gde, the Paseks of the Black Wood.

50. Ratu Magening

The deity of purification. This deity and #49 play an important role in the concept of a mandala of sacred waters supplying irrigation water to the *subak*s. On the floor of the crater near the lake is a subsidiary temple called Pura Jati. The principal deity enshrined at the Pura Jati is #49. Beside the lake is a small shrine to Ratu Magening, where water for holy water is sought. It is said that Ratu Magening causes the waters of the lake to circulate, and so decides how much water will flow in a given direction. The main *odalan* (festival) at the Pura Jati occurs at the Full Moon of the First Month, in the midst of the dry season, and is well attended by the *subak*s.

51–55. Offerings shrines and statues for #49

56–64. The following nine shrines form a group:
56. Ratu Sumampat
57. Ratu Bunut
58. Ratu Manukan
59. Ratu Ayu Mas Magelung
60. Ratu Ayu Tusan
61. Ratu Mas Sakti
62. Ratu Bangun Sakti
63. Ratu Ayu Kentel Gumi
64. Pesamuan #61–#63
Ratu Ayu Kentel Gumi, Lord of the Thick Earth, is the ruler of this group. The first shrine in the row (#56) is used for offerings to control agricultural pests. Bunut is a type of tree. Manuk means bird. Mas Magelung is a dancer's golden headdress. Tusan is the name of the legendary smith who created metalworking. Mas sakti means sacred gold. Bangun sakti means sacred building.

65. Ratu Pekiisan
Pekiisan comes from the word for a procession to seek holy water (*mekiis*). This deity provides holy water to candidates for priesthood at the temple.

66. Ratu Ayu Jelung

67. Ratu Gde Makolem
Makolem means sleep. Offerings for couples planning marriage are made here.

68. Ratu Gulem
Gulem means rain clouds.

69. Ratu Gde Baturrenggong

70–95. The remaining shrines constitute a separate temple, the Pura Puseh Batur (Navel Temple of the village of Batur). A single exception is #83, the drum tower, which is struck forty-five times every morning in honor of the forty-five principal deities of the temple.

78. Ida Iratu Dalem Majapahit
79. Ida Iratu Tambang Layar
80. Ida Iratu Gde Dalem Mesim
81. Ida Iratu Gde Dalem Mekah
82. Sanggar Agung: Surya, Chandra, Bayu
83. Bale kulkul tengeran Ida Bhatara
84. Pretiwi Ulun Bale Agung
85. Divider
86. I Ratu Rambut Sedana
87. I Ratu Bhatari Cri
88. Pepelik Bhatari Cri
89. Ratu Paumbukang
90. Pepelik
91. Bale Agung Bedanginan solas lobang
92. Bale Pesamuan Agung
93. Bale Agung Bedauhan siu lobang
94. Bale Perebuan
95. Apit lawang

Figure A.2. The Mandala of Waters

According to the Jero Gde Alitan, the mandala of waters consists of eleven springs:

1. "Holy water from the summit" (*tirtha puncak* Gunung Batur) comes from the caldera.

From the center of the lake come three types of holy water:

2. Siwamurti
3. Sadasiwamurti
4. Sunyamurti

The center of the lake is called *tengahing segara*, the center of the ocean. Near the Pura Jati temple complex is the spring called (5) Magening, which is the place from which the goddess sends water in every direction. Other springs around the lakeside are

6. Danu gadang (to south central Bali)
7. Danu Kuning (to south Bali)
8. Reijang anyar (to the north)
9. Bantah anyut (to the southeast)
10. Telaga wajah (to the west)
11. Pelisan seked (to Pakisan, and via underground tunnels to the western lakes)

There are no springs along the eastern shore of the lake because it lies within the domain of Ida Bhatara ring Gunung Agung, the God of Mount Agung.

Technical Report on the Ecological Simulation Model

THE SIMULATION MODEL was developed by James N. Kremer as a tool to investigate the role of water temple networks in the management of rice terrace ecology along two rivers in south-central Bali, the Oos and the Petanu. The original goal of the research was to develop a computer simulation model of hydrology, rice growth, and pest population dynamics. Using this model of the watershed, various management scenarios could be explored. The hypothesis to be tested was whether an optimum scale of spatial coordination existed to balance two conflicting goals: efficient use of water for irrigation and control of insect pests and insect-borne diseases.

For the simulation model, the most fundamental level of information is the geographical description of the area. The physical facts of hydrological interdependency dictate that the total watershed of a river is the appropriate scale of analysis. The Gianyar region of Bali includes the watersheds of the Oos and Petanu rivers (fig. 1 of chap. 6). In our approach, all information is organized in relation to the catchment basins and the hydrology that connects them.

Based on topographical maps, we divided the Oos-Petanu watershed into 12 subsections specifying the catchment basins for each dam for which hydrological data was available. For each of the 172 *subaks* located in these basins, we specified the name, area, basin in which it resides, the dam from which it receives irrigation water, and the dam to which any excess is returned. We also defined the real spatial mosaic connecting these *subaks*. Thus, for each one we specified the neighboring *subak* on all four sides, or whether it is bounded by another kind of boundary, such as a river, road, or city.

Given this geographical setting, the simulation model computes the growth and ultimate harvest of rice. The computer program consists of three submodels: hydrology, rice growth, and pest dynamics.

HYDROLOGY

The hydrological model is based on daily rainfall and stream flow records for the Gianyar regency in south-central Bali. Data for the flow rates of springs are not included in the model at present.

Rainfall

A statistical analysis enabled us to define a seasonal pattern for rainfall by elevation based on daily precipitation records from metering stations in Gianyar. Average monthly rainfall values are drawn from a table appropriate for each of the catchment basins. For the low rainfall option, a similar table was constructed based on the 80 percent probability value used for calculations by the Bali Irrigation Project. The high rainfall option given in a third table exceeds the average rainfall by the same proportion (e.g., 120 percent of average values).

Rainfall-Runoff Relationship

Lacking the geological data that would be required for a detailed hydrological model of each watershed, we sought an empirical statistical description to define the relationship between rainfall and river flow by elevation for each catchment basin:

$$Runoff = (Rain_{elev} - ET)*A_{ews}$$

where

$Rain_{elev}$ is the rainfall specified as a function of average elevation for each weir's watershed;

ET is the empirical intercept from the plot of raw data, roughly interpreted as evapotranspiration; rain less than ET does not result in any rainfall to rivers;

A_{ews} is the area of the effective watershed in hectares.

CROP MODEL

By choosing among the various management scenarios, the user specifies crop planting patterns to be followed by each of the 172 *subak*s included in the model. The growth dynamics of the crops are formulated in a simplistic way designed to focus directly on the rice harvest and its potential reduction by water stress or pest damage. Detailed physiological data that might be used to formulate a mechanistic rice model are not available for the traditional varieties, and, in any case, such a detailed model of growth is inappropriate for this purpose.

The model presently provides five crop options including a fallow period, vegetable crops (*palawija*), and three rice varieties. Padi del or padi tahun is the traditional first crop, planted during the rainy season to mature in about five to six months in the dry season. Padi Cicih is the traditional second crop. This type of rice is assumed to mature in four months. High-yielding rice varieties are assumed to mature in three months. For each crop, data specify the time from planting to harvest, normal maximum yield, water demand, and potential maximum effect of pest damage on harvest yield.

Water demand is set at the values used for these calculations by the Bali Irrigation Project: 5 liters per second per hectare for rice crops and 1 liter per second per hectare for vegetables. Values for the remaining parameters were chosen whenever possible to be consistent with the available scientific literature, but we also used rough estimates given by Balinese farmers. Although these values are, therefore, preliminary, they are reasonable. In any case, results within any series of simulations make the same assumptions and are directly comparable.

Rice Stage and Time to Harvest

At the start of a planting cycle, the crop code for each *subak* is set to define the rice variety being grown. Water demand is specified and remains constant for the duration of the crop until harvest. If adequate water is available to meet the calculated demand, the crop is assumed to grow normally, and the model output parameter *Rice Stage* progresses linearly toward a value of 1.0 at harvest. After the specified period, the crop is harvested and the results are tabulated. The yield is calculated at 5 tons per hectare for traditional rice varieties (del/cicih) and 10 tons per hectare for high-yielding varieties, less any effects due to water stress or pest damage.

Water Stress

If the total demand for water by the *subaks* in a catchment area exceeds the volume available from the weir plus any direct rainfall, the calculated deficit is assumed to be shared equally by all affected *subaks*. Presently, the model simply reduces the calculated growth towards full harvest by the fractional water stress deficit. Water stress is linearly related to this fraction, and the effect is equal throughout the growth period. Future versions of the model are planned to include the varying sensitivity of the plants to water stress at different stages of growth and development.

For example, given the four-month growth duration of padi cicih, the normal sequence would calculate 25 percent growth each month. If the region received only one-half of the specified demand for any one of the four months, this water stress would reduce the growth that month by half, to 12.5 percent, resulting in a final growth of 87.5 percent at harvest rather than the maximum of 100 percent.

Pest Damage

The pest submodel represents the dispersal and growth of insect pests and the damage they may cause the rice crops directly or as carriers of bacterial and viral diseases. Despite voluminous information on pests in the agronomic literature on rice, it proved difficult to formulate a composite, generalized model of dispersal, growth, and damage rates by using the mechanistic approach. Instead, we chose to model the pest population directly in terms of the reduction in rice yields caused by pests.

In each *subak*, the pest density is assumed to start at a low background level. For example, the usual background level of pests is 0.001, which signifies a pest level that would reduce the harvest yield by 0.1 percent. During the simulation, the pest density changes owing to migrations (immigration, emigration), and local growth. Migration is computed as a simple diffusion. That is, the direction and magnitude of any exchange depends on the gradient in concentrations between a *subak* and each of its neighbors.

$$\frac{dP}{dt} = kD\frac{(d^2\,P)}{dx^2}$$

For a *subak* surrounded on all four sides by other *subaks*, the rate of change in pest level by migration may be approximated by the finite difference equation

$$\frac{dPest_x}{dt} = \frac{D}{dx}\,(Pests_{x-1} + Pests_{x+1} + Pests_{y+1} + Pests_{y-1} - 4*Pests_x)$$

where $Pest_x$ is the density of pests in *subak* x; D is a coefficient of simple diffusion, dx is the distance in meters between the centers of two *subaks* (assumed here to be the average 1000 meters).

In addition to migration, pests are assumed to increase. As an initial approximation, we have assumed a constant rate of instantaneous increase (G) depending on which crop is grown:

$$\frac{dPest}{dt} = G(Pest)$$

This equation causes unlimited exponential increase of pests as long as rice is being grown in the *subak*. However, because the unit of pest density is expressed as potential pest damage, the effect of the pest population grows from the background level (.001) to a maximum of 1.0. When rice is not the crop, the parameter G is less than 1, and the pest level declines, rapidly during a fallow period and more slowly if vegetables are being grown.

Values of the Pest Growth Rate, G, for Different Crops

Crop	Growth Rate (per month)
Fallow	0.1
Del rice	2.0
Cicih rice	2.0
HYV rice	2.0
Vegetables	0.33

MANAGEMENT SCENARIOS

The key to the present application of the model is the choice of management scenarios. Six choices are supplied that span the range of coordination in cropping patterns from all 172 *subaks* setting independent cropping patterns to a single cropping pattern for everyone. These choices assume that the *subaks* plant and harvest together in groups that parallel to various degrees the subdivisions of the temple hierarchies.

Management Scenarios

1 group	172 *subaks*
2 groups	Highlands and lowlands offset one month
7 groups	Pairs of temples offset by one month (uplands plant earlier)
14 groups	Masceti temples set cropping patterns
28 groups	Ulun Swi temples offset
172 groups	Each *subak* is autonomous

For the first two choices, the user has complete control over which crops are planted. For the remaining choices, the crop choices specify the crops that may be planted, and the computer generates the appropriate number of distinct planting schedules from a set of twenty-two schedules stored in the program, which are constructed to reflect plausible and realistic permutations of all possible cropping patterns. Once the various cropping schedules have been assigned to all *subaks*, the program simulates the rainfall, river flow, irrigation demand, rice growth stage, and pest levels for all watersheds and *subaks*. At the appropriate times, the harvest is adjusted for cumulative water stress and pest damage, yields are tallied, and the next crop cycle is initiated.

ADDITIONAL INFORMATION

This model can be downloaded from the author's Web site, http://press.princeton.edu/titles/8394.html. A self-organizing version of the model is analyzed in a new book about the water temples of Bali: J. Stephen Lansing, *Perfect Order: Recognizing Complexity in Bali* (Princeton University Press, 2006).

Notes

ARA   Algemeen Rijksarchief
KITLV Koninklijk Instituut voor Taal-, Land en Volkenkunde
Mailr.   Mailrapport (official government correspondence)
Nr.   Number
TBG   *Tijdschrift van het Bataviaasch Genootschap* (Journal of the Batavian Society)

Introduction

Epigraph: Virgil, *Georgics* 2:490, 493.

1. Karl A. Wittfogel, *Oriental Despotism: A Comparative Study of Total Power* (New Haven, Conn.: Yale University Press, 1957), 53–54. Karl Marx, in Shlomo Avineri, ed., *Karl Marx on Colonialism and Modernization* (New York: Anchor Books, 1969), 456.

2. Clifford Geertz, *Negara: The Theatre State in Nineteenth Century Bali* (Princeton, N.J.: Princeton University Press, 1980), 69.

3. "La religion fondamentale de la société khmère, sous son brilliant manteau indien, fût le culte des eaux et du sol." Bernard Groslier, *Angkor et le Cambodge au XVIe siècle d'après les sources portugaises et espagnoles* (Paris, 1958), 116.

4. According to Lando, "The supernatural order mirrors the human one in the control of irrigation." Richard P. Lando, "The Spirits Aren't So Powerful Any More: Spirit Belief and Irrigation Organization in Northern Thailand," *Journal of the Siam Society* 71 (1983): 142.

5. Theodore G. Th. Pigeaud, *Java in the Fourteenth Century* (The Hague: Martinus Nijhoff, 1960), 4:483 and passim.

6. See chapter 6 for an extended account.

7. N. Sutawan, M. Swara, W. Windia, G. Pitana, and W. Sudana, "Gambaran Umum Sistem Irigasi Pada Aliran Sungai: Sungai Ho, Kabupaten Tabanan; Sungai Sangsang, Kabupaten Bangli; dan Sungai Pati, Kabupaten Karangasem" (Denpasar, Bali: Universitas Udayana, stenciled typescript, 1985), 4. The Indonesian text is as follows: "Namun sebegitu jauh, belum diketahui secara jelas bagaimana sistem hierarkis pura-pura subak dalam kaitannya dengan letak sumber-sumber air dan pola koordinasi antara subak dalam melakukan upacara-upacara maupun dalam pengelolaan sistem irigasi. Pengetahuan mendasar dan menyeluruh tentang hal ini akan sangat membantu usaha-usaha untuk lebih memahami serta menghayati masalah-masalah persubakan."

8. Jelantik Sushila, "Peningkatan Jaringan Irigasi dan Wadah Koordinasi Subak di Bali" (Dinas Pekerjaan Umum Propinsi Dati I Bali, Bagian Pengairan, Denpasar, Bali, 1984), 233.

9. Georges Condominas, "Ritual Technology in Swidden Agriculture," in Irene Norlund, Sven Cederroth, and Ingela Gerdin, eds., *Rice Societies: Asian Problems and Prospects* (Riverdale, Md.: Curzon Press, 1986), 29.

10. Condominas, "Ritual Technology," 40.

11. Valerio Valeri, *Kingship and Sacrifice: Ritual and Society in Ancient Hawaii* (Chicago: University of Chicago Press, 1985), 156.

12. Jürgen Habermas, *Lifeworld and System: A Critique of Functionalist Reason*, vol. 2 of *The Theory of Communicative Action* (New York: Beacon Press, 1987), 400.

13. In a sense, of course, Wolf intended to remedy our lack of appreciation for the history of the non-European world. But Wolf follows the Marxist view that for the non-Western world, history begins with the spread of Western capitalism. I return to this point later in the introduction.

14. Marshall Sahlins, *Culture and Practical Reason* (Chicago: University of Chicago Press, 1976), 207.

15. Karl Marx, *Das Kapital*, 3 vols. (Berlin: Dietz, 1867, 1893, 1894); English translation, *Capital* (New York: International Publishers, 1967) 1:47.

16. Eric Wolf, *Europe and the People without History* (Berkeley: University of California Press, 1982), 20.

17. Marx, *Capital* 1:185.

18. Karl Marx and Friedrich Engels, *Historisch-Kritische Gesamtausgabe* (hereafter cited as *MEGA*) (Berlin and Frankfurt am/Main, 1927–1932) 3:84, 122.

19. Habermas observes, "While epistemologically we must presuppose nature as existing in itself, we ourselves have access to nature only within the historical dimension disclosed by the labor process." Jürgen Habermas, *Knowledge and Human Interests*, Jeremy Shapiro, trans. (London: Heinemann Educational Books, 1971), 34.

20. Habermas, *Knowledge and Human Interests*, 39.

21. Karl Marx, *Economic and Philosophical Manuscripts of 1844* (Moscow: Foreign Languages Publishing House, 1961 [1844]), 71.

22. Marx and Engels, *MEGA*, 1: sec. 3, 44.

23. For a survey of Marx's observations on nature, see Alfred Schmidt, *The Concept of Nature in Marx* (London: New Left Books, 1971).

24. Anthony Giddens, *A Contemporary Critique of Historical Materialism* (Berkeley: University of California Press, 1981), 59. William H. Shaw makes the same point in *Marx's Theory of History* (Stanford, Calif.: Stanford University Press, 1978), 152, "The development of the productive forces through history tells the story of man's evolving dialectical intercourse with nature."

25. Stephen Toulmin and June Goodfield, *The Discovery of Time* (Chicago: University of Chicago Press, 1965), chaps. 6–10.

26. Giddens, *Contemporary Critique*, 36.

27. It is interesting, in fact, to turn the question around and consider the claim that the linear historical view of time has special scientific status. When social scientists refer to linear historical time, presumably they have in mind the chronological sequence of important historical events, such as the French Revolution.

But in science, as distinct from social science, time has nothing to do with the French Revolution; time measures the duration and analysis of periodicity. Intervals such as the lunar period or the span of a human generation do not depend on history or progress. Indeed, from the perspective of modern physics, the idea of "progress" would appear to be a distinctly metaphysical concept. If human society were a single entity undergoing a process of development at a rate that exactly matched the progression of calendar years, we could express the concept of linear history by the predictive equation

$$Y = k\,T$$

where Y is society, k is the constant of progressive development, and T is time, in this case the solar year. Given these assumptions, the concept of linear historical time would indeed be both rational and scientific. But if society were progressing at a rate twice as fast as the earth's sidereal period, the parameter of linear historical change would be $Y = 2k\,T$. If different parts of society were developing at different rates, we would need an expression like

$$Y_i = a_i\,k\,T$$

that would enable us to track different growth rates for different components of society. As we will see, this comes close to the representation of time in the Balinese calendrical systems.

28. Marx, *Capital* 1: chap. 14, sec. 4; quoted in Shlomo Avineri, *Karl Marx on Colonialism and Modernization* (Garden City, N.Y.: Anchor Books, 1969), 40.

29. Avineri, *Karl Marx on Colonialism and Modernization*, 456.

30. Ibid., 456.

31. G. W. F. Hegel, *The Philosophy of History*. (New York: Dover Publications, 1956), 139.

32. Avineri, *Karl Marx on Colonialism and Modernization*, 11.

33. Ibid., 90.

34. Ibid., 13.

35. On the "invention of tradition," see Talal Asad, ed., *Anthropology and the Colonial Encounter* (London: Ithaca Press, 1973); Nicholas B. Dirks, *The Hollow Crown: Ethnohistory of an Indian Kingdom* (Cambridge: Cambridge University Press, 1987); Edward Hobsbawm and Terence Ranger, *The Invention of Tradition* (Cambridge: Cambridge University Press, 1982); Ann Stoler, "Rethinking Colonial Categories: European Communities and the Boundaries of Rule," *Comparative Studies in Society and History* 31 (1) (January 1989): 134–61.

36. Nicholas B. Dirks, *The Hollow Crown: Ethnohistory of an Indian Kingdom* (Cambridge: Cambridge University Press, 1987).

37. H. Schulte Nordholt, *Een Balische Dynastie: Hierarchie en Conflict in de Negara Mengwi 1700–1940* (Ph.D. diss., Vrije Universitet van Amsterdam,

1988). Geertz, *Negara*. James Rush, *Opium for Java* (Ithaca, N.Y.: Cornell University Press, 1989).

38. Ann Stoler, "Rethinking Colonial Categories: European Communities and the Boundaries of Rule," in *Comparative Studies in Society and History* 31 (1) (Jan. 1989): 134–35.

39. Geertz, *Negara*, 82.

40. Michel Foucault, *L'Impossible Prison: Recherches sur le système pénitentiaire au XIXe siècle réunies par Michelle Perot* (Paris: Éditions du Seuil, 1980), 47.

Chapter One
"Income to Which No Tears Are Attached"

Epigraph: Ida Pedanda Ngurah of Mengwi, the conclusion to *Bhuwana winasa*, written in 1918, ten years after the fall of the last Balinese state.

1. For a historical overview, see C. van Vollenhoven, *De ontdekking van het adatrecht* (Leiden: Koninklijk Instituut voor Taal-, Land- en Volkenkunde, 1928) (hereafter cited as KITLV). For prominent examples of Adatrecht scholarship in Bali, see the publications of F. A. Liefrinck (see chap. 1, n 26) and V. E. Korn (see chap. 1, n 48).

2. Wertheim adds, "And was the expansion of the opiumregie perhaps not only a result that followed, but also one of the background motives for the expansion of power?" (my translation). W. F. Wertheim, Foreword in Ewald Vanvugt, *Wettig Opium* (Haarlem: Knipscheer, 1985), 11.

3. See J. van Swieten, *Krijgsbedrijven tegen het eiland Bali in 1848* (Amsterdam: Doorman, 1849); A. W. P. Weitzel, *De derde militaire expeditie naar het eiland Bali in 1849* (Gorinchem: Noorduyn, 1859); J. O. H. Arntzenius, *De derde Balische expeditie in herinnering gebracht* (The Hague: Belinfante, 1874); G. Nypels, *De Expedities naar Bali in 1846, 1848 en 1849* (Haarlem: Vandorp, 1897).

4. E. Utrecht, *Sedjarah Hukum Internasional di Bali dan Lombok* (Bandung: Penerbitan Sumur Bandung, 1962), 340. The passage quoted is a translation of article 15 of an agreement between the kingdom of Klungkung and the Dutch government, dated July 13, 1849.

5. For an overview of Balinese-Dutch relationships of this era, see Alfons van der Kraan, *Lombok: Conquest, Colonization and Underdevelopment 1870–1940* (Singapore: Heinemann, 1980). The correspondence between the controleurs of North Bali and Batavia is preserved in the Algemeene Rijksarchief in The Hague. See especially M.v.K. 1850–1900, Inventaris 6059, December 31, 1874 (Geheim); M.v.K. 1850–1900, Inventaris 6448, Mailr. 1885; M.v.K. 1850–1900, Inventaris 6496, Mailr. 1892 Nr. 872; Mailr. 1 July 1902, Mailr. no. 546.

6. Van der Kraan, *Lombok*, 97.

7. Ibid., 99.

8. G. F. de Bruyn Kops, "Het evolutie tijdperk op Bali 1906–1915," *Koloniaal Tijdschrift* 4 (1915): 466.

9. Algemeen Rijksarchief, Kol. na 1900, Inventaris 77, October 12, 1906 (Geheim).

10. H. M. van Weede, *Indische Reisherinneringen* (Haarlem: H. D. Tjeenk Willink and Zoon, 1908), 462.

11. Ibid., 477.

12. Van Weede's account continues: "As soon as his coming was announced by messengers, the quarters of the general were prepared to receive him. Two platoons were therefore put in readiness but they had to wait for a whole hour in the rain, before they were informed by our outposts that the procession was in view. Soon the rajah, his son and successor Ngurah Arom, the rijksbestuurder, the pedandas (high priests) and other followers arrived on foot. The king was an old and honorable man with sharp aristocratic features; his son, approximately 22 years old, looked brave and sympathetic. The two princes seated themselves on the bale-bale, a sort of bamboo bench, across from the General, and the conference started. Seated around the king were his followers, with his priests beside him. Next to the General, Major van Rietschoten and the Assistant Resident Schwartz had seated themselves. The latter, who speaks Balinese fluently, had a conversation with the king, and first had to answer his question if he could not obtain the same position as the rajahs of Gianyar and Karangasem, who had been nominated as officials (ambtenaren) of the Dutch Indonesian government in the capacity of land-guardians (landvoogden). However, it was too late for such concessions, and it was indicated to the king that he had, for the moment, to surrender unconditionally. Then he wished to know if he could possibly stay in his country and asked a few other questions which could only be answered by the commisaris of the government, who was in Denpasar. Finally, he requested to be allowed to get some possessions from his puri, which of course was refused: others would take care of that. A short exchange of thoughts followed between the rajah and his followers and after that Gusti Ngurah Agung surrendered unconditionally [my translation]." Van Weede, *Indische Reisherinneringen*, 477–78.

13. *Bataviaasch Nieuwsblad*, 4 May 1908, Algemeen Rijksarchief (hereafter cited as ARA).

14. H. van Kol, *Uit onze Koloniën* (Leiden: A. W. Sijthoff, 1902), 519: "In vroeger jaren bedroeg de invoer van opium bijna twee derde van den totalen invoer à 3,400,000 gulden." See also ARA Mailr. July 1, 1902, Mailr. no. 546, "Vergelijkend overzicht van de Uitkomsten der opiumverpachtingen in eenige gewesten ter Bezittingen buiten Java en Madoera over de jaren 1901 en 1902," which reports total income from opium sales in Bali as Fl 102,240 in 1901 and Fl 108,060 in 1902.

15. In the years 1904, 1906, 1908, and 1911 the opium monopoly yielded respectively Fl 14,523,000; Fl 15,177,000; Fl 14,741,000 and Fl 16, 375,000: H. van Kol, *Weg met het Opium!* (Rotterdam: Masereeuw and Bouten, 1913), 18. In 1912, the Colonial Yearbook reports that a total of 1,599,928 thails of opium of an average purity of 41% yielded an income of Fl 23,262,000. Bijl. A. A. of the *Kolonial Verslag 1912*.

For a succinct and largely uncritical history of the opium monopoly during this era, see the entry under "Opium" in D. G. Stibbe, ed., *Encyclopaedie van Nederlandsch-Indië*, 2d ed., 3:155–67. (Leiden: E. J. Brill; The Hague: Martinus Nijhoff, 1919).

16. Geheim (Secret) letter to His Excellency the Governor General of the Netherlands Indies from W. G. de Bruyn Kops, Resident of Bali and Lombok, Singaraja, December 26, 1907, ARA, The Hague.

17. The administrative cost of the opium monopoly on Bali to the government was estimated by the Resident at Fl 32,280 per annum.

18. *Bataviaasch Nieuwsblad*, May 4, 1908, 1. See also the articles in the colonial newspaper *De Locomotief* beginning April 30, 1908.

19. Total opium revenues from the Netherlands Indies in 1911 were Fl 23,262,000 from the sale of 1,599,928 thail (one thail = 38.6 gm). Van Kol, *Weg met het Opium!* 13–16. Ten years later, the sale of opium in Bali alone was worth over one million guilders a year to the Dutch government. See the annual report of the opium controleur to the Resident of Bali, dated 31 January 1923; as well as report 435 (197) of the Korn Collection, KITLV, Leiden. The sale of opium was a steady source of income: in 1921, for example, income from opium in Bali was Fl 1,127,377.

20. Van Kol, *Weg met het Opium!* 1–2. Van Kol continues: "On Java alone, every year 16 million guilders are obtained from 150,000 Chinese and Javanese who could spend that money on better things than poppy juice. The native becomes poorer, and brings his jewelry, clothes and tools to be pawned. He pawns his land and would rather commit a crime than work. The unsafety of the village increases, and harms those who do not use opium, the police have more work, and order and peace are disturbed for all. . . . According to Dr. Groneman, 'Most of my patients were modest users for 16–50 cents a day, but it starved their families because the yearly income of a Javanese family is no more than 100 guilders a year or 30 cents a day [my translation].' "

21. Ibid., 10.

22. W. F. Wertheim, in Vanvugt, *Wettig Opium*, 10. Wertheim adds: "I researched the well-known handbooks of Netherlands Indies history, and had to conclude that in most of them the opium politics of the government are only mentioned casually. The same goes for the well-known handbooks of economics. You can find something there about the opium monopoly of the VOC and about the Chinese opiumpachters of the nineteenth century—but it is as if with the suspension of the opiumpacht and the introduction of the opiumregie, around the turn of the century, the question lost its interest."

23. Van Bloemen Waanders estimated the royal tax revenues for Buleleng in 1859:

tax on water of 1,400 pikuls of rice, valued at 3.5 guilders per pikul	Fl 4,900
tax on land (valued in money)	Fl 1,500
trade licenses to the harbormaster	Fl 4,200
other sources	Fl 2,050
Total	Fl 12,650

F. L. van Bloemen Waanders, "Aantekeningen omtrent de Zeden en Gebruiken der Balinezen, inzonderheid die van Boeleleng," *Tijdschrift van het Bataviaasch Genootschap* (hereafter cited as TBG.), 3d series, pt. 2 (Leiden, 1859), 8:168–169.

24. Because there are no records of the opium trade before the arrival of the Dutch, it is not possible to estimate the extent of opium addiction in Bali before 1855. However, it is clear that the amount of opium entering Bali through the Dutch-controlled "free port" of Buleleng increased steadily throughout the latter half of the nineteenth century.

25. Mailr. no. 546, July 1, 1902, ARA, The Hague.

26. F. A. Liefrinck, "Rice Cultivation in northern Bali," in J. L. Swellengrebel, ed., *Bali: Further Studies in Life, Thought and Ritual* (The Hague: W. van Hoeve, 1969), 3–4.

27. F. A. Liefrinck served as a controleur in Bali, 1874–1878, and as Resident of Bali and Lombok, 1896–1901. He was a major architect of the conquests of Lombok and the southern Balinese kingdoms and eventually became Councillor of the Indies.

28. "The Balinese rulers, although disposed to encourage the opening up of new ground, usually did no more than express a passive interest in such projects or accord certain privileges to those members of the community who were, despite the many difficulties, prepared to undertake the work involved. While land was sometimes opened up by order of the rulers for their own advantage, in general they refrained from taking any initiative as regards large-scale land clearance or the digging of new irrigation conduits" (Liefrinck, "Rice Cultivation," 4).

29. Ibid., 12.

30. The *sedahan agung* was assisted by lesser officials called *sedahan tembuku* (*tembuku* was the name for a wooden irrigation water-divider). Of the responsibilities of the *sedahan tembuku*, Liefrinck in Swellengrebel, *Bali*, 12 wrote: "One of their main responsibilities is to ensure the collection of the taxes traditionally levied on the sawahs. . . . Irrigation also comes within the scope of their authority, but their intervention does not usually extend beyond deciding the apportionment of the water in instances where one river is serving several of the subaks (local irrigation units) under their jurisdiction. . . . The sedahans tembuku are appointed by the sedahan agung after being first approved by the Dutch administration" (p. 11).

31. Verder bevindt zich in ieder poenggawaschap, zoo ook ter hoofdplaats Gianjar, een sedahan, de major domus van het districtshoofd en den Stedehouder. Hij is tevens belast met de ontvangst van de sawahbelasting en het beheer der domeingronden. De sedahan ter hoofdplaats met name Dewa Ktoet Oka Adji alias Dewa sandat ontvangt behalve de soewinih in het direct door den Stedehouder bestuurde district ook diens aandeel in de belasting der overige districten. Verder is hem opgedragen de inning der in- en uitvoerrechten op de havenplaats Lebah.

(Furthermore in each poeggawaship as in the capital Gianyar there is a sedahan, the major-domus of the district head and the Stedehouder. He is also in charge of receiving the sawah tax and is in charge of the domeingrounds. The sedahan in the capital, by name Dewa Ktoet Oka Adji alias Dewa Sandat, receives besides the soewinih in the area directly governed by the Stedehouder also the Stedehouder's share in the taxation of the other districts.

Furthermore he has been put in charge of the reception of the import and export taxes from the harbor of Lebah.) H. J. E. F. Schwartz, "Aanteekeningen omtrent het landschap Gianjar," *Tijdschrift voor het Binnenlandsch Bestuur* (Batavia: G. Kolff and Co., 1900), 19:172.

32. The importance of this point will be clarified in the ecological analysis presented in chaps. 2 and 6.

33. F. A. Liefrinck, "Rice Cultivation," 43.

34. Ibid., 8.

35. Ibid., 17.

36. Liefrinck, "Rice Cultivation," adds 24: "Formerly the unpaid labor required for the maintainence of the ruler's palace was furnished partly by subjects liable to compulsory labor service and partly by members of subak associations, particularly when deliveries of materials were required from the subaks. These obligatory deliveries would include straw for laying along the top of walls, roofing material, split bamboo for fencing, firewood and fencing, and were demanded only of the sawah owners, who formed the wealthier section of the population.

"Apart from these obligations the members of the subak associations might sometimes be called on by the ruler to assist with the digging of a conduit for a new subak when the work was beyond the capacity of the association concerned, or to help with the restoration of a damaged dam which could not otherwise be repaired quickly enough to save the crop. Such obligations . . . were, of course, imposed very infrequently."

37. Ibid., 30.

38. The conflict is apparent in the land surveys undertaken in Lombok after the exile of the king. The Dutch found that Balinese classed land rights as *druwe dalem*, which verbatim means "belonging to an insider or insiders," and *druwe djaba*, "belonging to outsiders." The "insider/outsider" distinction is a basic principle of Balinese ritual and social classification, as Gerdin notes. Thus *wong dalem* (insiders) is the usual Balinese term for high-caste aristocrats, and a common title for a king is simply *dalem*, the innermost insider, the royal center of the realm. The same distinction is mapped onto productive lands as seen from the perspective of the ruler: lands *owned* by the ruler are *druwe dalem* (druwe meaning "owned by"), whereas druwe djaba lands are "owned by outsiders." "Outsiders" in this context may not only refer to peasants but to peripheral princely houses— lesser aristocrats, who from the king's perspective are also outsiders. As Gerdin observes, in the context of land law, " 'Inside' and 'outside' refer to whether the rights to land and labour fell directly within the jurisdiction of the supreme ruling house or were allocated outside it."

But in the Balinese political universe, few ruling houses were supreme for very long, and relations of insider/outsider were quite impermanent: "Since the distinction between druwe dalem and druwe djaba was dependent on the political relations between houses, it was not defined once and for all. . . . The distinction . . . was one of relative sociopolitical position of the holders of the estates—but not one of different rights to the produce of the land." But this was a distinction the Dutch government could not afford to make: "The major Dutch studies on traditional land tenure were carried out just after the conquest by the colonial power. In these studies, a sharp distinction is drawn between druwe dalem and druwe djaba, since one of the aims of the Dutch investigations was to establish the exact extent of the land that had belonged to the supreme ruling house and could be taken over by the Dutch state as domeinground. They actually froze a complex system of interlocking, sometimes contradictory, claims into a clear-cut simplicity of two-way classification." Ingela Gerdin, *The Unknown Balinese: Land, Labor and Inequality in Lombok*, Studies in Social Anthropology (Gothenberg, 1982), 76.

39. A. J. van der Heijden, "Het waterschapswezen in de voormalige Zuid-Balische rijkjes Badoeng en Mengwi," *Koloniale Studiën* 9 (1925): 431.

40. The Balinese *druwe dalem* lands became the Dutch *domeingrond* (government land).

41. We have a firsthand account of the very first steps taken by the Dutch in the reorganization of irrigation in Badoeng, in the form of a report written in October 1907 by the officer in charge, an assistant resident. He describes his activities in the village of Sanur, along the coast of Badoeng where the invasion force had landed a few months earlier:

> In Sanur under the leadership of the assistant residents the reorganization of the subak system for the Pangloerahan Jeh Oongan was finished. Badoeng was divided into 12 pangloerahans, and each pangloerahan is now subdivided into subaks. For the institution of a governing system for these subdivisions, the former pekasehs were called together. It was explained to them that an improvement of the situation was extremely urgent. . . .
>
> At the end of some of the aforementioned meetings, the boundaries of the different subaks were walked around by the official, accompanied by the pangloerahs and both the newly appointed and former pekasehs, and the new appointees were requested to memorize these boundaries very firmly since later on they would have to tell the surveyor, when the soebak was going to be measured.

Not only were permanent boundaries established, but a new form of administrative control was created, based on an official called the *pekaseh*. The title pekaseh originally referred to the elected head of a *subak* association in the Gianyar area. But in the new system of *pangloerahans*, the *pekasehs* became appointed officials responsible to the *pangloerahs*, who were in turn placed under the authority of the sedahan agung. The 1907 report clearly defines this new structure: the "pekaseh has to file full reports on his activities to the pangloerah in question, who if necessary consults further with the sedahan agung." Anon., "Ontwikkeling van Desa- en Soebak-bestuur in Zuid-Bali," *Adatrechtbundel XXXVII* (The Hague: Martinus Nijhoff, 1934), 477.

42. Anon., *Adatrechtbundel XXXVII*, 473.

43. "Memorie van overgave" van den Assistant Resident van Bali en Lombok G. A. W. Ch. de Haze Winkelman, KITLV, Leiden, April 1937.

44. G. F. de Bruyn Kops, "Memorie van overgave (1909)," ARA, The Hague, 12. Here he refers to the situation in Klungkung immediately after the conquest.

45. For example, the 1938 assistant resident's report for Gianyar states: "At

the head of an irrigation area there is the pangloerah, an employee instituted by the Resident, who in exchange for a collection fee is in charge of the getting of the land taxes, the supervision of dams and canals, and the ruling of water sharing. At the head of the pangloerahs is the Sedahan Agung, who is in charge of taking care of the irrigation system for the whole area and is also the receiver of taxes." And in the former kingdom of Mengwi: "The sekehe subaks that were united under one sedahan did not always have common interests and often belonged to different irrigation areas." A. J. van der Heijden, "Het waterschapswezen in de voormalige Zuid- Balische rijkjes Bangli en Kloengkoeng," *Koloniale Studiën* 2 (1925): passim.

46. Ibid., 426.

47. V. E. Korn, *Het Adatrecht van Bali*, 2d ed. (The Hague: Martinus Nijhoff, 1932), 298–99.

48. Van der Heijden, "Het waterschapwezen," 9:426.

49. The religious character of the *soewinih* was also noted by Korn, with regard to the eastern kingdom of Karangasem: "From several village regulations from Karangasem, this opinion appears without doubt, that the water of the central Balinese lakes—Bratan, Batur, Buyung and Tamblingan—is in the hands of the gods, on whose good will it depends if the rivers will receive enough water through underground canals (a widespread belief). The water recognition, the soewinih upati toja, has to be dedicated to the gods of water." Korn, *Het Adatrecht van Bali*, 604.

50. Van der Heijden, "Het waterschapwezen," Bangli, 2:3.

51. Ibid.

52. Korn, *Het Adatrecht van Bali*, 271.

53. By 1938, the assistant resident for Badoeng, H. J. Hoekstra, repeated this thesis as though it were historical fact in the introduction to his annual report: "The irrigation that originally was the affair of one or a few villages had slowly spread to the bigger rivers, where the king had power over the water, and thus the king's influence increased. Cooperation among many was now necessary for the construction of big dams and long conduits. The king took over the ruling of some of this labor, and great irrigation areas were created under the guidance of the royal irrigation officials [author's translation]," H. J. Hoekstra, "Nota van Toelichtingen betreffende het in te stellen Zelfbestuurend Landschap Badoeng, 1938," ARA, The Hague, 32.

54. This investigation was made possible by the decipherment of an inscription engraved on a stone pillar near the beach in Sanur, which proved to be an inscription written by a Balinese king in A.D. 914. The Blanjong Pillar was a Balinese Rosetta Stone: the message was written on one side in the hitherto undecipherable "Old Balinese" language using a well-known Early Nagari script; on the other side, the message was repeated in Sanskrit using an indigenous Pallava-derived script called Kawi. Thus the local alphabet was used to write Sanskrit, an Indian language, whereas an Indian alphabet was used to write the message in Old Balinese. Dozens and ultimately hundreds of inscriptions were subsequently discovered and translated, providing detailed information on Balinese kingdoms from the ninth through the fourteenth centuries A.D. The inscriptions provide a great deal of information on taxation and the role of the kings in regulating village

affairs because the early Balinese kingdoms relied on a system of "tax farming," in which taxes were actually collected by the officials they were intended to support. See Roelof Goris, *Prasasti Bali: Inscripties voor Anak Wungcu* (Bandung: N. V. Masa Baru, 1954).

55. As Korn himself commented, during the seven-hundred-year period covered by the inscriptions "It does not appear at all that in Bali in the time of which we are speaking now, there was one kingdom with one overlord (oppervorst)" (Korn, Adatrecht, 10). This is clear from the fact that early inscriptions issued by different kings often overlap. Moreover, there are often indications in the texts of the inscriptions of the effective boundaries of a ruler's kingdom. Consider, for example, King Ragajaya, whose inscriptions were issued in the eleventh century. Based on the inscription of Dayankayu, discovered in 1964 by the head of the archaeological service on Bali, Dr. Sukarto Atmodjo, "Most probably his kingdom only covered the region north of Lake Batur (North Bali) and East Bali, mainly in the vicinity of Tejakula and Bugbug. If this surmise is correct, then Ragajaya had nothing to do with the southern region of Bali." Interestingly, the office of the sedahan is mentioned in a couple of inscriptions but not in the context of vast royal irrigation projects. Consider a typical inscription from the reign of the twelfth century Balinese king Jayapangus: "And furthermore it is allowed to cut down overhanging trees if they interfere with sawah, gardens, public buildings or roads; in these matters it is not necessary to request permission from Mpu Sthapaka [an important monk attached to the court] or from the king's sedahan at [the royal residence of] Dharmahanyar." M. M. Sukarto K. Atmodjo, "Prasasti Buyan-Sanding-Tamblingan dari jaman Rajah Jayapangus" (Gianyar, Bali: Lembaga Purbakala dan Peninggalan Nasional, stenciled typescript, 1972).

56. H. Schulte Nordholt, *Een Balische Dynastie, Hierarchie en Conflict in de Negara Mengwi 1700–1940* (Ph.D. diss., Vrije Universiteit, Amsterdam, 1988), 54.

57. Ibid.

58. Korn Collection, Doc. 138, in the KITLV, Leiden.

59. Michel Foucault, *An Introduction*, vol. 1 of *The History of Sexuality*, trans. Robert Hurley (New York: Random House, Vintage, 1980), 1:93.

Chapter Two
The Powers of Water

1. Marx, quoted in Avinieri, ed., *Karl Marx*, 7.

2. Ibid., 456.

3. Wittfogel, *Oriental Despotism*, 53–4.

4. Clifford Geertz, "Form and Variation in Balinese Village Structure," *American Anthropologist* 61 (1959): 991–1012; idem, "The Wet and the Dry: Traditional Irrigation in Bali and Morocco" *Human Ecology* 1 (1972): 34–9; idem, *Negara*.

5. Hunt, Robert, and Eva Hunt, "Canal Irrigation and Local Social Organization," *Current Anthropology* 17:389–411.

6. Roelof Goris, *Prasasti Bali I* (Bandung: N.V. Masa Baru, 1954), 55. The inscription is 002. Bebetin A1:IIb.4 *(undagi pangarung)*.

7. Eugene Odum, *Basic Ecology* (New York: CBS College Publishing, 1983), 490–1.

8. Shoichi Yoshida, *Fundamentals of Rice Crop Science* (Manila: International Rice Research Institute, 1981) 147–51; Surajit K. DeDatta, *Principles and Practices of Rice Production* (New York: John Wiley and Sons 1981), 297–8.

9. The basic unit of Balinese irrigation is the *tenah*: the amount of water that will pass through a small opening, which is cut into a wooden water divider called a *tembuku*. But the *tenah* unit is not only a measure of a share of water. One *tenah* of water will irrigate one *tenah* of land. Planted with one *tenah* of seedlings, it should yield one *tenah* of rice. If it should happen, as it does regularly in most villages, that vegetables rather than rice are grown in the terraces, the *tenah* measure is still used. A farmer does not receive a fraction of a *tenah* of water. Instead, for vegetable crops he will receive one *tenah* of water for his fields every third or fifth day. The *tenah*, in short, is the basic, irreducible unit. It is measured at the upstream corner of each farmer's field—the spot where the water flows into the terrace.

Upstream from his field, the farmer can trace a series of larger dividers that measure out shares of five or ten or several hundred *tenah*. There are also diversionary gates and canals for use in the rainy season when a sudden storm or minor flood could quickly wash out crops, fields, earthen dikes, canals, and gates. The problem of too much water flowing too fast is potentially much more serious than too little water—which at worst can only spoil one crop.

A block of terraces obtaining water from the same canal system is called a *tempek*. All farmers whose lands lie within a given *tempek* share responsibility for maintaining its irrigation works. One or more *tempeks* form a *subak*, which is distinguishable from the *tempek* because it is a ritual unit, as well as a corporation with legal standing within the framework of Balinese *adat*. *Tempeks*, in contrast, are simply work groups, with no special legal or ritual importance. The ritual standing of the *subak* derives from the fact that it is responsible not only for the irrigation works but for the health and well being—the continuing productivity—of its rice terraces. To this end, each *subak* has a temple for offerings and rituals intended to promote growth and fertility—a subject we will turn to in chapter 3.

10. Badruddin Machbub, H. F. Ludwig, and D. Gunaratnam, "Environmental Impact from Agrochemicals in Bali (Indonesia)," *Environmental Monitoring and Assessment 11* (1988): 1–23.

11. Translated from an interview tape recorded in Sukawati in 1976. Presumably he is counting the two *tempeks* of *subak* Cau as separate *subaks*.

12. Traditionally, this planting is timed so that panicle development occurs at "full moon of the tenth month." The relationship between the *tika* and the traditional cropping pattern are further discussed in Lansing, "Balinese Water Temples and the Management of Irrigation," *American Anthropologist 89* (1987): 326–41.

Chapter Three
The Waters of Power

1. Geertz, *Negara*, 124.
2. Ibid., 125.

3. Christiaan Hooykas, *Surya-Sevana: The Way to God of a Balinese Siva Priest* Verhandelingen Koninklijk Nederlandse Akademie van Wetenschappen, afd. Letterkunde, n.s. no. 3, (Amsterdam, 1966), 72:97.

4. This is the typical pattern along the Oos and Petanu rivers, and more generally, in Bangli, Gianyar, and Badung. Elsewhere, there are other patterns of water temples, which await investigation.

5. In this section, we are only concerned with the holy water associated with water temples. There are many other types of holy water in Bali. Brahmana priests (*pedanda*) create holy water that is sought by their clients for life-cycle rituals. For a description of the rituals by which *pedandas* create holy water, see Christiaan Hooykaas, *Surya-Sevana*.

6. David Stuart-Fox, *Pura Besakih, A Study of Balinese Culture and Religion*. Doctoral dissertation, Australian National University, Canberra, Australia, 1987.

7. Balinese terms for kinship temples are highly variable. By "clan temple," I mean *pura panti, pura dadia, pura paibon*, and so on. By "clan origin temple," I mean *pura kawitan*. For discussions of Balinese kinship temples, see Hildred Geertz, and Clifford Geertz, *Kinship in Bali* (Chicago: University of Chicago Press, 1975) or Lansing, *The Three Worlds of Bali* (New York: Praeger, 1983), 93–111.

8. "Mwah panungsungan dewane di masceti, mangraksa tikus, ikane wenang sungsung; mwah dewane di sakenan, mangraksa walang sangit, ika ne wenang sungsung. Yen ada cendela ring empelan, ring ulun swi wenang di balik sumpah." Ida Pedanda Made, Dewa Tattwa (original palm-leaf lontar manuscript, dated 1865 Icaka, housed in the collection of the Griya Taman Sari, Sanur, Bali).

9. Ratu Ngurah is often depicted as the famous *Barong*, a sacred costume worn by two men, which is animated by the birth spirits of the inhabitants of the village. When a child is born, four portions of the afterbirth are buried at the four sacred directions around the houseyard. Henceforth, they represent the *kanda empat*, the "four siblings" of the newborn. They may cause sickness or good fortune and are given offerings throughout a person's lifetime. While they are defined as the basic constituents of the inner self—the personal microcosm—they may take other forms. Ratu Ngurah, the Lord Protector, is animated by the "four siblings" of all of the members of a village. In this sense, he quite literally symbolizes the village as a microcosm. For further information about the Lord Protector, see Jane Belo, *Bali: Rangda and Barong*, American Ethnological Society monograph no. 22 (Locust Valley, N.Y., 1953); and J. S. Lansing, *Evil in the morning of the World: Phenomenological Approaches to a Balinese Community*, Michigan Papers on Southeast Asia no. 6, (Ann Arbor, Mich., 1974).

10. See note 9. The "Lord Protector of the Earth" is Ratu Ngurah.

11. He is sometimes allied with the kingdom of Klungkung. His offerings are placed in a special shrine outside the temple, facing the sea.

12. Claude Lévi-Strauss, *The Savage Mind (La pensée sauvage)* (Chicago: University of Chicago Press, 1966), 232–35.

13. See Paul Wirz, *Der Reisbau und die Reisbaukülte auf Bali und Lombok* (Batavia: Tijdschrift voor Indische Taal-, Land-, en Volkenkunde, 1927), 67:217–345; Korn, *Het Adatrecht van Bali*.

14. The ceremony is performed only for rice, not vegetable crops, and celebrates the initial clearing and flooding of the terraces. The actual date of the cer-

emony may not coincide perfectly with the flooding of the fields. But if there is not enough water, *muat emping* cannot be performed.

15. The correspondence between cyclical concepts of time and music in Java is explored by Judith Becker in her "Time and Tune in Java," in A. L. Becker and A. A. Yengoyan, *The Imagination of Reality: Essays in Southeast Asian Coherence Systems* (Norwood, New Jersey: Ablex Publishing, 1979), 197–210.

16. The relationship between the *tika* and the traditional cropping pattern are further discussed in Lansing, "Balinese Water Temples and the Management of Irrigation," *American Anthropologist* 89 (1987): 326–41.

17. This index of rank is repeated in multitiered cremation towers that display the caste status of the deceased: one to three tiers for a commoner, three to five for the lesser gentry, seven or nine for a prince, and eleven for a consecrated king.

18. Geertz, *Negara*, 120.

Chapter Four
The Temple of the Crater Lake

1. *Statistical Yearbook of Bali 1986* (Denpasar, Bali: Statistical Office of Bali Province, Jl. Raya Puputan), 8.

2. Rajapurana Ulun Danu Batur, (Denpasar, Bali: Bali Museum Library, stenciled manuscript, 1979), 2:24, 28.b.1.

3. This story is related in the manuscript "Babad Pasek Kayu Selem," about which more will be said in this chapter.

4. The priests of the Temple of the Crater Lake emphasize the uniqueness of many features of the temple, most of which have to do with its relationship to the Goddess of the Lake, Dewi Danu. For example, periodic rituals at Balinese temples often involve a ceremonial procession, in which the emblems and images of the deities (which are normally kept inside the temple shrines) are taken out and carried on a journey, usually to the sea. These images are usually placed at the head of the procession, except at the Temple of the Crater Lake, where the procession is led by the temple's large orchestra (the *gong gde*). According to the temple priests, this arrangement is because the supreme deity of the temple is a goddess of imperial rank, who is preceded by her orchestra like a sovereign queen.

5. The Balinese word that I have translated as virgin priestess is Jero Balian. There are two such priestesses at the temple, the Elder (*duuran*) and Younger (*alitan*). Each is chosen by a Jero Balian upon the death of her predecessor. Unlike the male priests of the temple, the virgin priestesses may not marry. They are the only priests of the temple who act as trance mediums (*balian*).

6. The Balinese term is *pedanda siwa*. For a description of the role of Brahmana high priests in the preparation of holy water, see Christiaan Hooykaas, *Surya-Sevana*.

7. Translated by the author from a transcript in Balinese of a conversation between the author and the Jero Gde, summer 1986.

8. This quote and the dialogue that follows are translated by the author from a transcript in Balinese of an interview he tape-recorded with the Jero Gde, summer 1986.

9. A partial list of *tenah* (a measure of both water and irrigated land) owned

by specific villages is included in the manuscript "Babad Patisora," part of the "Rajapurana Ulun Danu Batur," sections of which are translated below. However, this collection of manuscripts is in disarray, with many pieces missing. The temple scribe says that much of the collection was lost during the 1926 eruption of Mount Batur, which will be described in chapter 5.

10. Excerpts tape-recorded and translated by the author from a transcript in Balinese of a meeting in the village of Pengalu, 1986.

11. A "weir" (empelan) is a diversionary dam in the river, which channels all or part of the flow into an irrigation canal. Almost always in Bali, this canal begins as a tunnel because the rivers lie at the bottom of deep ravines.

12. Bali is divided for administrative purposes into eight administrative regions called kabupaten. At the head of each kabupaten is an official called the bupati, whose role with respect to his kabupaten is likened to that of the governor for the province of Bali. Each kabupaten is itself subdivided into half a dozen or so subdistricts called kecamatan. I have followed the usual practice of translating kabupaten as "regency."

13. Probably the Jero Gde meant that the flow from the spring amounted to about 100 liters per minute, produced by the watershed area above the spring.

14. The Balinese term is Jero Sinoman.

15. Bathing in springs is an essential purificatory rite for all major rituals of consecration in Bali.

16. Excerpts translated by the author from a transcript in Balinese of a tape-recorded interview with the Jero Gde in Duuran, Batur, 1986.

17. According to Van der Meij: "The word abiseka denotes one of the essential features of the ceremony, the sprinkling of water on the king . . . and also on Bali the word now denotes the consecration name given to the king during the ceremony. . . . Needless to say, the kings could only bear the abiseka name after they were consecrated, a fact not always understood. . . . The ceremony is intended to install the ruler in the place of his predecessor." Th. van der Meij, "A Balinese Account of the Royal Consecration Ceremony of I Dewa Manggis of Gianyar in 1903," in C. Hellwig and S. O. Robson, eds., A Man of Indonesian Letters: Essays in Honor of Professor A. Teeuw, (Dordrecht: Foris Publications, 1986), 258–59. See also J. L. Swellengrebel, Een vorstenwijding op Bali, vol. 2 (Leiden: Mededelingen van het Rijksmuseum voor Volkenkunde, 1947),

18. Excerpts tape-recorded and translated by the author from a transcript in Balinese of an interview with Brahman priests in Klungkung, 1986.

19. See Van der Meij, "Balinese Account"; Swellengrebel, Een vorstenwijding op Bali.

20. The rituals for the consecration of a pedanda involve a symbolic death and rebirth.

21. Excerpts tape-recorded and translated by the author from a transcript in Balinese of an interview with a temple elder at the Temple of the Crater Lake, summer 1986.

22. In Balinese, Pasek Kayu Selem.

23. From the Babad Pasek Kayu Selem, n.d., trans. author, library of the Griya Taman Sari, Sanur.

24. For an analysis of the role of performances in temple rituals, see chapters 3–5 of Lansing, *Three Worlds of Bali* (New York: Praeger, 1983).

25. For a thorough analysis of these rituals, see Hooykaas, *Surya-Sevana*.

26. The performances included *wayang wong* from Batuan, and *legong* and *topeng* from Peliatan.

Chapter Five
Chance Observations and
the Metaphysics of Taxation

1. *Journal of a Tour along the Coast of Java and Bali & with a Short Account of the Island of Bali, particularly of Bali Baliling* (Singapore: Mission Press of the Singapore Christian Union, 1930), 24.

2. References to the lake as *segara* are frequent in the manuscripts of the "Rajapurana Ulun Danu Batur" as well as in the conversation of temple priests.

3. Liefrinck, "Rice Cultivation."

4. P. A. J. Moojen, letter of 21 January 1919, 19–20, Stukken afkomstig van P. A. J. Moojen (architect, kunstschilder), "Kultuurproblemen," stukken voornamelijk betreffende de restauratie van tempels op Bali, met platte gronden, ca. 1930, 1 bundel. H 1169:17, archives of the KITLV.

5. *Journal of a Tour*, 33.

6. "Mangku ada sijang soedah tentoe lebih dahoeloe ada malem, micalnya sebab ada kalihatan soedah tentoe acal dari bangsa aloes."

7. "De roep van heiligheid, die van dezen tempel uitgaat, is, na de laatste uitbarsting van den Batoer in 1905 nog zeer gestegen door de wonderbare wijze, waarop hij toen is gespaard voor algeheelen ondergang. De gloeiende lava-stroom werd immers juist bij de hoofdpoort op niet te verklaren wijze gestuit!

"Wie eenmaal dezen tempel aan den voet van den somberen Vuurhaard Batoer heeft bezocht; wie slechts eenmaal van af den ouden kraterwand, langs den weg van Panalokan naar Kintamani, dit heiligdom heeft aanschouwd, gelegen temidden van de majestueuse schoonheid van het geweldige vulkanen landschap, het silhouet van zijn meroe teekenend in het bruin-zwart van den met diep blauw waas overtogen, gestolden lava-stroom, die zal niet vragen naar woorden om de schoonheid van deze plaats te roemen; de meest ongevoelige voor esthetisch genot zal hier met klaarheid kunnen erkennen de hooge beteekenis van de natuurlijke gave, die den Baliër in zoo hooge mate eigen is: het kiezen van de omgeving, waarin hij zijn kunstscheppingen weet te plaatsen en waardoor hij hen tot een klimax van vereering weet op te voeren.

"Ook uit een architectonisch oogpunt heeft het gebouwencomplex groote waarde en his het van meer beteekenis dan de tempels van Besakih." Stukken afkomstig van P. A. J. Moojen (architect, kunstschilder), "Kultuurproblemen," stukken voornamelijk betreffende de restauratie van tempels op Bali, met platte gronden, ca. 1930, 1 bundel. H 1169:17, KITLV, Leiden, 21, letter to His Excellency the Governor General of the Nederlands-Indies, January 21, 1919.

8. Ibid., 38

9. "In meerdere streken bestaat de gewoonte dat de waterschappen door het zenden van deputaties, aan de vereering der aan de goddinnen der bergmeeren

(Batoer, Bratan, Boejan en Tamblingan) gewijde sanctuaria deelnemen. Het tijdens de tempelfeesten door de afgezanten van de *soebak* verkregen wijwater wordt in plechtigen optocht tegemoetgetreden en op ceremoniëele wijze onder de verenigingsleden verdeeld, die er hunne velden mede besprenkelen, om zoodoende den zegen deelachtig te worden, die de meergodin, als behoedster van het bevloeiingswater aan de landman toebedeelt.

Opgemerkt wordt nog dat de feestkalender van de *soebak* met de organisatie der ten laste van de dorpsgemeenschap komende religieuze ceremoniën, geen- of ten hoogste slecht incidenteel- verband houdt." Memoire van overgave van G. A. W. Ch. de Haze Winkelman, Resident van Bali en Lombok, April 1937, ARA, The Hague.

10. Korn, *Het Adatrecht van Bali*. (The Hague: G. Naeff, 1932).

11. Van der Heijden, "Het waterschapswezen in de voormalige Zuid- Balische rijkjes Bangli en Kloengkoeng." *Koloniale Studiën*, tweede deel (1925), page 431.

12. Ibid., page 426.

13. The text continues:

Leaf 29.a.4. "The people of the villages of srongga and abyanbase are obliged to offer 55 copper-measures of rice belonging to the Goddess of Batur;

Leaf 29.b.1. and the village of Wubatu must pay 40 copper-measures of rice belonging to the sacred ruler of Batur; and each household

Leaf 29.b.2. of the village of Batur must provide fruit and a coconut; and the village of Telepud must provide 10 copper-measures of rice, and coconut(s) from each household, and the village of Nira

Leaf 29.b.3. Ked must provide 10 copper-measures of rice, and the villages of Kebon and Kedisan must provide 20 copper-measures of rice, and the village of Ponggang must provide contributions (*pajeg*) of

Leaf 29.b.4. 20 copper-measures of rice, and the village of Taro must provide 10 copper-measures of rice, and the village of Panempahan must provide 30 copper-measures of rice;

Leaf 30.a.1. and after harvest all the Batur villages may offer coconuts."

Commentary (to the end of leaf 28.a) by the Lesser Temple Scribe
(Translated by the author from their tape-recorded interview)

SCRIBE: This much first. The Deity's possessions at Batur, the rice terraces—if they deviate, if they don't bring the fruits here to Batur every year, and for as long as ten years they fail to do so, they will be struck with a curse. "Everything they plant will fail"—this is given as a reminder. Pests like brown planthoppers or rodents—as soon as they store the rice in the barn, it becomes empty. But after they return this tax, after they make an offering for the ceremonies, then they can work the land successfully. This is true up to the present day. It's still in force. . . .

The offerings for the rituals of the Tenth Month here are in accordance with the contents of the "Rajapurana." Like "10 copper-measures of rice" [leaf 29.b.3] those are the "seeds."

LANSING: But is this saved nowadays?

SCRIBE: Stored in the temple ricebarns. Some for seeds, some for food and ceremonies. Here it refers to the copper measure used to measure the quantities of rice. We keep an identical copper measure here at Batur. . . .

LANSING: Like "Village of Bulian, ten tenah?"

SCRIBE: Those are seeds. Whatever grew on those ten tenah, whether it is 5 quintal or a ton, is sent here. Always, every year. Here, we store it. But nowadays, within three months the new rice starts to rot. So we turn it over, we turn it into money, for example, and use the money for repairing the temple, the shrines, or [for] the monthly ceremonies. After all, that uses up money! So we use this rice. And also we can use whatever remains of the labo temple lands. The labo lands produce something too.

LANSING: These village contributions in the manuscript—they're not labo?

SCRIBE: No, they're different. *Labo* means temple lands. Lands that belong to the Deities. The produce of the *labo* lands can be divided among the citizens of Batur, but the "possessions of the Goddess of Batur" (druwen ida bhatari ring batur) may not be divided. They're strictly for ceremonies!

LANSING: How much rice do they amount to?

SCRIBE: Every Tenth Month, about 13 tons. It's a lot because it comes from the whole congregation.

LANSING: Is there any left after the ceremonies are over?

SCRIBE: In my experience, there are usually about five and a half or six tons of rice left over after the festival. . . . We divide it up and sell it to the citizens of Batur at a reduced price. Everyone can buy about 10 kilograms. We also sell ducks for 1,000 rupiah apiece, chickens for 450 rupiah, peanuts for 350, and betel supplies for 100 rupiah.

LANSING: What about other contributions to the temple?

SCRIBE: If people come requesting holy water (*tirtha pakuluh*) to combat pests or for water opening or temple (*ngusaba*) festivals, they bring offerings called *pejati*.

LANSING: These are separate from the deities' possessions?

SCRIBE: Completely different! These are for special blessings or rituals. The other contributions belong to the temple by right to be used in ceremonies here. This is different. These are requests—but without them, no matter how much work is done, it won't bear fruit. But it isn't a great deal—if you valued it in money, it costs only 15,700 rupiah (in 1986, about $10). In fact, a *subak* can just bring the money, and we will prepare the offerings here.

LANSING: You make them here?

SCRIBE: Yes. Let's say a *subak* is having trouble; their fields are unproductive. Their leaders collect a contribution, bring it here, and we prepare the offerings for them. That's the easy way—very easy.

LANSING: What about feeding all the *subak* delegations? Who decides which *subaks* are fed? Is it voluntary? (A great deal of the offerings brought to the temple appear to be returned directly to the *subaks*, who are usually invited to eat en masse after they have made their offerings, prayed, and received holy water.)

SCRIBE: No, it's organized. When a delegation arrives, the *subak* head goes to the speech pavillion and reports, "I'm from the *subak* kelepud. We are twenty-five people and bring, for example, one pig, two quintals of rice, fifty coconuts." Then they go off and receive their blessings and holy water. Then they're summoned—after they have received their holy water. And they eat, and then go home.

LANSING: What about those who don't report?

SCRIBE: It's private. They're embarrassed to report; they bring nothing extra, usually.

LANSING: Extra contributions?

SCRIBE: Extra. What is written in the "Rajapurana" manuscript and the scribe's accounts book is required. Every year these instructions must be followed. Any additional contributions are a private matter. Even if the *subak* has already met its obligations, they want to add more—well, go ahead! It's according to their individual means. And there are those who can't manage more than basic offerings—then it is enough. They're not forced.

14. Memorie van overgave der onderafdeeling Kloengkoeng, door Controleur J. C. C. Haar, May 27, 1926 to February 3, 1930, ARA, The Hague, no. 817, 22–24.

15. Ibid., 22. The text continues: "The village people on the whole were not farmers, for around the village were lava fields. The Batur inhabitants were dealers in pigs, cows, cloth, tobacco, fruit, coffee, corn, etc."

16. Ibid., 22–24. The text continues:

"At 11:00 P.M. a huge mountain of cinders, under which the lava was hidden, reached the border of the village. At 1:00 P.M. the first house began to burn; trees were slowly pushed over, walls collapsed and everything within fifty meters of the lava stream was on fire. The lava stream was moving at about 200 meters per hour. But as yet the mountain of lava, which was about 8 meters tall, was not too hot on the outside. You could approach the edge of the lava to about 3 or 4 meters, while slowly being pushed back by the huge wall of moving cinderblocks.

"In the meantime a number of people had cleared out their houses, and installed themselves on the path, in expectation of further events. I had ordered the military patrol to fetch 200 prisoners from the prisoner's camp in Bantang, and with the help of these troops the populations prepared their exodus."

17. "Ibid. At ten in the morning, after consultation with the anak agung (prince) of Bangli, the Temple of Batur was abandoned. All precious possessions were taken to safety after a brief ceremony by the Jeros and Mangkoes (temple priests). The market, the Bale Banjar, and the big pavillion (*wantilan*) were on fire. Above the loud noise of the 50-meter-high flames, the sound of the twenty-one erupting craters could still be heard. . . .

"Up above on the rim, a good piece of land was found, near the hamlet of Kalanganjar, which belongs to the village of Batur. The land was bought and divided among the Batur members. Every family was given a house yard; here and there little corridors were made; a piece of land for the temple, the banjar assembly building, wantilan pavillion, and new market were also appointed. Funds came in from all sides—the smeroe fund helped—and food was given by sympathetic people. The pity on Bali and Lombok was general."

18. Fortunately, the rains also improved in the months following Panca Wali Krama!

19. Haar, Memorie van overgave, passim. "Op het oogenblijk zijn de lieden der nieuwe Batoer desa (Batoer Kalanganjar) bezig het terrein voor een nieuwen tempel in orde te brengen. Een verzoek om geheel Bali in dezen nieuwbouw te doen deel hebben, door middel van leveren van bijdragen werd reeds gedaan, doch zal nader door den Anak Agung van Bangli voorbereid en daarna opnieuw voorgebracht worden. Gedacht werd een bijdrage van geld van vijf cent per gezinshoofd te heffen."

20. According to Korn, elsewhere the *soewinih* "was spent by the king mostly in offerings in water temples. Only where a king had given himself the trouble to construct water works was the soewinih paid to him, but used for offerings" (Korn, *Het Adatrecht van Bali*, 299).

21. The version translated here is a passage from the Dewa Tattwa translated by Ida Pedanda Made of Griya Taman Sari, Sanur, who transcribed it in 1937 from an original of unknown date.

Chapter Six
Massive Guidance

1. Mark Poffenberger, and Mary S. Zurbuchen, "The Economics of Village Bali: Three Perspectives," *Economic Development and Cultural Change* 29 (1) (October 1980): 109.

2. For a historical overview of the Green Revolution in Indonesia, see I. Palmer, *The New Rice in Indonesia* (Geneva: UNRISD, 1977); E. Utrecht, "Land Reform and BIMAS in Indonesia," *Journal of Contemporary Asia* 3 (1973): 149–64; W. F. G. Blankenheim, "Groene Revolutie en verarming op Java," in W. F. Wertheim, E. Utrecht, and J. M. Pluvier, eds., *Tien jaar onrecht in Indonesia: Militaire dictatuur en internationale steun* (Amsterdam: Van Gennep, 1976); A. Stoler, "Rice Harvest in Kali Loro: A Study of Class and Labor Relations in Rural Java," *American Ethnologist* 4 (1977): 678–98; W. Collier et al., "Recent Changes in Rice Harvesting Methods," *Bulletin of Indonesian Economic Studies* 2 (1973): 36–45; Muriel Charras, *De la forêt maléfique à l'herbe divine. La transmigration en Indonesie: les Balinais a Sulawesi*, Études insulindiennes/archipel 5, Éditions de la maison des sciences de l'homme, Paris. (Paris, 1982).

3. Laporan Statistik Pertanian (Reports on agricultural statistics), Dinas Pertanian Daerah Bali, Kantor Statistik Pulau Bali, Renon, Bali.

4. IRRI estimates an average growth of 105 days for IR-36, whereas the fastest-growing native Balinese varieties take about 135 days. However, as we will see, the rapid growth of high-yielding varieties of rice is not an unalloyed benefit but a question of trade-offs. Native Balinese rice takes longer to mature and puts more of its energy into the whole plant rather than the seeds. Consequently, it is more resistant to disease and other stresses in its environment.

5. "Depuis 1970, les riz hybrides à croissance rapide, de 109 à 120 jours, se sont imposés dans la plaine du Sud-Parigi. Astina a, dès ses débuts, adopté le rythme de cinq récoltes en deux ans. . . . Le fait que les cultures se succèdent sans

interruption favorise aussi la propagation rapide des insectes predateurs, en particulier le wereng," Charras, *De la forêt maléfique à l'herbe divine*, 221–22.

6. Anon., Bali Irrigation Project Feasibility Study Pt. 2, Vol. 5A, Subak Improvement Schemes (Manila: Asian Development Bank, 1981). Consultant's report prepared by Electroconsult International, Milano, Italy, and Agricultural Development Corporation, Seoul, Korea, for the Directorate of Irrigation, Ministry of Public Works, Republic of Indonesia, January 1981.

7. Ibid., 1–7.

8. Bali Irrigation Project Feasibility Study, Pt. 2, 1–2, the economic evaluation described in this study assumes that the project will generate $15,360,000 per year in increased rice production (p. 8).

9. Project Performance Audit Report, Bali Irrigation Project in Indonesia. Asian Development Bank Post-Evaluation Office PE-241 L-352-INO, Manila, Philippines, May 1988, 47.

10. Tukiman, "Pengalaman dalam Merumuskan Pola Tanam di Kabupaten DATI II Tabanan" (Experience of formulating a cropping pattern for the Tabanan regency). Irrigation Division, Government of the Province of Bali, Denpasar, Bali: Jalan Beliton no. 2, 1985, p. 1.

11. Tjokorde Raka Dherana, "Pengalaman Melaksanakan Pola Pergiliran Tanaman Lahan Sawah didaerah Kabupaten Gianyar" (Experience of carrying out a rotational cropping pattern in rice terraces of the Gianyar regency). Office of the Bupati of Gianyar, Gianyar, Bali: April 25, 1985, p. 4.

12. Ibid., p. 5.

13. Bali Irrigation Project Feasibility Study, Pt. 2, app. 2D: Sociology, January 1981.

14. Project Performance Audit Report, Bali Irrigation Project in Indonesia, PE-241 L-352-INO, 47.

15. Personal communications from various officials at the Asian Development Bank and Bali Irrigation Project, 1984–1988.

16. Nyoman Sutawan, Made Swara, I Wayan Windia, I Gde Pitana, and I Wayan Sudana, "Gambaran Umum Sistem Irigasi Pada Aliran Sungai" (Denpasar: Universitas Udayana, 1985), 91. This report was prepared with support from the Ford Foundation in Jakarta.

17. Ibid., 50–51.

18. Project Performance Audit Report, Bali Irrigation Project in Indonesia. PE-241, L-352-INO, 48–50.

19. Ibid., 47.

20. Ibid., 50.

21. Ibid., 49.

Conclusion

1. Marx, MEGA 3:86–89.

2. Ibid., 161. Marx argues that alienation has its source "within the producing activity itself," of which the objective world is only a "resume." (MEGA 3:155).

3. Foucault, *History of Sexuality*, 93.

4. Stephen Toulmin and June Goodfield, *The Discovery of Time* (Chicago: University of Chicago Press, 1965), chaps. 6–10.

Afterword

1. Geertz, *Negara.*
2. Ibid., 82.
3. Ibid., 85.
4. Swellengrebel, *Bali,* 22.
5. Wolters' "men of prowess." Oliver Wolters, *History, Culture and Region in Southeast Asian Perspectives* (Singapore: Institute for Southeast Asian Studies, 1982), 6.
6. Cf. Antony Reid, *Southeast Asia in the Age of Commerce: The Lands below the Winds* (New Haven, Conn.: Yale University Press, 1987), 136.
7. Janet Hoskins, "Doubling Deities, Descent, and Personhood: An Exploration of Kodi Gender Categories," in *Power and Difference: Gender in Island Southeast Asia,* ed. Jane Monnig Atkinson and Shelly Errington (Stanford, Calif.: Stanford University Press, 1990), 323–42.
8. Monni J. Adams, "Myths and Self-image among the Kapunduk People of Sumba" *Indonesia* 10 (1970): 81–106; idem, "Symbols of the Organized Community in East Sumba, Indonesia," *Bijdragen tot de Taal-, Land- en Volkenkunde* 130 (2–3) (1974): 324–47; Gregory Forth, *Rindi: An Ethnographic Study of a Traditional Domain in Eastern Sumba* (The Hague: Nijhoff, 1981), 237, 245, 254.
9. Clark Cunningham, "Order and Change in an Atoni Diarchy," *Southwestern Journal of Anthropology* 21 (1965): 359–83; James Fox, "The Ceremonial System of Savu," in *The Imagination of Reality,* ed. Alton L. Becker and Aram Yengoyam (Norwood, N.J.: Ablex, 1979), 145–73; James Fox, "Obligation and Alliance: State Structure and Moiety Organization in Thie, Roti," in *The Flow of Life: Essays on Eastern Indonesia,* ed. James J. Fox (Cambridge, Mass.: Harvard University Press, 1980), 98–133; H. G. Schulte-Nordholt, *The Political System of the Atoni of Timor* (The Hague: Nijhoff, 1971).
10. It would also be possible to argue, however, that there is not much evidence that it did not control it either. Arguments a silentio are intrinsically fragile.
11. Swellengrebel, *Bali,* 64–65; Geertz, *Negara,* 36–37; Jean-François Guermonprèz, "Rois divins et rois guerriers: Images de la royauté à Bali," *L'Homme* 25 (1985): 36–39; and, for qualifications, Peter J. Worsley, "Preliminary Remarks on the Concept of Kingship in the *Babad Buleleng,*" in ed. Antony Reid and Lance Castles, *Pre-Colonial State Systems in Southeast Asia,* Monographs of the Malayan Branch of the Royal Asiatic Society, no. 6, 1975, pp. 108–13, Kuala Lumpur.
12. Cf. Avineri, *Social and Political Thought of Karl Marx,* 65–95.
13. Cf. Habermas, *Knowledge and Human Interests,* 41–42, and passim.
14. Valerio Valeri, *Kingship and Sacrifice.*

Index